The Great Eastern Railway

The Great Eastern Railway

The Early History, 1811–1862

Charles Phillips

PEN & SWORD
TRANSPORT
AN IMPRINT OF PEN & SWORD BOOKS LTD.
YORKSHIRE – PHILADELPHIA

First published in Great Britain in 2023 by
Pen and Sword Transport
An imprint of
Pen & Sword Books Ltd.
Yorkshire - Philadelphia

ISBN 9781399024709

A CIP catalogue record for this book is available from the British Library.

Typeset in INDIA by IMPEC eSolutions
Printed and bound in England by CPI Group (UK) Ltd, Croydon CR0 4YY

Pen & Sword Books Ltd incorporates the imprints of Pen & Sword Books Archaeology, Atlas, Aviation, Battleground, Discovery, Family History, History, Maritime, Military, Naval, Politics, Railways, Select, Transport, True Crime, Fiction, Frontline Books, Leo Cooper, Praetorian Press, Seaforth Publishing, Wharncliffe and White Owl.

For a complete list of Pen & Sword titles please contact

PEN & SWORD BOOKS LIMITED
47 Church Street, Barnsley, South Yorkshire, S70 2AS, England
E-mail: enquiries@pen-and-sword.co.uk
Website: www.pen-and-sword.co.uk

or

PEN AND SWORD BOOKS
1950 Lawrence Rd, Havertown, PA 19083, USA
E-mail: Uspen-and-sword@casematepublishers.com
Website: www.penandswordbooks.com

FSC
www.fsc.org
MIX
Paper | Supporting responsible forestry
FSC® C171272

Contents

Introduction

This is the first volume of a short history of the Great Eastern Railway (GER) and its constituents and its successors. I have written this book because I live in the territory of the former GER and I like the Railway and the Eastern Counties of England. I am old enough to just remember the last days of steam on the former GER and travelled on it behind steam.

This volume covers the period from the first proposal for a railway in the Eastern Counties in 1811, which was for an Essex Iron Railway, to the formation of the GER in 1862. It covers the history of all of the constituent companies of the GER.

Within the book will be found details of how the Eastern Counties (ECR), Northern and Eastern (N&ER) and London and Blackwall (L&BR) railways were originally built to a gauge of 5ft but were later converted to the standard British gauge of 4ft 8½in. The L&BR was originally worked by cable haulage as opposed to steam traction – the failure of the ECR to complete its main line to Norwich and Yarmouth beyond Colchester resulted in the formation of the Eastern Union Railway and this is dealt with later. The Newmarket Railway, which saw one of the first railway closures in Britain, the East Anglian Railway (which nearly became part of the Great Northern Railway) and the Norfolk Railway and its constituent companies are all covered in the later chapters.

I have tried within this book to include illustrations relevant to the subjects covered in it. In this and any other material that might be deemed copyright I have made all efforts to trace the copyright holders. Where it has not been possible, the publishers and I apologise for the omission.

I am a member of the GER Society to whose members I apologise for asking awkward questions on the internet group. The GER Society is the premier railway historical society of England and has produced CDs of a number of magazines which I have used in the writing of this book. These are the *GER Magazine*, *Railway and Travel Monthly* and *The Locomotive Magazine* for the period 1896 to 1923. The Society also inspired the North Eastern Railway Association to produce a CD of the *North Eastern Railway Magazine* which was also used in the writing of this history. The GER Society has for the record also produced CDs of the *London and North Eastern Railway Magazine*, the *British Railways Eastern Region Magazine* and the Directors' Report to Shareholders of the Eastern Counties, Great Eastern and London and North Eastern railways.

Charles Phillips

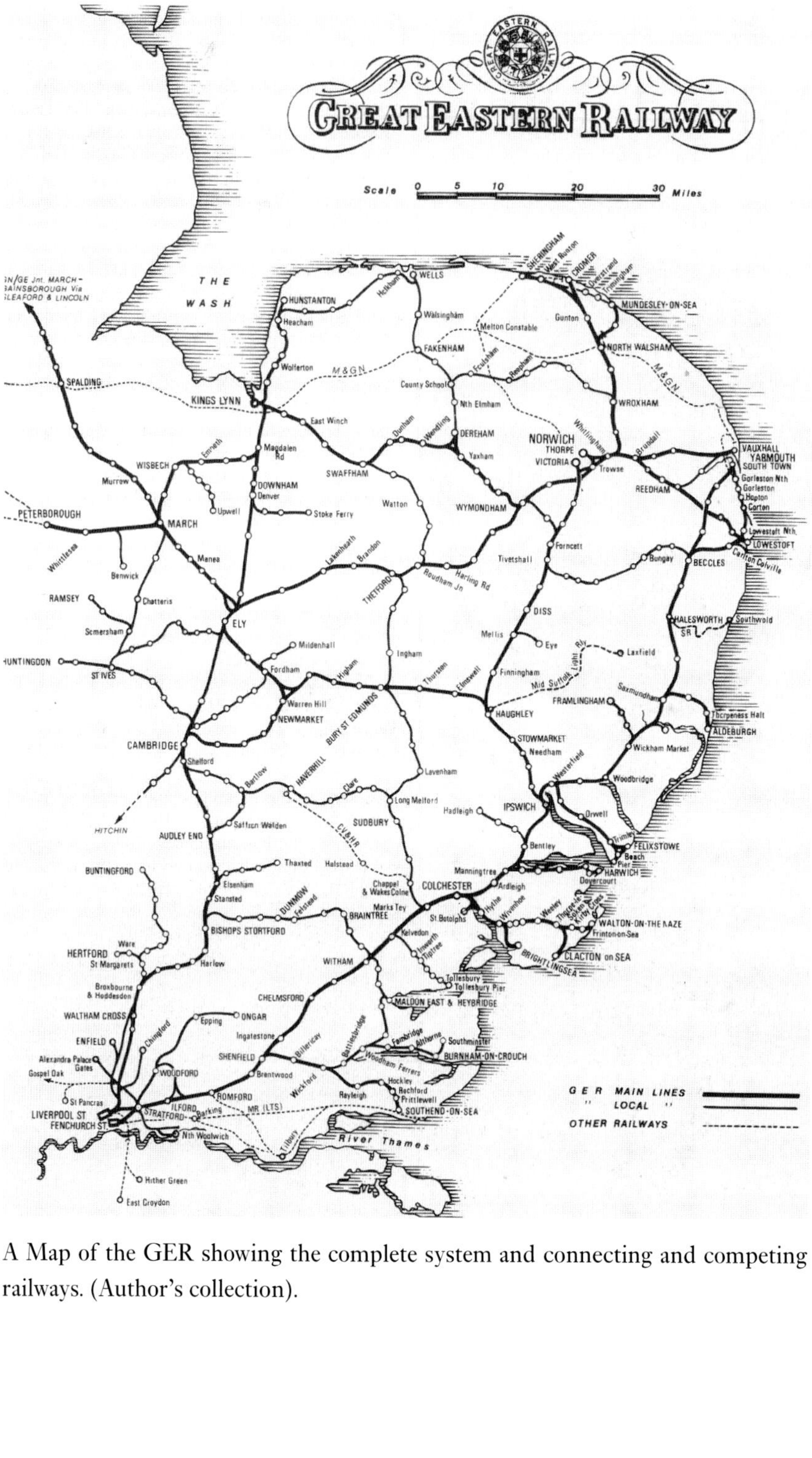

A Map of the GER showing the complete system and connecting and competing railways. (Author's collection).

Chapter 1

Ancestry

The ancestry of the GER can be traced back as far as 1811, when a plan for an iron railway from Islington to Wallasea Island with a branch to Mucking Creek on the River Thames was deposited with the Clerk of the Peace for Essex. The promotion of the proposed railway was inspired by the successful Surrey Iron Railway and the linking Croydon, Mersham and Godstone Railway which had been opened in 1803 and 1805 respectively. The railway, which would have been worked by horse power, did not come to fruition. It can be held to be the ancestor of both the New Essex Lines of the GER and of the London, Tilbury and Southend Railway (LT&SR).

In 1821, William James made a survey for an 'Engine Railroad from Bishop's Stortford to Clayhithe Sluice with a branch to Waddon and an estimate thereof' which he submitted to the Earl of Hardwicke. This also came to nothing and indeed no plan was ever, as far as is known, deposited with the Clerks of the Peace for Hertfordshire, Essex or Cambridgeshire. The idea would appear to be an alternative to the suggested but ultimately unsuccessful proposal to build a canal from the Stort to the Cam.

In 1825 the brothers John and George Rennie, who were well known civil engineers, proposed a railway to run from London through Hoddesdon, Ware, Braughing and Barkway to Cambridge. In an advertisement in the *Cambridge Chronicle* of 11 November 1825, a Bill would be deposited with parliament for the construction of the railway in the Session of 1827 and that it was to be called the Northern Rail Road Company. The ultimate destination of the railway was to be

Cromford in Derbyshire, where it would join the High Peak Railway and then go to Manchester. Nothing came of this.

At the end of 1824, there was a proposal for a Norfolk and Suffolk Rail Road Company to construct a railway from London to Norwich via Chelmsford, Colchester and Ipswich with branches from Colchester to Harwich, Ipswich to Bury St Edmunds and Norwich to Yarmouth and Lynn. A prospectus was issued but only a handful of shares were taken up and in consequence the proposal died. In November 1825 it was revived in a truncated form as a railway to run from Whitechapel in London to Ipswich via Ilford, Brentwood, Chelmsford, Witham, Colchester and Brantham. A plan of the proposed railway, which was to be worked by horse traction, was deposited with the Clerk of the Peace for Essex. Although 10,000 shares were issued, only 3,346 were taken up and this proposal lapsed.

Failed proposals are a big part of the history of the GER. For example, in 1825 there had been a proposal for an Ipswich and Suffolk Railway to run from Ipswich to Diss via Eye. Nothing came of this. In 1829 there was a proposal for a railway or railways from Whitechapel to Poplar with two branches, one of which was wholly within Poplar and the other was to Bromley by Bow, but nothing came of this either.

Chapter 2

The Eastern Counties and Northern and Eastern Railways to August 1845

The ancestry of the ECR can be traced back to 1834 when surveyor Henry Sayer went to solicitors Dimes and Boyman with a plan for a railway from London via Cambridge and York to Edinburgh. Following consultations between those gentlemen and two others, John Clinton Robertson and John Braithwaite of the engineering firm of Braithwaite and Kirk, it was decided instead to build a railway from London via Colchester and Ipswich to Norwich. That is not to say that the original proposal did not receive some attention in the press. The *Bury and Norwich Post* of 20 August 1834 reported that notice had been given to parliament that it was intended in the ensuing session to introduce a bill for constructing a railway from London to Edinburgh via Cambridge, York and Leeds with branches to Norwich and Bury St Edmunds, Nottingham, Lincoln, Sheffield and Hull. The estimated cost was £4 million. However, by the end of the month the direction of the railway had changed as the *Chelmsford Chronicle* of 29 August reported that Messrs Dimes and Boyman had given notice to parliament to promote a railway from London to Norwich and Yarmouth via Romford, Chelmsford, Colchester, Ipswich and Eye.

The ECR was promoted in the summer of 1834 to build a railway from London to Norwich and Yarmouth via Romford, Chelmsford, Colchester, Ipswich and Eye and was originally called the Grand ECR. The engineer of the proposed railway was John Braithwaite, who, with Captain John Ericsson, had constructed the locomotive *Novelty* which had taken part in the Rainhill Trials in 1829.

The bill for the construction of the railway was introduced into parliament on 19 February 1836 and following a rather stormy passage as a result of serious opposition from landowners and other parties, the bill received its royal assent on 4 July. Interestingly, the Company's Act contained no mention of the gauge of the Railway. According to B.D.J. Walsh, writing in the *Railway Magazine* in February 1956, at this time Brunel's Great Western Railway (GWR) with its gauge of 7ft ¼in had aroused considerable interest and the directors of the ECR were in favour of building their Railway to the same gauge. Braithwaite, who was the engineer of the Company, opposed this and the Company's directors after a full discussion decided that Brunel's gauge should not be adopted. It would appear though that the directors were somewhat doubtful of their decision as they stipulated that provision should be made for converting the railway to Brunel's gauge should that be subsequently proved desirable. Braithwaite, when asked by the directors for his preference of gauge, pronounced in favour of 5ft, his reason being that it gave more space for the boiler and for the working parts. He assumed that the Railway would have a monopoly of the traffic in East Anglia and that it would not seek to extend northwards and therefore there would be no problems arising from the change of gauge.

Construction of the railway commenced in the latter part of March 1837. The *Chelmsford Chronicle* of 31 March 1837 reported that 'The ECR Company have commenced operations at Brentwood by sinking shafts for the tunnel, which is to be cut through the hill at that place', although it was a cutting rather than a tunnel that was built at Brentwood.

The *Suffolk Chronicle* of 15 April 1837 reported that the works of the first division of the railway out of London were in full progress.

The *Norfolk Chronicle* of 22 July reported that on 12 July the directors of the railway, accompanied by a large number of shareholders and also a considerable number of scientific gentlemen, had inspected the works over the River Lea and Stratford Marshes.

The owners of land that was taken for the building of the railway were required to submit claims which comprised of two elements of which one was the market value and the other was compensation. To give an example of this, when the ECR proposed to pass through seven miles of Lord Petre's land at Shenfield, Mountnessing, Ingatestone and Margaretting, he claimed £20,000 for the market value of the land and £100,000 in compensation.

Unfortunately, claims were open to fraud. The *Hertford Mercury and Reformer* of 21 November 1837 reported that a Mr Hubbard had demanded £1,156 for damage to a villa in West Ham of which he was only the yearly tenant, but which he alleged he had paid £750 for in expectation of being undisturbed and would be put to a further expense of £600 for fixtures. As the railway would not pass within a mile of the house and the Company had bought the house from the owner, he was only awarded £5 for the land taken away and £5 for damage.

Building the railway, which was almost entirely done by hand using picks and shovels, was dangerous. The *Chelmsford Chronicle* of 6 October 1837 reported the death of a young man named Bond who was employed as a labourer and who was killed on 30 September. He was clearing away the loose earth from the excavations in progress for the formation of a bridge in Angel Lane, Stratford when a large quantity of earth fell on him whilst in the act of stooping and forced his head against a pile of brickwork, so killing him.

Whilst construction of the first stage of railway east of Stratford was relatively easy, that of the railway west of Stratford to the London terminus at Shoreditch was not. Much of the line had to be built on a brick viaduct which was costly to build. The marshes between Bow and Stratford were of an unstable character and the adjacent River Lea was prone to flooding.

Even whilst the railway was under construction there were proposals for connecting lines and branch lines. The *Suffolk Chronicle* of 24 February 1838 reported that it was intended to make an application to parliament to build a railway from Colchester to Harwich.

Progress on building the railway was such that according to the *Essex Herald* of 6 February 1838 it was expected that the railway would be open to Ilford in the coming June or July.

There was corruption amongst the contractors' men as the *Essex Herald* of 20 March 1838 reported. Mr Webb, a foreman to Mr Sherwood, one of the contractors of the railway, had been in the habit of supplying the workmen with goods and deducting the amount from their wages. This was known as the 'truck system'. The matter had reached the Ilford magistrates, who told Webb that he had made himself liable to heavy penalties by an act of parliament designed to stop the practice. The Railway's board of directors heard about this and indicated their displeasure of the interference of their foreman with the established tradesmen of the district and passed a resolution that in future they would not employ any contractors who either directly by themselves or indirectly concerned themselves in supplying goods to their workmen. A copy of the resolution was ordered by the board to be forwarded to all the contractors.

Unfortunately, sufficient progress had not been made by the end of June to open any part of the railway. The *Essex Herald* of 17 July said that the works of the ECR were proceeding very rapidly and that a gentleman had travelled over a part of it at fourteen miles per hour. Meanwhile, the first locomotive arrived on the uncompleted railway. The *Railway Times* had reported that the previous week, the locomotive made its appearance on the completed part of the line between Maryland Point and the Abbey and that it had been built by Messrs Braithwaite and Milner and seemed very efficient and powerful and that it was employed to drag fifty wagons loaded with materials. According to the *Norfolk Chronicle* of 28 July, the contracts for the construction of the works to Romford had been signed and the time stipulated for their completion was three months and two weeks.

The *Essex Standard* of 3 August told its readers that the construction works of the Railway had advanced to the outskirts of Romford. The *Railway Times* was quoted as saying that in addition to the locomotive named *Essex* already employed at work on the building of the railway, another one was expected to be 'launched in the next few days'. At Stratford, the embankment over the marshes was proceeding 'with the help of a new embanking machine invented by the engineer (of the railway) with a degree of rapidity not often seen in constructions of that sort'.

The *Essex Standard* of 21 September reported that the ECR was making great exertions to complete its line to Romford. Two sets of men, one working in the day and one at night, were forcing the work forward at Stratford, Ilford and Chadwell. Whilst work was going on constructing the line at the London end of the Railway, there was a lack of progress at the other end, which was causing concern in that area. The *Norfolk Chronicle* of 8 September said that it wished it could see some movement at that end of the line and that works according to the practice of the other lines were going on at several points simultaneously. The distance from Norwich to Yarmouth, which was level country and consequently less expensive, might have been made a source of income to the company in a short period. The *Chronicle* said that it was alleged that Norwich and Yarmouth people, having evinced little interest in the matter, were not entitled at the present to much attention from the directors, although the *Chronicle* said that it could not gainsay that remark.

There was concern beyond Colchester that the railway would not be built beyond that town. The *Essex Standard* of 2 January 1839 reported that on 24 December there had been a meeting at Harwich to apply to parliament to bring forward a bill for the formation of a Harwich Railway (HR) Company to connect that town with the ECR at Colchester.

Regarding the extending of the ECR, the *Essex Herald* of 12 February reported that the Railway Company had agreed to promote the undertaking to construct the railway to Harwich. The *Suffolk Chronicle* of 9 February mentioned the same thing and said that it would be advantageous to Harwich but implied that the failure of the

ECR to extend its line to Norwich and Yarmouth would be injurious to those places unless it was intended to continue there as contemplated by its act. The *Chronicle* said it did not think that that would happen, as the Railway had no intention of continuing beyond Colchester. The *Essex Standard* of 15 February announced the formation of a Provisional Committee and a Local Committee for the promotion of a railway from Harwich to Colchester.

By the early part of March 1839, the contracts for extending the railway from a temporary London terminus in Devonshire Street to Shoreditch had been let, according to the *Essex Standard* of 8 March. The *Standard* also said that on 2 March, the directors of the company had made an inspection trip down the line from Mile End to Ilford and a little bit beyond to inspect the state of the works.

According to the *Bury and Norwich Post* of 20 March, it was expected that the ECR would be open to Chelmsford the following year and that a bill to extend the Railway from Colchester to Harwich was before parliament.

It was in the early spring of 1839 that the directors of the ECR decided to build the railway no further east than Colchester. According to the *Essex Herald* of 2 April, a writer from Liverpool said that all the Liverpool directors and most of the London directors were of the opinion that the railway should not be constructed further than Colchester because it would not pay to build it any further, whilst most of the local directors were of the opinion that it should be constructed as far as Norwich and Yarmouth. Understandably, this did not go down well in Norfolk and the *Norfolk Chronicle* of 6 April contained a short article saying that that was what had only been expected and that the Norwich and Yarmouth shareholders would be aroused to the sense of injury inflicted on them by the northern shareholders before it was too late. Earlier the concern of the inhabitants of Norfolk regarding the failure of the Railway to commence building work at the eastern end of the line was mentioned in the comments section of the *Norfolk Chronicle* of 2 March.

The failure of the railway to build its line beyond Colchester resulted in the railway company being taken to court. The *Chelmsford Chronicle* of 10 May 1839 recorded the case of the Queen versus the ECR Company. In the Bail Court on 6 May, the Attorney General said that he had been instructed to make an application to the Court to compel the Railway Company to complete the railway beyond Colchester to Norwich and Yarmouth. In giving judgement, Mr Justice Williams said that the case being of great novelty, he would rather that it be made to the full Court. The Attorney General said that because of the quantity of business before the Court and the case was one that pressed, he hoped that the application would be granted. The case was mentioned in the *Norfolk Chronicle* of 11 May. According to the *Norwich Mercury*, the rule nisi if made absolute (which would happen unless the other party could show cause why it should not) would compel the directors of the Railway to complete the whole railway as authorised. The *Essex Herald* of 21 May carried a copy of rule nisi which said that the Railway Company were ordered at the start of the Trinity Term of the Court to show why a writ of mandamus (a writ from a superior court to an inferior court or to an officer or corporation commanding that a specific thing be done) should not be issued to it to complete the railway as authorised – that is, an order compelling the Company to do so. The *Railway Times* of 25 May reported that the case had come before the Queen's Bench Court and the rule had been made absolute, but the same publication of 30 May then said that that had been an error and that the rule would be argued in the courts in the course of the Legal Term. The *Essex Herald* of 4 June recorded that the previous week it had given two versions of the decision, but the *Railway Times* furnished an explanation. This was that the rule had been made absolute, but an agreement had been made that the rule should not be drawn up but should be argued on such day as both sides should agree and that 'an immediate return as of this term being agreed, should the rule be made absolute on being argued'. According to the *Bury and Norwich Post* of 5 June, the rule had been made absolute. According to the *Essex Standard* of 28 June, decision was finally granted in the Queen's Bench Court on Saturday, 22 June in which Lord Denman said that 'the mandamus must issue, leaving to the defendants to make what return they might deem to be advisable. Rule absolute'. A decree absolute. The *Essex Chronicle* of 26 July reported that the directors of the Railway were proceeding with setting out the line of the railway between Colchester and Yarmouth. The same newspaper of 16 August recorded that the company intended to apply for a bill in the next session of parliament to enable it to raise further capital by way of shares, mortgages, etc. to enable it to carry it out into effect. The *Essex Standard* of 18 October reported that an application was intended to be made to parliament for the purpose of a bill to complete the Railway to Yarmouth including the raising of money to do this. The failure of the ECR to extend its line beyond Colchester was still giving grievance and the *Suffolk Chronicle* of 26 October quoted the *Railway Times* as saying that the failure had induced other parties to turn their attention to a railway into Norfolk. The new engineer of the N&ER, Robert Stephenson, the son of George Stephenson, was quoted as saying that Bishop's Stortford in Hertfordshire was well suited as a terminus for the accommodation of traffic from the north and the east and that a line to accommodate the agricultural districts of Norfolk and Suffolk should be made in the not too distant future. The *Norwich Mercury* of 14 December reported that an application had been made to parliament for the purpose of completing the railway from Colchester to Great Yarmouth. Judgement was finally given in the Court of the Queen's Bench on 17 June 1840 and was in favour of the Railway Company.

The *Essex Standard* of 7 June 1839 reported that the railway would be open to the public from London to Romford on 20 June and that times and fares would be announced shortly.

The ECR, as announced, formally opened from its temporary London station in Devonshire Street, Mile End to Romford on Tuesday, 18 June. The *Chelmsford Chronicle* in its edition of Friday,

21 June carried an account of the opening ceremony which was well attended and included a dinner held in Romford.

With the opening of the first section of the railway came the first accident when on Friday, 21 June, the day after the public opening, a derailment occurred between Stratford and London which resulted in the death of the engine driver, John Meadows, and the fireman, Charles Leech. The cause of the accident was speeding. The accident was reported in several local eastern counties newspapers.

The ECR was also involved in a Sabbath-breaking dispute by running trains on Sundays. The *Essex Standard* of 12 July 1839, in an account of rowdy scenes at the Fairlop Fair held between 5 and 7 July amongst other things, mentioned that the Railway had run trains on Sunday, 7 July to Ilford which was the nearest station to Fairlop. The *Standard* quoted the *Morning Herald*, saying that it was hoped that the magistrates would, before another fair, take steps to abolish the 'recurrence of scenes so disgraceful to the metropolis of a Christian country'.

The *Chelmsford Chronicle* of 19 July reported that a total of 29,052 passengers had been conveyed by the ECR between Devonshire Street and Romford in the period 20 June to 10 July. Clearly the railway was proving popular as the *Essex Herald* of 9 July reported that on 30 June 3,656 passengers had travelled by train on the railway and that as there was not enough room in the passenger carriages, some had decided to travel in cattle trucks. This suggests that some of the trains conveyed goods or at least cattle as well as passengers – or that there were not enough passenger carriages available.

On 21 February 1840, the *Essex Standard* reported that an application would be made in the following session of parliament to build a railway between Harwich and Colchester to be called the Harwich and Colchester Railway. The anticipation of the expected railway to Harwich caused a Mr Bagshaw to purchase land and property in Dovercourt according to the *Cambridge Independent Press* of 4 April. Whilst the people of Harwich were thinking in practical terms of building their own railway, the bankers, merchants and others of Ipswich, Norwich and Yarmouth still frustrated with the failure of the ECR to build its line no further east than Colchester had petitioned parliament about this failure and hoped that something could be done. This was reported in the edition of the *Standard* of 28 February. In March, Sir Charles Broke Vere and Edmond Wodehouse brought to parliament a bill compelling the ECR that when the London end of the line was completed as far as Chelmsford, an equal extent of the railway from Yarmouth must be completed towards London. Also, when the railway was completed to Colchester from London at the other end, it should next be completed from Yarmouth to Ipswich. The section from Colchester to Ipswich to be safely let to the discretion of the Company. Agitation for the completion of the railway beyond Colchester continued and on 24 April, a meeting was held in the town hall in Ipswich to consider what steps could be taken by the inhabitants of Ipswich and its neighbourhood towards promoting the extension of the railway from Colchester to Norwich and to consider the position of Ipswich. The outcome was that it was decided to form a committee and a petition to be presented in favour of the bill. Unfortunately, the bill failed at its second reading in the House of Commons on 11 May with a majority of 137 against. The frustration at the eastern end of the railway as originally authorised as well as the Northern and Eastern was such that the *Essex Standard* of 8 May reported that a Great Eastern Railway was being floated, the course of which was to run from London to Norwich and Yarmouth via Woodford, Dunmow and Bury St Edmunds with a branch from the latter place to Ipswich.

1840 saw an extension of the railway at both ends. The *Essex Standard* of 17 April said that the date of opening of the extension from Devonshire Street to Shoreditch and Romford to Brentwood had been fixed for June. The *Norwich Mercury* of the 11th of the month reported that the first locomotive had reached Brentwood the previous Tuesday. The *Chelmsford Chronicle* of 17 April reported a different story, saying that it did not think that the opening would take place before September. Even the claim that the first locomotive had reached Brentwood was challenged as, according to the *Essex Standard* of 17 April, several parts of the embankment were incomplete and that the previous Saturday one of the locomotives being drawn by fourteen horses on its way to the Brentwood end of the line to haul earth wagons was overtaken on the high road near Brook Street by the Yarmouth mail coach. The extensions were not opened in June. The date fixed instead was 1 July and the line was duly opened from Devonshire Street to Shoreditch and from Romford to Brentwood on schedule. The *Chelmsford Chronicle* amongst other newspapers gave an account of the opening of the two sections of railway and the journey of the train from Shoreditch to Brentwood conveying some of the directors, who were later joined by other directors who had come from London and all dined in the White Hart at Brentwood.

With the opening of the Railway between Shoreditch and Brentwood, at least some of the stagecoaches plying the roads to Colchester, Ipswich and Norwich were conveyed between the capital and Brentwood and vice versa by railway by having the coaches loaded on to flat wagons attached to a passenger train. On Wednesday, 19 August, a train conveying two stage coaches in addition to its passenger carriages was involved in a fatal accident shortly after leaving Brentwood. According to the *Chelmsford Chronicle* of 21 August, on the evening of the fatal day a train comprising an engine, a tender, a third class carriage, a second class carriage, a first class carriage, a third class carriage and two wagons on which were the *Norwich Times* and *Colchester Defiance* coaches left Brentwood at seven o'clock in the evening. There were twenty-three passengers in the railway carriages and in the *Norwich Times* coaches were the two coachmen – Palmer and Tabor. According to the *Chronicle*, whilst the train was descending the 'inclined plane which commences at Brentwood Hill' the driver of the engine neglected to shut off steam, contrary to the orders issued to all the Company's drivers. The *Chronicle* said that they started to reach a speed of 60-70mph and near Patwell's Gate began to rock in a fearful manner. After about 150 yards, the engine, tender and leading three carriages left the rails and went down a 12ft high embankment. The accident resulted in the death of four people, including the driver of the train, Mr Foster, and injuries to others. One person died in September. There were other accidents occurring on the ECR and this seems to have given concern to the government, which had recently established its Railway Accident Inspectorate. The *Cambridge Chronicle and Journal* of 26 September reported that Lt Col Thomson of the Royal Engineers had been sent by the Board of Trade to inspect the ECR, with instructions to make a full report on the accidents that had been occurring.

There is a mention of the railway being used to reach Brentwood from London by Elizabeth Fry aged 15 of Warley Lodge in 1842. Elizabeth was the granddaughter of Elizabeth Fry the prison reformer. Thus: 'Janry. 18th. This morng we three came by railroad to Warley, I must say to our pleasure for home always has indescribable charms.' And April 21st: 'Returned home this evening with Papa by the railroad, heartily delighted to leave the bustle [and] dirt … of London.'

Having reached Brentwood, work now re-started on building the rest of the railway to Colchester. The *Norwich Mercury* of 12 September reported that the previous Monday work had recommenced at Springfield (Chelmsford).

By the middle of June 1841, work on building the Railway was in hand at the Colchester end of the line. The *Essex Herald* of 15 June reported that the Railway had commenced operations at Mott's Farm and Newbridge in the parish of Lexden. The *Norfolk Chronicle* of 26 June said that work was about to commence at Colchester.

In 1841 there was a development regarding connecting Harwich to the railway network. In the General Election of that year, John Attwood, a railway speculator, was elected as one of the Members of Parliament for Harwich. Apart from spending quite a bit of money in bribes to get himself elected, he announced that if he was elected he would advance £20,000 for a railway to the town. Having been elected he did not immediately make good his promise.

The autumn of October 1841 appears to have been very wet as the *Essex Standard* of 29 October reported that because of bad weather the works on building the railway at Chelmsford had been suspended, putting a large number of men out of work. The *Ipswich Journal* of the following day also said that because of the weather the railway works were going very slowly and that a large number of men were out of work. By the end of November, the weather had cleared up as the *Chelmsford Chronicle* of 26 November said that workmen were being employed night and day in concreting the foundations for the viaduct which would cross Duke Street in the town and that throughout the line the return of better weather had been attended by a spirited renewal of work. The return to work after the rains caused problems as at Kelvedon where a contractor had seized on the opportunity to speed up the brick work on a viaduct over the River Blackwater with unfortunate but fortunately not fatal consequences. The contractor persisted in running the rings out of one of the arches although forbidden to do so. Whilst keying the last ring, the centrings gave way and collapsed. The brickwork followed as did all those working on the arch but without loss of life. Eleven men were more or less bruised but not seriously injured according to the *Norwich Chronicle* of 18 December and *Chelmsford Chronicle* of 17 December.

There was concern in Chelmsford about the lack of progress in opening the Railway to that town. According to the *Chelmsford Chronicle* of 26 November, a correspondent pointing to the course adopted by the N&ER for completing their works as they advanced observed that if the workmen employed in building the Railway between Chelmsford and Colchester had been employed in building the Railway between Brentwood and Chelmsford, trains might have been running to the town.

Whilst not caused by bad weather, there was another collapse of a viaduct on the railway. The *Chelmsford Chronicle* of 18 February 1842 reported that the timber viaduct on which the earth had been carried to form the embankment carrying the railway over the river Chelmer had collapsed the previous Friday, taking with it five empty earth wagons which were on it at the time. A number of workmen who for several days had been working to remove some of the piles for the purpose of first letting it down at one end prior to its total removal were at work on it but all escaped injury. There was little loss to the contractor as the collapse, although unplanned, had ended up with the desired result.

In either 1841 or 1842, the exact date is not clear, the Railway built workshops just east of Romford, the actual location being east of what is now Gidea Park station and on the opposite side of the running lines from Gidea Park sidings. The works lasted until 1848 when they were closed, and the ECR moved its works to those of the N&ER at Stratford.

In late 1842, there was a proposal which ultimately proved unsuccessful by the Thames Haven Railway to build a railway from the ECR at Romford to Thames Haven, where there were plans to build a dock. In order to tell the story, it is necessary to go back first to 1835. The Thames Haven dock proposal had originated in that year with a proposal by the Thames Haven Dock and Railway company to build a direct railway line from London or a line from the recently promoted ECR to Shell Haven on the River Thames. Shell Haven was to be renamed Thames Haven. Here a dock would be built by which means ships would be able to avoid the dangers and the delays occurred in navigating the crowded upper reaches of the river towards London. The Company received its Act in 1836 – the same year that the ECR received its Act. Under the Act the Company's railway was to join the ECR, the junction with which was to be made under the directions of the ECR Engineer. Things did not progress very well. Although work had started on building the dock in 1836, there were difficulties with the ECR. When the Thames Haven Company's bill was progressing through parliament, the ECR Provisional Committee had promised that if the Thames Haven would give up the idea of an independent route to London, it would grant especially favourable rates for running Thames Haven trains between Romford and Shoreditch. Disagreement arose in regard to the tolls that the Thames Haven would pay to the ECR and in 1838 it was thinking of building an independent railway to London. In February 1839, notices of a parliamentary application for a line from the Minories was served but because of the failure of the shareholders' meeting of March 1839 to take place, nothing came of this. The problem seems to have been the state of the money market at that time. As the powers of the original Act were due to expire in July 1843, a new Act was obtained which received its Royal Assent on 30 June 1842. This Act revived the Romford line powers. However, by the end of 1842 the Thames Haven had given up on the ECR and the idea of an independent railway again came to the fore. In November 1842, plans were deposited for a Thames Haven Railway Extension to run from an independent terminus at Jubilee Street in Stepney to join the alignment of the route of the proposed 1839 line from Thames Haven near Orsett between Thames Haven and to London, plus a branch line at Stepney to link with the L&BR. The line authorised from Romford to Orsett in the Act of 1842 was to be abandoned. However, nothing came of this. Things get very complicated and to cut things short the authorised line from Romford to Thames Haven was not built. I will briefly mention this again in the chapter on the L&BR.

In the early days of the railways, signalling was by red and white flags carried and exhibited by railway policemen at certain distances. These had been found inadequate for the purpose. In the autumn of 1841, Mr Hall, the Managing Director of the ECR, invented a system of signals. The new signal which was called the fan or panel signal had when in operation the appearance of an upright pole about twelve feet high surmounted by a piece of woodwork resembling in shape a closed fan. The two were joined by a strong iron framework. In the upper woodwork there were encased three panels, worked by machinery, which when they were brought down to the iron framework assumed the appearance of crimson quadrant which would be visible in a straight line from two miles away. When a train was due to start, the man in charge of the signal lowered the three panels. As soon as the train had started and reached the signal, the man in charge operated a piece of machinery which worked up the three panels in the space of fifteen minutes so that at the end of that time it was back to its original appearance. According to the *Suffolk Chronicle* of 16 October, by that arrangement engine drivers would be able to accurately calculate the time since a train had passed. One panel being five minutes, two ten minutes and three fifteen minutes. The new signal would be put into operation within a few days on the ECR.

On 12 May there was the collapse of another bridge under construction at Kelvedon with, unfortunately, the loss of one man and injuries to six others. The reason for the collapse was not established, according to the *Chelmsford Chronicle* of 13 May.

The *Essex Standard* of 17 June reported that the first two locomotives had recently arrived at Chelmsford for work on the construction of the railway. The locomotives had been drawn by horse over public roads. According to the *Chelmsford Chronicle* of 1 July, the first of the locomotives was put to work on 29 June. The name of the locomotive was given as *Essex* and it was working at the Springfield end of the town. The *Chronicle* said that the second locomotive, named *Middlesex*, would be working at the Widford end of the town in a few days.

At Colchester, work had started on the construction of a temporary terminus at the northern edge of the town which, according to the *Essex Standard* of 26 August, was to be finished by 1 October. At Chelmsford, according to the *Essex Standard* of 23 September, the temporary station had been brought down to the town ready framed and was being erected on the eastern side of the viaduct in Duke Street. On a different note, it said that the general opinion was that it would be impossible to open the line to Colchester on 1 October.

1 October came and went and the line was not opened beyond Brentwood to Colchester. At the General Meeting of the Company held at Shoreditch station on 1 October, the Chairman said that it was fully expected that the line would be opened on the 28th. However, by the 27th, an experimental trip which was to have been taken on the Railway from Colchester was postponed as it was found that it had been impossible to complete the works. The *Norfolk Chronicle* of 22 October said that the works of the Railway were going well but that some weeks 'must elapse before the line is completed'. The question of the delay in the opening of the Railway to Colchester came up at the adjourned General Meeting of the Railway at Shoreditch station on 28 October. Mr Braithwaite the Engineer said that with fine weather the line might be opened with a single line of rails for goods traffic only in three weeks from the time of the meeting and entirely for passengers at the expiration of three months from the time of the meeting. The *Ipswich Journal* in its account of the meeting quotes a report by Mr Braithwaite given at the meeting in which he had said that the Mountnessing and Shenfield embankments, the Brentwood Hill cutting and the Cann embankment could not be brought to a sufficient forward state to complete the line of continuation over the Colne viaduct owing to recent unfavourable weather. It was perhaps better that the works should not be hurried for the temporary gratification of having trains run to Colchester only to close again because of the subsidence of some of the embankments. In this, a great number of shareholders concurred. The *Essex Standard* of 9 December, in a report about the great anxiety felt in Essex about the delay in opening the line to Colchester, said that Mr Braithwaite had said that if there was fair weather or a little frost, the line to Colchester would be open for goods traffic on 1 January. According to the *Standard*, the line was now so far completed so that a train could run from Mountnessing to Colchester. The *Suffolk Chronicle* of 10 December said that on Wednesday, the Directors had made an experimental trip from Mountnessing to Colchester. The reason for Mountnessing and not

Brentwood was that the line between those two places was not quite ready. The feeling that not all was well with the railway was borne out by the *Cambridge Independent Press* of 10 December which said that it had been necessary to take down and rebuild several of the bridges. The third Kelvedon bridge had exhibited symptoms of insecurity and the Boreham bridge was shored up to prevent it falling.

By the end of February 1843, work had progressed such that on 27 February a special train was arranged to leave Shoreditch with the Directors, proprietors and their friends over the supposedly completed railway to Colchester. Unfortunately, the trip did not go to plan. On Brentwood Hill, it was found that, because of the weather affecting the state of the rails, the locomotive did not have sufficient power to haul the train up the hill and another locomotive had to push the train up the hill now known as Brentwood Bank. This caused some delay. Eventually it was decided to press on to Chelmsford, but finding that there had been subsidence of the timber viaduct at Mountnessing it was decided not proceed any further. The special train to Colchester with the Directors, proprietors and their friends did successfully run on 1 March.

The *Essex Standard* of 10 March 1843 reported that General Pasley had made his final inspection of the new section of the Railway the previous Wednesday (7th) and he told the directors that he felt that it should be opened immediately. According to the *Bury and Norwich Post* of 8 March, the Directors of the railway decided on 6 March that goods traffic would start on 7 March, which it did. It seems, though, from the evidence of William Wire of Colchester, who will be mentioned shortly, that goods trains started running on 2 March prior to the Directors of the Company giving their approval for goods traffic to start.

The railway to Colchester opened to passenger traffic on 29 March. With the opening of the railway from Colchester, some stage coaches east of the town were now conveyed by train to and from London and the fare table for the Railway included the fares for stage coaches.

The opening to Colchester was a fairly low-key affair. There was a special train carrying the Directors and their friends to Colchester.

Chelmsford was reached in one hour and forty minutes and Colchester in two hours and forty minutes. At various stations and bridges along the line, crowds gathered and cheered the passing train. At Witham, a band of musicians who had been in attendance there went into one of the roofless carriages and played some agreeable airs for the rest of the journey. At Colchester, the directors and their friends went to the Moot Hall where they were received by several members of the Corporation and sat down to an entertainment provided by Mr Chaplin, the host of the Three Cups Hotel. In this they were joined by a large number of the principal inhabitants of the town. The *Essex Standard* of 31 March in its account of the event said that there was not enough room for everyone.

There is quite a bit about the railway in Colchester in 1842 to 1843 in the diary of William Wire, a watchmaker, but later a postman of Colchester. Wire was interested in archaeology:

> June 17 1842 – Purchased of a railway labourer, who found it near the viaduct, Lexden, a silver gilt hand-in-hand medieval ring with the following legend engraved on it, JESUS NAZARENE.
>
> August 30 1842. Went to the rail road, found they were getting on with the station, which appears from its slight construction to be but for a temporary purpose. The 'navvies' continue digging but find nothing.
>
> September 16 1842. Went to the railway and was informed by one of the company's police that persons not engaged on the work was not permitted to visit them and he told me that the day before he had ordered Mr Green, the banker, off.
>
> October 31 1842. Mr Braithwaite, engineer in chief to the Eastern Counties Railway, kindly sent me a pass so that I can inspect the works at any time.

November 20 1842. Went to the railway on Tuesday last, when I was informed that the day before that a fluted Roman Urn had been discovered in a field south of the station.

December 26 1842. Went for a ride to the railway viaduct, Lexden; walked on the top which is covered with a pitch-like substance to prevent any damp penetrating the brick work. Down each arch is a funnel, opening near the bottom, for carrying off the surface water.

February 6 1843. It is currently reported that a railway train, drawn by an engine, is to arrive at the station, but no such thing took place.

February 10 1843. A train drawn by an engine arrived at the Station here.

February 14 1843. Went to the railway viaduct, Lexden, and saw an engine drawing the muck waggons.

February 24 1843. Went to the railway station and saw the directors arrive per rail, accompanied by General Pasley, the Government Inspector, before whose inspection and approval as to tis completeness no railway can be used for public conveyance.

February 27 1843. The town in a state of excitement and the bells ringing in consequence of a report that the railway directors and shareholders were coming by the rail in four carriages drawn by the engine. Went to the station and after waiting there two hours, finding they did not make their appearance, came home, after which it was reported that a bridge at Mountnessing was not considered safe to cross.

Daresay there was two thousand people collected ... And much disappointment prevailed.

March 1 1843. The Railway Directors arrived from London by rail, walked in procession headed by a band of music and flags flying, bells ringing and other demonstrations of joy to the Three Cupps Hotel where they partook of a cold collation.

March 2 1843. No 64 Railway Policeman informed me that luggage trains commenced running this morning for the conveyance of goods to and from London and intermediate stations.

March 15 1843. A party of ladies and gentlemen came down by the rail, the former proceeded to see St Botolph's Priory ... then returned to the station where the two carriages they came in were set out, dinner spread, and they enjoyed it during their return to London.

March 29 1842. Opening of the railway for passengers through to London; the first train . . . left the station at nine o'clock . . . A great number of people went to the station to see the trains arrive and depart.

July 13 1843. Went to the station ... The seven o'clock train, coming at a rate of 25 miles an hour, the brake not answering left it to pursue its rapid course past the station, when it ran into the engine which was standing at the extremity of the rails and drove it down the bank. Providentially no injury was sustained ... except a little fright to the passengers.

In regard to Harwich, the *Chelmsford Chronicle* of 18 November 1842 reported an application had been made to parliament for a Bill to promote and build a railway to that town; the *Essex Herald* of 10 January 1843 reported that there were two parties promoting a railway from Colchester to Harwich. One was for a line from Harwich to Colchester with a branch to the ECR at Lexden and the construction of a pier or jetty at Harwich whilst the other was from Harwich to Colchester to connect directly with the ECR – the HR.

Following the completion of the Railway to Colchester, the leading inhabitants of Chelmsford gave a banquet for the Directors and the Engineer of the Railway in the Assembly Room at the Saracen's Head Hotel in the town on Wednesday, 9 May.

The Royal Mail was soon being carried on the railway from Colchester and the *Essex Standard* of 2 June announced that a mail train would commence running on the railway on 6 July.

Meanwhile, the directors of the Railway were looking at building a branch line from Stratford to the River Thames and in February 1843 had deposited with parliament a bill with plans for such a line. The line was to terminate at the River Thames at its junction with the River Lea and was to be worked by horse traction. The length of the line was about 2¼ miles long. Its sole purpose was to be for the conveyance of coal. The bill received its Royal Assent on 4 July.

Not all the stations on the railway were successful. Forest Gate, which at that time was in open country, was very unsuccessful and does not appear in the Railway's timetables commencing 1 June. The service provided was rather bad, being just one train a day in each direction. The station reopened on 31 May 1846.

In Ingatestone, the inhabitants were unhappy about the fact that they did not have a railway station despite the railway running through the parish. The nearest stations were at Brentwood six miles to the west and at Chelmsford six miles to the east. With the opening of the railway almost all of the coaches which used to travel through the town had ceased to do so. It was not only the inhabitants of Ingatestone who suffered but also those of the nearby parishes of Stock, Buttsbury, the Hanningfields, Margaretting and Fryerning. The cause of the

EASTERN COUNTIES.—Colchester Line—50¼ Miles.

Stations.	3rd cl.	Down Trains.								mail.
Trains leave	a.m.	a.m.	a.m.	3rd cl	p.m	p.m	pm.	p.m	p.m.	p m.
Shoredtch	7 45	8 30	11 0	12 30	2 0	3 0	4 15	5 0	6 30	8 30
Mile End ..	7 50	8 34	..	..	2 4	..	..	..	..	..
Stratford ..	8 3	*	11 11	12 46	2 13	..	4 26	5 11	6 41	8 40
Ilford ..	8 15	8 48	11 18	1 0	2 20	3 16	4 33	5 18	6 48	8 46
Romford....	8 35	9 0	11 30	1 22	2 32	3 28	4 45	5 30	7 0	8 56
Brentwood ..	9 20	9 15	11 45	1 46	2 47	3 43	5 0	5 45	7 15	9 11
Ingatestone	9 40	9 31	Friday	..	..	..	5 16	..	..	9 35
Chelmsford .	10 6	9 44	12 12	2 34	3 14	4 12	5 29	6 12	.	9 49
Hatfield .. .	10 18	..	..	..	3 27	..	..	6 25	..	..
Witham ..	10 40	10 5	12 34	3 10	3 38	4 33	..	6 34	..	10 13
Kelvedon ..	10 58	10 15	12 44	3 26	3 48	4 43	..	6 44	..	10 23
Marks Tey..	11 25	..	..	..	3 58	..	..	6 54	..	..
Colchestr	11 40	10 43	1 11	4 5	4 16	5 11	..	7 15	..	10 49

Stations.	mail.	Up Trains.						3rd cl.		3rd cl.
	a.m.	a.m.	a.m.	a.m.	a.m.	p.m.	p.m.	p.m	p.m	p. m.
Colchstr	2 45		..	9 0	11 0	2 0	4 0	5 0	6 0	7 0
Marks Tey	..	frm Colchester on Mondays at 7 5	..	9 10	..	..	..	5 12	..	..
Kelvedon..	3 10		..	9 22	11 22	2 22	4 22	5 34	6 22	7 36
Witham ..	3 20		..	9 32	11 32	2 32	4 32	5 49	6 32	7 52
Hatfield ..	..		..	9 45	..	..	..	5 58	..	..
Chelmsford	3 45		8 45	9 59	11 54	2 54	4 54	6 24	6 54	8 28
Ingatestone	4 3		8 54	..	12 8	Friday	..	6 50	7 8	..
Brentwood	4 23	8 40	9 10	10 25	12 23	3 22	5 22	7 26	7 23	9 14
Romford ..	4 38	8 56	9 26	10 41	12 39	3 37	5 37	7 53	7 39	9 33
Ilford	4 48	9 6	9 38	..	12 49	3 47	5 47	8 6	7 50	9 58
Stratford ..	4 54	9 14	9 46	..	*	3 55	5 55	8 34	7 58	10 14
Mile End	..	..	9 52	..	*	..	..	..	8 4	..
Shordtch	5 4	9 27	10 3	11 11	1 11	4 11	6 11	8 50	8 15	10 35

On Sundays.—From London to Colchester, 8½ a.m., 4, & 8½ p.m.; to Brentwood, 9¾ a.m., and 2 p.m. From Colchester to London, 2¾ & 8½ a.m., and 6 p.m.; from Brentwood, 1 and 7 p.m.—* On Wednesdays only.

Stations.	FARES.—From London. 1st clss.	2nd clss	3rd clss.	From Colchester 1st clss.	2nd clss	3rd clss.
	s. d.	s d.	s. d.	s. d.	s. d.	s. d.
LONDON	..	..	..	12 6	9 6	4 3
Stratford	0 9	0 7	0 4	11 9	8 10	3 11
Ilford................	1 4	1 0	0 7	11 2	8 6	3 8
Romford	2 6	1 9	1 0	10 0	7 9	3 3
Brentwood	3 6	2 9	1 6	9 0	6 9	2 9
Ingatestone	5 6	4 6	2 0	7 0	5 0	2 3
Chelmsford	7 0	5 0	2 6	5 6	4 6	1 9
Hatfield	8 0	5 9	2 11	4 6	3 9	1 4
Witham	9 0	6 6	3 2	3 6	3 0	1 1
Kelvedon..	10 0	7 6	3 6	2 6	2 0	0 9
Colchester	12 6	9 6	4 3	..	..	..

The timetable of the ECR Colchester line for July 1845 taken from *Bradshaw's Railway Guide* for that month. Note that only some trains carried third class passengers and that some trains only called at some stations on certain days of the week. (Author's collection).

failure of the railway to provide a station was a difference of opinion between Lord Petre and the Company, according to the *Essex Standard* of 21 July 1843. A public meeting attended by about sixty people was held in the Spread Eagle on 22nd of July. There was a debate as to where the station should be with some favouring Hall Lane and some Stock Lane. At a show of hands, Stock Lane came out first by twenty-two votes to twelve. The following week, the *Standard* quoted the part of the Eastern Counties' act which gave cause to the contention. What it said was that Lord Petre's consent was needed for the erection of a station at Ingatestone. The *Essex Standard* of 25 August carried a letter from Lord Petre saying why he felt that the station should be in Hall Lane rather than Stock Lane, his argument being that it was better to have a station on the level in Hall Lane than in a cutting as in Stock Lane and for that reason he refused his consent for the station to be in the latter place. He said that a memorandum had been signed by the principal inhabitants of Ingatestone asking for the station to be in Hall Lane and added that he offered to give the Railway half an acre of land to erect a station in Hall Lane but the Directors refused the offer. The Railway Company then erected two long platforms and stairs in the cutting in Stock Lane. Lord Petre said that he was then compelled to obtain an injunction ordering the Company to remove the platforms and the stairs and to pay the costs to dissolve the injunction. The dispute carried on into September. The *Chelmsford Chronicle* of 22 September carried a letter from Richard Hall, the Manager of the ECR, in which he said that the Directors of the Company were unaware of a stipulation that the station at Ingatestone had to be in Hall Lane and that it was permissive but not compulsory. According to the letter, trains were stopping at the station in Stock Lane. Hall also said that the Station Clerk at Ingatestone had said that, since 1 August, no goods or parcels had been taken or delivered to Ingatestone by train. From the time of trains stopping at Ingatestone to 1 August, only six small parcels had been delivered by train. The injunction was dissolved following an affidavit made by the Station Clerk confirming that the injunction was dissolved. Although not mentioned as such, it is clear that access to the railway at Ingatestone was rather perilous and it seems that Lord Petre had made things rather awkward – and dangerous, as a letter to the *Essex Standard* of 3 November states. According to the letter, it was highly dangerous particularly in wet weather and impossible for women without the assistance of men friends. The letter, which was signed by 'One of the People', placed the blame on Lord Petre. It appears from other sources that there was no proper stairway to the line from Stock Lane. Tickets were sold in one of the former Petre Almshouses. When the railway was built, some of the almshouses had to be demolished and new ones erected elsewhere in Ingatestone. Lord Petre, having given land to the railway, was very determined by all means that the station should be where he wanted it.

At least Lord Petre allowed the public to use Ingatestone station. Sir John Tyssen Tyrell, who lived at Boreham House about 3½ miles east of Chelmsford, had his own private station built for him, which opened when the line was extended to Colchester in 1843 and not infrequently exercised his rights wrested from the ECR as part of his compensation to stop any train at will.

It is in mid-August that we find the first mention of the ECR taking a lease of the N&ER and working the latter with a view to reducing operating costs. The *Chelmsford Chronicle* of 25 August reported that the directors of the former had been in communication with the latter about this. The *Chelmsford Chronicle* of 13 October reported that the ECR was going to take a lease in perpetuity on the N&ER. The *Essex Standard* of 20 October reported that at a special general meeting of the proprietors of the ECR, negotiations had proceeded so far for an amalgamation of the interests of both companies on an equal footing. The terms of the proposed amalgamation had been approved by both Boards and had been signed by them conditionally that the sanction of the proprietors of both companies be obtained ratifying the arrangement. Under the lease, two thirds of the profits would go to the ECR Company and one third to the Northern and Eastern Company,

The second Ingatestone station opened at its current location in 1844. The location of the station was determined by the insistence of the then Lord Petre who had given land to the ECR to build the railway. The station is an architectural gem. (Author).

the Board to consist of twelve ECR directors and six Northern and Eastern directors. On 25 October at a meeting of the shareholders of the ECR at Shoreditch station to consider the amalgamation, or rather the lease, was approved. The *Essex Standard* of 28 November reported that an application was to be made to parliament in the ensuing session to alter, amend, change and extend the provisions of several Acts relating to the ECR and the N&ER, including to enable the former to lease the latter either for a term of years or in perpetuity. The *Essex Standard* of 3 November reported that the ECR and N&ERs had agreed to amalgamate the meetings of their special boards on 1 November. Notices appeared in newspapers in November announcing the intention of the ECR to apply to parliament to make an act enabling it to lease the N&ER. The *Hertford Mercury and Reformer* of 30 December reported that the amalgamation of the two railways would take place on 1 January 1844.

The provision of a hotel at Shoreditch station came up at the end of September. The *Chelmsford Chronicle* of 29 September said that it understood that an extensive hotel was to be erected at the Shoreditch terminus of the ECR. The idea for a hotel seems to have dated back to the meeting of the Board of the Railway in February 1842 when the Board resolved that the Manager and the Engineer applied to the 'most likely parties' to erect a hotel at the London terminus. No one seems to have been found, so in April 1843 the Committee of Management was given full powers to make arrangements with a view to erecting a hotel and opening it. Although a contractor to do the job was found by May of that year, he must have regretted the error of this and started using delaying tactics, saying that there were unspecified difficulties in the construction of the hotel. The Board was clearly upset and told him to get on with the job or withdraw. He did the latter. Some years later, in 1849, a Mr Bacon was proposing to lease a hotel to be erected at Shoreditch, but nothing came of this.

Soon after the opening of the Railway, it was realised that goods traffic provided the means of acquiring much needed income and so a small site was acquired at what was then Hare Street, but later became Cheshire Street and Duncombe Street and the north side of the viaduct into Shoreditch about 700 yards east of the terminus. The name of the goods station was Brick Lane, although it was not situated in Brick Lane as that was several streets westwards.

An interesting side piece is a mention of a steam excavator being used on the ECR quoted in the *Essex Herald* of 26 September. The *Herald* quotes what seems like an American newspaper, *Galignani's Messenger*, which uses the word Railroad as opposed to Railway. This suggests that the machine in question was used prior to the completion of the railway to Colchester. Possibly the newspaper article in question was referring to events of earlier in the year.

It was at this time that the ECR first officially heard about the proposed Eastern Union Railway (EUR) which intended to build a line from Colchester via Ipswich to Norwich with branches to Bury St Edmunds and Harwich Harbour. Following a meeting held at Ipswich on 8 August to promote the formation of a railway company to build a line beyond Colchester, at which a Provisional Committee was formed for this purpose, a letter was sent by the Mayor of Ipswich to the

Board of Directors of the ECR annexing the resolutions passed at the meeting of 8 August and requesting that they nominate any gentleman from their number to be added to the Provisional Committee. The ECR replied that the communication would be laid before the next monthly meeting of the Board of Directors. The Directors' reply to the Provisional Committee was to refuse the invitation to nominate a Director to the Provisional Committee and they added that a line of railway from Colchester through or near Hadleigh and Bury St Edmunds (to Thetford) with a branch to Ipswich would best unite and promote all interests and hoped that they, the ECR, would have the support and assistance of the Ipswich interests. Although the Railway had no intention of going further than Colchester it had purchased land as far as Ardleigh, four miles beyond Colchester.

The Harwich Railway came up in late October 1843. On 24 October there was a meeting in Harwich town to discuss the Railway. A company having been formed, at the meeting there was much discussion about whether the proposed railway should be leased to and worked by the ECR or not, the consensus being that it should be. The *Essex Standard* of 28 November recorded that an application was to be made to parliament to enable the company to construct the Railway.

It was in November that the ECR along with the N&ER first thought about changing its gauge from 5ft to 4ft 8½in, which was the gauge of most other railways north and south of the Thames other than the Great Western which had a gauge of 7ft ¼in. The *Chelmsford Chronicle* of the 10th of the month quotes the *Railway Magazine* as being the source of this. The only other railway in the vicinity of the ECR and N&ERs having a gauge of 5ft was the L&BR, which at that time did not connect with either.

The proposed ECR line via Hadleigh and Bury was naturally of concern to the embryonic Eastern Union. The *Bury and Norwich Post* of Wednesday, 15 November reported that the Provisional Committee of the Railway had held a meeting in Ipswich on 'Saturday week' at which a motion was passed which was deprecatory of the Hadleigh and Bury line as injurious to the trade of Ipswich and that it was the duty of the Town Council and its inhabitants to prevent the line being built. At the meeting it was resolved to apply for powers to build the Railway as far as Ipswich. The same newspaper reported the previous Thursday that the Ipswich Dock Commissioners held a special meeting at which a motion was passed opposing the carrying through in parliament of any railway which would in their opinion have the effect of diminishing the returns of the Dock Commissioners.

The *Essex Standard* of Friday, 22 December reported that on Wednesday, 13 December there had been a meeting held in Bury St Edmunds in support of the proposed ECR's line from Colchester to Norwich through Bury St Edmunds. The *Ipswich Journal* of 30 December reported the ECR had abandoned its proposed railway from Colchester to Norwich via Bury St Edmunds.

The N&ER originated with a project for a railway from London to York via Cambridge and Lincoln with a branch from Cambridge to Norwich. The London terminus was to be in Islington. Unfortunately, the Company's Act of Incorporation, which received its Royal Assent on the same day the ECR's Act received its Royal Assent, only authorised the construction of the Railway as far as Cambridge. Even this proved too much for the Company and it was also forced to abandon the section between Tottenham and Islington and, having first thought of building a line from the former place to join the L&BR, instead decided to divert its line to join the ECR at Stratford. The Act authorising this received its Royal Assent on 19 July 1839. In joining the ECR at Stratford, the N&ER was forced to adopt the 5ft gauge of the former Company. As the L&BR was also built to the gauge of 5ft, had the N&ER built a connecting line to that Railway it would still have to adopt that gauge. As the L&BR was at that time using cable haulage, it would entail N&ER trains using that method of propulsion between its junction with the former Railway and its London terminus. Bishop's Stortford had now become the intended northern terminus of the railway.

Robert Stephenson, who had succeeded James Walker (the original Engineer of the N&ER) as the Engineer of the Company, had somewhat different ideas from John Braithwaite of the ECR and did not make allowance for conversion of the Railway to a wider gauge. Whereas on the latter railway, the Up and Down tracks were 6ft 5in apart and a space of 6ft 9½in on each side of the tracks thus forming a roadbed with a total width of 30ft on the former, there was a space of only 5ft on each side of the outer rails so that the total width of the roadbed was only 26ft 5in.

It was not until the spring of 1838 that work on building the Railway started. This is implied by an advertisement for the lease of property land at Puckeridge quoted in the *Cambridge Chronicle and Journal* of 5 May which said that the first stage of constructing the railway was in progress. The *Huntingdon, Peterborough and Bedford Gazette* of the same day was more precise, quoting the (original) *Railway Magazine* which said that work had started on 19 March between Broxbourne and Tottenham Mills and that on 23 April the contractor had laid two miles of railway and that notices for the contract to continue the line to Bishop's Stortford had been given.

By the end of October 1839, work on building the Railway had progressed to the point where, according to the *Essex Standard* of 1 November, the line from Tottenham Mills to Broxbourne was complete except for one half of the ballasting for receiving the permanent way. Work at the Stratford end of the line seems to have been started in the spring of 1840 as the *Essex Standard* of 1 April that year says that the Company had started their works at the intended junction with the ECR. According to the *Hertford Mercury and Reformer* of 9 May, 500 men and 36 boys were employed in building the line to Stratford.

Although the N&ER was no longer interested in getting to Cambridge, even before construction had started the idea of connecting it to Hertford had been mooted. In the summer of 1836, there had been a proposal for a Hertfordshire Grand Union Railway to connect the London and Birmingham Railway (L&BR) to the N&ER

by way of the towns of Watford, St Albans, Hatfield, Hertford and Ware. However, nothing came of that scheme.

The idea of connecting Hertford to the N&ER did not die, as the *Essex Herald* of 24 December 1839, quoting the *Herts Reformer*, reported that the subject of promoting a line to connect the towns of Hertford and Ware with the N&ER had again been mooted and that some steps had been taken to promote it.

Things moved fairly fast as the *Hertford Mercury and Reformer* of 14 March 1840 reported that notice had been given to parliament that it was intended to bring forward a Bill in the following session for making and maintaining a railway from Hoddesdon on the N&ER to Hertford.

The *Hertford Mercury and Reformer* of 15 August 1840 reported that the Railway would be open from Bishopsgate Street to Broxbourne on 15 September and that proposals had been made by a separate company to build a railway from Broxbourne to Hertford at an estimated cost of £50,000, but that at that point nothing had been decided. On Tuesday, 15 September the Railway was opened from Stratford to Broxbourne. The event was recorded in all the local newspapers, the *Hertford Mercury and Reformer* giving a good description of the Railway. The opening of the Railway reduced the time between London and Cambridge by 1½ hours.

An account of an accident to an N&ER train on 23 September recorded in the *Chelmsford Chronicle* of the 25th of the month gives a little insight in to how trains of the Railway were worked over the ECR between London and Stratford. According to the *Chronicle*, as a matter of accommodation the ECR locomotives worked some of the early N&ER trains to Stratford combined with the former Company's trains where the Northern and Eastern Company's locomotives took them over. On the day in question, the first train of the day was worked to Stratford in that manner and when it was about a quarter of a mile from Stratford, the Eastern Counties' locomotive and carriages were detached from the Northern and Eastern's carriages and the former proceeded on its journey. That part of the railway was on a 1 in 300 incline. The detached train as usual travelled for some distance by gravity and its own velocity and, the points having being changed immediately once the ECR train had passed over them, the Northern and Eastern train went on to the lines of the latter company. In this instance, the driver of the Northern and Eastern locomotive placed his locomotive too near to the points and disregarding the instructions of the train's guard to move forward as the latter could see that a collision was going to take place, the carriages hit the locomotive with a violent crash. Although some of the passengers were slightly bruised, none was seriously injured and shortly afterwards the train proceeded on its journey. The blame for the accident rested with the engine driver for the placing his engine too near to the points and disregarding the guard's signal.

At Stratford, the locomotives were maintained at the Robert Stephenson-designed Polygon, a roundhouse which had been built between July and September 1840. The Stratford works can be said to have begun at this point, after which the ECR moved its locomotive maintenance to Stratford, from its workshops at Romford, in 1848. Presumably, there was a period between 1844, when the ECR took over the working of the N&ER, and the move in 1848 when locomotives were maintained at two workshops. At the beginning of 1841, the idea of building a branch railway off the N&ER to Hertford took a step further. According to the *Cambridge Chronicle and Journal* of 30 January, the Company intended to make an application to parliament for leave to bring forward a Bill to construct and maintain a railway from Hoddesdon to Hertford. The *Hertford Mercury and Reformer* of 6 February carried a notice dated 28 January which said that plans and sections of the proposed branch had been deposited with the Clerk of the Peace for Hertfordshire at St Albans.

The idea of extending the line beyond Bishop's Stortford to Cambridge, Norwich and Yarmouth had been considered at a meeting held in London on 30 December 1840 and a Company was formed for this purpose at the meeting. On 7 January, a large meeting was held in Norwich to consider the expediency of constructing the Railway and a committee was formed to take into consideration the plans and specifications of John Rastrick, the engineer of the proposed railway, and report to a further meeting. The fact that a company had been formed at the London meeting was not mentioned. The *Norwich Mercury* of 30 January carried a copy of the report of the committee about the proposed railway in which they said that they had been in contact with the N&ER and urged the county of Norfolk not to support any company which would not undertake to carry out the whole of the line from Bishop's Stortford to Yarmouth. By the middle of February things had advanced to the point where the Railway had decided to apply to parliament for powers to extend its line beyond Bishop's Stortford to Cambridge and the *Hertford Mercury and Reformer* of the 20th of the month carried a notice to this effect. According to the *Essex Herald* of the 23rd of the month, at the General Meeting of the Company held on the 18th, the report of the Company said that application was going to be made to parliament to enable the Railway to construct and maintain a branch railway to Ware and Hertford and a survey had been directed to be made from Bishop's Stortford to Cambridge. Meanwhile, the *Cambridge Chronicle* of the 20th carried an announcement from the East Anglian Railway that it intended to apply to parliament to build a railway from Bishop's Stortford to Great Yarmouth via Cambridge and Norwich. The *Hertford Mercury and Reformer* of 27 February carried a notice dated the 13th of the month for a proposed railway from London to York which would have connected with the N&ER.

There was severe flooding in the Leytonstone marshes effecting the Railway at the beginning of 1841 and according to the *Essex Standard* of 22 January, for a time the trains were suspended. The *Standard* said that the damage caused could not have been anticipated by the engineers of the Railway. The flooding caused a depression in the embankment between Lea Bridge and the ECR, which had caused the sleepers to come adrift from the ballast. During the time that the trains were suspended, the Company provided conveyances for the passengers who used the Railway.

There were still problems with getting the Hertford branch into Hertford and a public meeting was held in the town on Saturday, 5 June to ensure that it did happen. According to the Mayor, who took the chair, there had been an endeavour in the Commons to stop the line going further than Ware. Fortunately, this had been frustrated. The bill was now with the House of Lords and would come up the following week. Mr J.M. Carter moved that a petition be delivered to the House of Lords making it compulsory to take the railway into Hertford. The resolution was passed unanimously. Its Act was passed in June 1841.

There was a further opening in August. The *Essex Standard* of 30 July, amongst other newspapers, said that the line to Harlow would be opened on 9 August and according to the *Cambridge Independent Press* of the 14th, the extension of the line was opened on the day in question, the *Essex Standard* of the previous day reporting that the occasion attracted a large number of people to the station. The day passed without incident.

At the General Meeting of the company on 19 August, a report was read which said that the company intended to have works to Spelbrook completed early in October. Several newspapers in September announced that the opening to Spelbrook, which was two miles from Bishop's Stortford, would take place then. It was not to be, as the *Essex Standard* of 8 October reported that the opening to Spelbrook would take place the following month. According to the *Essex Standard* of Friday, 26 November, the Railway opened to Spelbrook the previous Tuesday, but the *Cambridge Independent Press* of the following day says that the opening took place on the previous Monday. The latter date is borne out by the *Norfolk Chronicle* of Saturday, 20 November which stated that the opening of the Railway to Spelbrook would take place on Monday 22nd.

There was a meeting in Cambridge on 14 January 1842 to consider the various proposals for railway communication to the town. At the end of the meeting, a vote was carried in favour of John Rastrick's line, mentioned earlier. The *Essex Standard* of 11 November reported that a survey to connect Norwich to Cambridge so as to connect with London by means of the N&ER was in progress but that there were several landowners who opposed the scheme.

It is clear that there were problems regarding tolls on the conveyance of goods traffic over the ECR. It would seem that when the Railway opened to Stratford and thence worked over the ECR into Shoreditch station, only passenger trains were allowed. At a meeting of the Railway Company in early February 1842, it was reported that negotiations were afoot with the ECR about the conveyance of goods to the London terminus. It is also clear that the terms that the latter offered the N&ER for access to its London terminus were of concern as, according to the meeting, although the latter company would not take part in the construction of a west end branch, the fact of it being built by others would show a prospect of competition as would bring the ECR to reasonable terms. At a meeting of the ECR reported in the *Chelmsford Chronicle* of 26 August, it was reported that the N&ER were to rent and convert at their own expense for their goods traffic a number of arches in the Brick Lane viaduct. There also seems to have been problems in regard to the short distance traffic from Ponders End to London in regard to omnibus competition. According to the report, an arrangement was also made to secure this traffic. On 19 January 1843, the N&ER started running goods and cattle trains to Shoreditch.

According to the *Chelmsford Chronicle* of 29 April 1842, amongst the bills before parliament was one extending the N&ER to Cambridge. Another notice to this effect appeared in the *Bury and Norwich Post* of 16 November. The notice also mentioned the formation of a railway from Norwich to Cambridge via Thetford and Mildenhall. Obviously not everyone was happy with the extension of the railway and particularly from Cambridge to Norwich and according to the *Cambridge Chronicle and Journal* of Saturday, 17 December 1842, 'At a congregation on Thursday last, the following grace passed the

Senate: – "To affix the University Seal to a notice of dissent to the proposed extension of the N&ER."' The proposed route of the line passed through a field purchased by the University for the purpose of forming a new botanical garden. If the dissent was effectual, it would not interrupt the proposed line from Trumpington to Norwich.

On 16 May 1842, the Railway was opened from Spellbrook to Bishop's Stortford. According to the *Chelmsford Chronicle* of 27 May, no parade was made and only ordinary passenger trains were run. In the evening the directors and officers of the Company dined together.

The *Hertford Mercury and Reformer* of 11 June expressed concern about the lack of interest in making a branch railway to Hertford and said that it was about time that there was another meeting to induce the directors of the railway to carry out their intention of building the railway there. According to a report in the same newspaper of 27 August of a half yearly meeting of the Company, a Mr Crawshaw, who was the previous Chairman of the Company, proposed that the Company be leased, to whom he did not say. Amongst other things he said that the Directors of the Company should complete the Ware and Hertford branch within twelve months. The announcement took the meeting by surprise and the Chairman said that a special meeting could be called to discuss the matter. The meeting to discuss this and the sale of 3,186 forfeited shares took place on 7 September. At the meeting, the proprietors were in favour of leasing the Railway for a term of years and formed a committee. At a meeting of the shareholders on 5 October to receive the report of the committee, it was decided against any further negotiations on the subject of a lease. On the subject of the Ware and Hertford branch, it was said that that was in abeyance because of a lack of funds.

At a meeting of the Directors of the Railway on 14 February 1843, adjourned from a meeting held on the 9th of the month, authorisation was given for the Railway to be extended from Bishop's Stortford to Newport in Essex, a distance of 9½ miles and which was 16¾ miles short of Cambridge. The same meeting also authorised the construction of the Ware and Hertford branch. As the Hertford branch had already been authorised by parliament, all that was needed was authorisation by parliament for the Railway to build the extension to Newport and various newspapers carried a notice of the Company's intention to bring to parliament a bill authorising it to do so. The decision to only extend to Newport did not please everyone, including the inhabitants of Saffron Walden who, wishing to get a station as near to the town as possible, held a meeting in March of 1843 which resulted in the appointment of a committee to effect that object. On 23 March there was a public meeting in Cambridge principally to support the proposal for a railway from Blisworth on the L&BR to Peterborough but also to ensure additional support to the extension of the N&ER from Bishop's Stortford to Cambridge and northwards to Peterborough. At the meeting, a resolution put forward by the Mayor of Cambridge and seconded by the Master of Clare Hall that the extension of the N&ER to the town would be of great benefit to the landed and trading interests of Cambridgeshire and of great convenience to its inhabitants was passed. On 31 May, the bill for the Railway's extension to Newport received the Royal Assent. According to the *Chelmsford Chronicle* of 30 June, it was stated that it had now been arranged for the Railway to build to Cambridge and thence to Ely, from which it was expected that a branch would be built to Norwich. The *Cambridge Chronicle and Journal* of 3 June reported that in the debate in the House of Lords on the 1st of the month on the Northampton and Peterborough Railway bill, the Marquis of Salisbury had presented a petition against the bill from the N&ER. The *Cambridge Independent Press* of 15 July said arrangements had been made for bringing the N&ER to Cambridge. The *Ipswich Journal* of 19 August said a different thing. According to the *Journal*, the N&ER showed no anxiety to extend its railway to Cambridge. By the end of September we find that things had changed, as the *Cambridge Independent Press* announced that a special general meeting of the Company would be held on 25 October for the purpose of determining the expediency of applying to parliament for powers to extend the Railway from Newport to Cambridge and thence to Brandon in Norfolk where it would join, according to newspaper reports, an extension of the Norwich and Yarmouth Railway by a new company. At the meeting, a scheme would be proposed for raising the money to complete this undertaking. Notices appeared in newspapers in November announcing the intention to put forward to parliament a bill enabling an act to allow the extension to be built.

On the already authorised Ware and Hertford branch, the *Cambridge General Advertiser* of 12 April reported that the Company was preparing to extend the line and that notices had been sent to parties to treat for the properties required for the line. Progress seems to have been quite fast as the *Cambridge Chronicle and Journal* of 13 May reported that the Company had landed sleepers, wagons and materials at different points on the line and would be ready to begin as soon as they had bargained for the land required. Notices had for some weeks previously been sent to owners and occupiers of the property required and it was expected that within a few days, contracts would be arranged so as to allow operations to commence. The *Essex Standard* of 7 July, quoting the *Herts County Press*, said that work on building the Ware and Hertford branch had commenced. The *Essex Herald* of 17 October said that the work on building the branch was progressing very fast and that the workmen were working night and day. It was expected that public trains would start running on the 30th of the month, or at the latest, 6 November. The branch line to Hertford was opened on 31 October as a single track. The *Herts Mercury and Reformer* of 4 November carried details of the passenger train times.

It was at the beginning of August 1843 that we first hear of the offer made by the ECR to lease the N&ER. According to the *Essex Herald* of the 8th of the month, quoting the *Railway Magazine*, it had heard of the offer which had promptly been rejected by the latter Company. It understood that the offer would be very advantageous to the Company. According to the *Chelmsford Chronicle* of 18 August, it was at the half yearly meeting of the Company held on the 10th of the month that the offer of the lease had been received and had been rejected. The ECR version was given at the half yearly meeting of the Company on the 24th. At the meeting, the Chairman said the offer had been made with a view to reducing the cost of working its line. As mentioned in connection with the ECR, a meeting of that company was held on 25 October. The N&ER had held a meeting on the 12th of that month at which the proposed union and amalgamation (as it was termed) of the Railway with the ECR was discussed. According to a report on it the union and amalgamation had been conditionally approved by the boards of both companies, but the sanction of the proprietors might be obtained for the arranged lease and that a special meeting would be called for the purpose. As mentioned, it was at the meeting of the Eastern Counties' shareholders that that Company approved the lease. On the same day, a meeting of the N&ER shareholders was held which approved the lease. As mentioned in connection with the ECR, notices appeared in newspapers in November announcing the intention of the ECR to apply to parliament to make an act enabling it to lease the N&ER. The lease took effect from 1 January 1844. Just prior to this, the *Cambridge Independent Press* of 30 December reported that at the united board meeting of the ECR and N&ERs on the 21st of the month, it was determined that the latter's line should be carried forward to Cambridge.

There were hopes in October of a royal journey on the Railway. The *Chelmsford Chronicle* of Friday, 20 October said that the following Wednesday morning the Queen and Prince Albert would leave Windsor Castle and proceed by the GWR to Paddington where a military escort would accompany the royal couple to the terminus of the N&ER from which they would proceed to the nearest station to Cambridge, at which town they were expected to arrive at between two and three o'clock. The *Cambridge Chronicle and Journal* of the 21st said that from Bishop's Stortford, the royal couple would proceed in carriages. After a reception by the University and Town Council the royal couple would spend the night in Cambridge and the following day, after spending time in the town during which Prince Albert would be presented with an honorary degree, would leave the town for Wimpole, the seat of Lord Hardwicke, where they would stay until Saturday after which they would repeat the journey to Windsor, travelling, it was believed, by the Northern and Eastern and Great Western railways. Unfortunately, there was a change of plan and the royal couple did not use the N&ER on their journey to Cambridge. The route that was chosen was reckoned to be quicker. Understandably, the directors of the Railway were not very happy about this as they had started preparation for conveying the royal couple in suitable style.

As mentioned in connection with the ECR, it was in November that that railway and the N&ER first contemplated changing their gauge from 5ft to 4ft 8½in.

On 1 January 1844, the ECR took over the N&ER on a lease. For some time following this, the Company still remained active in the promotion of an extension. According to the *Bedfordshire Mercury* of 6 January 1844, an application was to be made by the Company in the ensuing session of parliament for an extension of the Railway to Cambridge and Ely to Brandon to join the Norwich and Brandon Railway with a branch from Ely to Peterborough from the already authorised extension from Bishop's Stortford to Newport. Unfortunately, things did not go quite to plan. Both Bills were passed by the House of Commons on 6 May. It was reported that the Bill for the ECR leasing the N&ER had been passed by the House of Lords. The Brandon and Peterborough Extension Bill was however opposed and as there was a possibility of both parties reaching a settlement, consideration of the Bill by the House of Lords was postponed. What happened was that, by mistake, the second Bill instead of the first Bill was included in the list of Bills to be given the Royal Assent on 10 May and so the wrong Bill received the Royal Assent. This necessitated a new Bill to rectify the mistake by annulling the Brandon and Peterborough Bill and providing

Sec., A. Bulkeley, Shoreditch, London. **EASTERN COUNTIES—Cambridge Line.** Engr., R. Stephenson.

	Down Trains	1	3 Cls.	Exp.	4	5	6	7	8	9	10	Fares.		
Mls	Trains leave	a.m	a.m.	a.m.	a.m.	a.m.	p.m.	p.m	p.m	p.m	p.m	1st C.	2d C	3d C.
	Shoreditch..	8 0	9 0	9 15	9 30	11 30	3 30	4 30	5 30	7 0	8 30	s. d.	s. d.	s. d.
$3\frac{3}{4}$	Stratford	8 8	9 12	..	9 38	..	3 38	..	5 38	7 8	8 38	0 9	0 7	0 4
$5\frac{3}{4}$	Lea Bridge	..	9 20	..	9 44	..	..	..	5 45	7 14	..	0 10	0 8	0 6
$7\frac{3}{4}$	Tottenham	8 17	9 28	..	9 49	11 45	3 47	..	5 49	7 19	8 47	0 10	0 8	0 8
9	Marsh Lane	..	9 34	..	..	..	..	..	5 53	..	..	0 10	0 9	0 9
$9\frac{1}{2}$	Edmonton......	..	9 38	..	9 54	..	..	..	5 56	7 25	..	1 0	0 10	0 10
$11\frac{3}{4}$	Ponder's End ..	8 27	9 47	..	10 1	11 55	3 57	..	6 3	7 32	8 57	1 3	1 0	1 0
$14\frac{1}{2}$	Waltham	8 34	9 58	..	10 10	12 2	4 4	4 58	6 10	7 40	9 6	2 0	1 6	1 3
19	**Broxbourne**	8 44	10 10	..	10 21	12 13	4 15	5 9	6 23	7 50	9 17	3 6	2 6	1 7
22	Saint Margaret's	..	10 30	..	10 34	..	4 28	5 22	..	8 10	..	4 6	3 6	1 10
$24\frac{1}{4}$	Ware	9 4	10 35	..	10 39	12 33	4 33	5 31	..	8 15	9 37	4 6	3 8	2 0
26	Hertford ..	9 10	10 42	..	10 46	12 40	4 40	5 38	..	8 22	9 44	5 0	4 0	2 2
22	Roydon	8 54	10 36	..	..	12 22	..	5 18	..	..	9 27	4 6	3 6	1 10
$24\frac{1}{2}$	Burnt Mill	..	10 45	..	..	..	..	5 25	..	..	..	5 0	3 9	2 1
$26\frac{1}{4}$	Harlow	9 5	10 56	..	..	12 31	4 33	5 31	..	..	9 37	5 6	4 0	2 3
$28\frac{1}{2}$	Sawbridgeworth	..	11 7	about	10 44	..	..	..	..	8 11	..	6 0	4 6	2 5
$32\frac{1}{4}$	**Stortford....**	9 19	11 22	10 0	10 54	12 45	4 47	5 45	..	8 23	9 53	7 0	5 6	2 8

	Up Trains.	1	2	3	4	Exp.	6	7	8	3Cl.	10	Fares.		
Mls	Trains leave	a.m.	a.m.	a.m.	a.m.	a.m.	a.m.	p.m.	p.m	p.m	p.m.	1 C	2 C.	3 C
	Stortford....	6 15	..	8 15	9 30	11 0	11 30	2 30	4 30	5 40	6 15	s.d	s.d.	s.d.
$3\frac{3}{4}$	Sawbridgeworth	..	..	8 23	..	..	..	..	..	5 55	..	1 3	1 0	0 4
6	Harlow	..	..	8 28	9 41	..	11 41	2 41	4 41	6 6	6 26	1 8	1 6	0 6
$7\frac{3}{4}$	Burnt Mill......	..	..	..	9 46	..	..	..	..	6 16	..	2 0	1 6	0 8
$10\frac{1}{4}$	Roydon	..	..	8 40	9 52	..	11 50	..	4 50	6 25	..	2 6	2 0	0 11
$16\frac{1}{4}$	Hertford	..	..	8 30	9 40	..	11 40	2 35	4 30	6 0	6 25	3 6	3 0	..
$15\frac{3}{4}$	Ware	..	..	8 34	9 44	..	11 44	2 39	4 34	6 10	6 29	3 6	3 0	..
14	Saint Margaret's	..	..	..	9 48	..	..	2 43	4 42	6 20	6 33	3 6	3 0	..
$13\frac{1}{4}$	**Broxbourne**	6 44	7 50	8 50	10 3	..	12 1	2 59	5 1	6 35	6 44	3 6	3 0	1 2
$17\frac{3}{4}$	Waltham	6 53	8 0	8 59	10 13	..	12 11	3 9	5 11	7 5	6 54	5 0	4 0	1 6
$20\frac{1}{2}$	Ponder's End ..	..	8 8	9 7	10 21	..	..	3 17	5 19	7 14	7 2	5 9	4 6	1 9
$22\frac{3}{4}$	Edmonton......	..	8 15	9 14	..	..	12 24	..	..	7 22	..	6 0	4 8	1 11
$23\frac{1}{4}$	Marsh Lane	..	..	9 17	..	..	..	..	..	7 26	..	6 3	4 10	2 0
$24\frac{1}{2}$	Tottenham	..	8 21	9 22	10 32	..	..	..	5 30	7 32	7 15	6 3	4 10	2 1
$26\frac{1}{2}$	Lea Bridge	..	8 26	9 27	..	..	..	..	5 35	7 40	..	6 3	4 10	2 3
$28\frac{1}{2}$	Stratford	7 15	8 31	9 33	10 40	about	12 37	3 35	5 40	7 48	7 22	6 6	5 0	2 5
$32\frac{1}{4}$	**Shoreditch..**	7 25	8 43	9 45	10 52	11 45	12 49	3 47	5 52	8 0	7 34	7 0	5 6	2 8

Sundays.—London to Hertford and Stortford 9 a.m. third class, $2\frac{1}{2}$, and $8\frac{1}{2}$ p.m. From Stortford to London $6\frac{1}{4}$, and $8\frac{1}{2}$ a.m. third class, and 6 p.m. From Hertford 8 40 a.m. and 6 10 p.m.; stopping at all the stations except the $6\frac{1}{4}$ a.m. up train. All the Sunday trains have second class open carriages attached.

Alterations.—These arrangements, together with those of the Colchester Line, will change on the 8th instant, in consequence of an extended opening of the Line from Bishop Stortford to Cambridge and Norwich.

LONDON AND BLACKWALL.

Sec., J. F. Kennell. Supt., A. Wightman.

Trains every day to and from London and Blackwall, and the intermediate stations of Cannon-street road, Shadwell, Stepney, Limehouse, West India Docks, and Poplar, every quarter of an hour from $7\frac{1}{2}$ a.m. until 10 p.m.

FARES.—first class 6d., 2nd class, 4d.

Passengers may take tickets at the Fenchurch-street, Minories, Cannon-street, Shadwell, and Stepney stations, for Woolwich, 1st class 10d; 2nd class 8d.: such tickets being available by the boats of the Woolwich and Watermen Companies.

On **Sundays** the trains cease running from $10\frac{1}{2}$ till 1, being the hours of church service.

Fast Steamboats start for Gravesend frequently throughout the day.

South Eastern,

GREENWICH BRANCH.

The trains run each way every ¼ of an hour from 8 a.m. till 10 p.m.; on Sundays from 8 till ¼ to 11, and from ¼ past 1 till 11.

FARES.—1st class 8d.; 2nd class 6d.; 3rd class 4d.; and if with return ticket, 1st class 1s. 2nd class 10d.

Annual Tickets may be had on the following terms:—1st class, £10 10s.; 2nd class, £7 7s.

An extra train leaves London at a ¼ past 10 p.m. calling at all the stations.

The timetable of the ECR Cambridge line for July 1845 just prior to the opening from Bishop's Stortford to Cambridge, Ely and Norwich, taken from *Bradshaw's Railway Guide* for that month. Also the timetable for the L&BR. (Author's collection).

that the Bill for the lease on the N&ER receiving the Royal Assent be effective from 10 May. Both the rectifying Act and the leasing Act were obtained on 23 May, whilst the Act for the extensions to Brandon and to Peterborough received the Royal Assent on 4 July. Under the terms of the lease, the whole of the rolling stock of the N&ER was taken over by the ECR.

Meanwhile work on extending the N&ER to Newport was well under way in January 1844, as the *Chelmsford Chronicle* of the 26th of the month reported, the works were proceeding with great rapidity in Stansted Mountfitchet, Elsenham and Birchanger. The *Bury and Norwich Post* of 3 April reported that works on the extension of the Railway from Bishop's Stortford to Newport would commence on the 23rd day of the month and it was expected to be open in March the following year. This contradicts what the *Chelmsford Chronicle* of 26 January said about the construction of the extension.

In building the Railway to Cambridge, Ely and Brandon Lord Braybrooke, the owner of the Manor at Audley End, insisted that there would be two tunnels. These were at Audley End (456 yards) and Littlebury (407 yards) and were separated by an open section of 352 yards. The tunnels are little more than enclosed cuttings.

The *Chelmsford Chronicle* of 18 April 1845, in a report on the construction of the railway, implied that the construction of the tunnel at Lord Braybrooke's had been a bit of a problem.

The projected extensions to Brandon and Peterborough raised for the first time the question of physical connections with other railways – the Norwich & Brandon Railway at Brandon and the London & Birmingham Railway at Peterborough – and this naturally led to a reconsideration of the gauge question. In Norfolk, the Yarmouth and Norwich Railway, which will be described in the next chapter, opened on 1 May 1844 and the connecting Norwich and Brandon Railway, which received its Act in 1844, were constructed to the gauge of 4ft 8½in. The Act for the London and Birmingham Railway's Blisworth to Peterborough branch line via Northampton had received its Royal assent on 4 July 1843 and (going slightly ahead) was opened to Northampton on 13 May 1845 and Peterborough on 2 June 1845. This was built to the same gauge.

So much store was apparently still set by the 5ft gauge, however, that Robert Stephenson and Braithwaite actually considered the feasibility of altering the Northern & Eastern Railway to the standard gauge, while retaining the 5ft gauge for the ECR line to Colchester and having mixed gauge by laying a third rail down between Stratford and London with a difference of 3½ inches between the gauges! Not surprisingly, Stephenson relates that they 'found it was impracticable to adopt a third rail, when they came to consider the combination of the two gauges in the station at Shoreditch.' In addition, they 'found that the two lines would require two completely separate carrying establishments. We could never make use of the carriages of one line upon the line of the other'. As a result, therefore, Stephenson and Braithwaite presented a report in favour of conversion to the standard gauge, and this course was adopted.

The *Norwich Mercury* of 23 March 1844 reported that the N&ER intended changing their gauge to that of the Yarmouth and Norwich and London and Birmingham railways i.e. the 4ft 8½in gauge.

Work on changing the gauge of the ECR and N&ERs to 4ft 8½in commenced on 5 September 1844 and was completed on 7 October. Prior to the start of the work of converting the gauge of the track, some train alterations were introduced on 2 September. The work of conversion involved one line of rails at a time. Traffic was operated on a single line whilst the adjoining line was being converted. Temporary sidings were constructed to enable trains to pass one another on the single line. Only the Hertford branch was closed whilst the conversion took place, from 23 to 30 September. During that time, a replacement coach service was put on from Broxbourne. The reason for the closure was, as mentioned earlier, that the branch line was only single track and so, unlike the other lines being converted, it was not possible to maintain a service. To maintain the service two sets of locomotives and rolling stock were maintained, one broad gauge and the other converted to narrow gauge for use as soon as the new line was ready. The change-over was made in one night after which the remaining broad gauge stock was converted. Because of their limited size, the conversion merely consisted of altering the wheels and axles of the locomotives and rolling stock. In cases where the wheels and axles could not readily be converted, they were replaced by new ones previously manufactured. The whole conversion was carried out without incident or interruption of the passenger service, although some delays did occur. The goods service was only stopped for two nights. The *Suffolk Chronicle* of 19 October quoted a report in the *Railway Times* which said how well the conversion of the gauge had been carried out without a single loss of life or limb and without stoppage of traffic.

Until the Act for the Regulation of Railway of 1844, there was no obligation for railway companies to provide either seated or covered accommodation for third class passengers. Under the Act, all companies had to run on their lines at least one train a day conveying third class passengers in carriages provided with seats and protection from the weather at a speed of not less than 12 miles per hour, including stoppages and at a fare not exceeding one penny per mile for adults with half fare for children under 12 and children under 3 free. 56lb of luggage was to be allowed without charge. The *Essex Standard* of Friday, 25 October reported that on the previous Monday, the ECR had started running such a train in each direction on the line between London and Colchester. It is clear that second class passengers were not treated very well on the ECR, as the *Essex Standard* of 6 December reported that the Railway had greatly improved its accommodation for these passengers and adopted closed carriages instead of cold and uncomfortable open ones as previously used.

The London terminus at Shoreditch was somewhat inconvenient for the ECR and the N&ER and both companies sought an alternative terminus – even after the former took over the working of the latter. The *Chelmsford Chronicle* of 22 November mentions in a list of projected railways one by the ECR for an extension to Old Street, St Luke's and one by the N&ER from Tottenham to Farringdon Street, Holborn.

It was in November 1844 that we first find mention of George Hudson, who the following year would become Chairman of the ECR. The *Norfolk Chronicle* of 23 November reported that the proposed project for a Cambridge and Lincoln railway had been taken up by the ECR and that Hudson had consented to join them. Six ECR directors had been placed on the committee of the Cambridge and Lincoln. The other Company involved was the Midland Railway (MR). It was possible that two or three Hudson directors would join them in the management.

By the end of 1844, work was progressing well on extending the Railway. The *Norwich Mercury* of 14 December reported that work on connecting the City with the N&ER at Newport near Bishop's Stortford was in such a state of forwardness that the whole line would be open to the public early the next summer. If the predictions of Samuel Peto (the contractor) were correct, the journey time between London and Norwich would be 4½ hours. By the end of January 1845, work was well in hand in the area of Cambridge. The *Chelmsford Chronicle* of 31 January reported that the piers of the bridge over the Paper Mills turnpike were in the process of erection and that the river at the bridge over it had been deepened to allow a tow path inside the timbers which supported the main arch on the Chesterton side of the bridge. From Chesterton to Waterbeach, the rails for the permanent way were being rapidly laid down. It was expected that within a few days, an engine would be on the line to facilitate the work. Everything gave promise of a great portion of the line being opened on 1 July.

On 30 July 1845, the N&ER was opened from Bishop's Stortford to Newport. Beyond Newport to Brandon was opened by the Eastern Counties where a connection was made with the Norfolk Railway. There was now direct railway communication between London and Cambridge and Norwich. The *Chelmsford Chronicle* of 1 August carried a rather lengthy article on the opening of the railway. Other local newspapers appearing shortly after the opening also carried articles of various lengths. The distance from London to Norwich via Cambridge and Ely was 126 miles. There was a service of four trains a day in each direction on Mondays to Saturdays and three trains in each direction on Sundays.

The ornate south portal of Audley End tunnel on the section of line from Bishop's Stortford to Cambridge. The reason for the ornate design was to harmonise with the amenities of the estate of Lord Braybrooke, the owner of Audley End house, whose land the railway passed through. (Author's collection).

A contemporary drawing of Cambridge station at the time of its opening in 1845. According to *Bradshaw's Railway Guide*, the station was served by seven trains a day each way on Mondays to Saturdays and three from London and four to London on Sundays. (Author's collection).

An early illustration of Weddon, later Audley End station. From the illustration it would seem that the up and down platforms were at separate locations as the locomotive is clearly taking water on the down (or is it the up) line. (Author's collection).

Chapter 3

The Yarmouth and Norwich and Norwich and Brandon Railways to the End of July 1845

The failure of the ECR to complete its railway beyond Colchester to Ipswich, Norwich and Yarmouth in mid-1840 led some people in Norwich and Yarmouth to contemplate building a railway between them. The *Norfolk Chronicle* of Saturday, 18 July 1840 carried a notice that an application was intended to be made to parliament to construct and maintain a Norwich and Great Yarmouth Railway which was called the Yarmouth and Norwich Railway. The same newspaper of Saturday, 15 August reported that considerable interest had been shown in the project. On 30 December, a meeting was held at the East India and Colonial Club Room in London for the purpose of establishing a railway from the N&ER at Bishop's Stortford to Cambridge, Newmarket, Thetford and Norwich to Yarmouth. The engineer of the proposed railway was John Rastrick, who was one of the engineers who had worked on the promotion of the London and Brighton Railway, which was then in the course of being constructed. At the end of the meeting, a company was formed to build the railway and a large number of shares were taken up. This railway was called the East Anglian Railway. A meeting of the inhabitants of Thetford on 5 January 1841 declared in favour of the EAR. According to the *Norfolk Chronicle* of 6 March 1841, the plans and books of reference were deposited with the Clerks of the Peace for the counties of Norfolk, Suffolk, Cambridgeshire, Essex and Hertfordshire, the city of Norwich and the boroughs of Great Yarmouth, Thetford, Cambridge and Saffron Walden on 1 March, so enabling the inhabitants of those districts to be in a position to go to parliament in the session of 1842.

On 7 January 1841, a meeting was held in the Swan Inn in Norwich of the landowners of Norfolk who were favourable to the construction of a railway from Norwich to London. The result of the meeting was that a committee was formed to consider the advantages of a communication by railway between Norwich and London. The *Norwich Mercury* of 30 January 1841, in a report on the committee of landowners formed to consider the advantages of a communication by railway between Norwich and London, mentioned that it had also had laid before it the report of a survey made by Robert Stephenson for a railway from Norwich to Yarmouth. The *Hertford Mercury and Reformer* of 6 February, quoting the *Norfolk Chronicle,* said that the railway projected by Rastrick from Yarmouth via Cambridge to Bishop's Stortford was contended as clearly being the best one for the interests of Norfolk as not only connecting the county with the metropolis, but also approximating towards the railways in the centre of the country with which a branch might thereafter be profitably made to connect with it. The *Norwich Mercury* of 20 February 1841 carried a notice of the intention to apply to parliament to construct and maintain a railway between Norwich and Yarmouth. According to the *Norwich Mercury* of 3 April, Robert Stephenson had visited Norwich on 30 March and, after spending two days in the city examining the line of the railway laid down under his direction, left the city on 1 April. It was understood that his personal inspection had confirmed his original opinion of the cheapness of its construction and the advantages to be gained from it by the public and the shareholders. According to the newspaper of 18 September, the proposal for the railway was to be brought before the Commons. According to the *Essex Standard* of 22 October, the length of the railway would be 20½ miles, expense was computed as £10,000 per mile and traffic was calculated to yield 12 per cent on a capital of £200,000. Stephenson's line would have followed a different route between Yarmouth and Norwich to Rastrick's.

On Friday, 19 November, there was a meeting held in Great Yarmouth at the town hall, convened by circulars for the purpose of considering the propriety of supporting the proposed railway between Norwich and Great Yarmouth that had been surveyed by Robert Stephenson. The outcome was support for the proposed railway, but it was suggested by G.D. Palmer that as it was not a public meeting it could not be considered as expressing the opinions of the town. This was concurred with by the Railway's promoters. It was suggested by them that a public meeting for that purpose should be held in the following January.

The fact that the ECR was no longer going to build their railway from London to Yarmouth via Norwich beyond Colchester did not mean that it did not have the power to do so. Merely that the power to compulsorily purchase land between Colchester and Yarmouth had been dropped, as was stated at the annual general meeting of the company on 25 February 1841. At the meeting it was also stated that the directors, with the view of assisting any independent company that might be formed to construct a line from Norwich to Yarmouth and ultimately to connect with the ECR, had directed that the plans and sections of the old line of the Railway should be lodged before Parliament before 1 March so as to comply in respect to that line also with the standing orders of parliament.

Not all the owners of land on the line of the proposed Norwich and Yarmouth Railway were happy with the route chosen and according to the *Norwich Mercury* of 25 December 1841, they had called a meeting to which other dissenters were invited to be held at the Royal Hotel in Norwich on 8 January 1842. The same newspaper, in an advertisement, calls it the Yarmouth and Norwich Railway.

The *Norfolk Chronicle* of 18 December reported that Robert Stephenson had said that the Norwich and Yarmouth Railway could be constructed for £150,000 and the railway was expected to produce a revenue of upwards of £40,000 per annum. The siting of the Norwich terminus of the railway was a cause of objection to the route chosen by Robert Stephenson, the objection being that any extension southward of the railway could not be conveniently made. Stephenson, in a letter published in the *Norfolk Chronicle* and the *Norwich Mercury* of 8 January 1842, said that the position of the line from Norwich to London had not yet been adopted and therefore he felt it prudent to adopt the route proposed of the Norwich and Yarmouth as being the most convenient for traffic between those two places.

The committee appointed by the inhabitants of Yarmouth to watch the proceedings of the two rival companies promoting the building of a railway believed that a union of the two in building the line would materially advance the public interest, so suggested a meeting between the rival promoters. This took place on Thursday, 10 February and it was agreed that the portion of the line from Yarmouth to Norwich of the proposed railway from Yarmouth to Bishop's Stortford would be withdrawn, abandoned in favour of the rival line from Norwich to Yarmouth. The *Norwich Mercury* of 19 February reported that the provisional committee of the promoters of the Yarmouth and Norwich Railway had the pleasure to announce that at the request of the committee appointed to watch the rival lines being promoted from London to Yarmouth, the EAR had withdrawn its opposition to the Yarmouth and Norwich Railway's line between those two places and that the latter's bill would now proceed to parliament.

The *Norwich Mercury* of 26 February reported that all the necessary preliminaries had been performed and the petition to introduce the bill into parliament for the formation of the Yarmouth and Norwich Railway had been presented by Edmond Wodehouse the previous Friday evening. The *Essex Standard* of 4 March recorded that it understood that the necessary measures had been taken for complying with parliament's standing orders, the petition for the Yarmouth and Norwich Railway bill had been presented the previous Friday (25th February) by Mr E. Woodhouse, the member for the Eastern Division of Norfolk. The same newspaper of 25 March reported that the previous Tuesday, on the motion that the Yarmouth and Norwich Railway bill be read the second time, Lord Dalmeny moved an amendment that the bill be read a second time that day six months hence, the reason being that the railway company did not have the power or the funds to carry the objects of the company into operation; another objection was that there was a navigable river which rendered 'the measure altogether unnecessary'. Following a debate, the House divided and the votes were 75 for the second reading and 16 against, a majority of 59. The bill was then read a second time and was ordered to be committed.

The Railway's progress through parliament did not go totally smoothly. At a special meeting of Norwich City Council on 12 April, the River and Tonnage Joint Committee reported that they had considered certain clauses suggested by them to be inserted in the Yarmouth and Norwich Railway bill for protecting the Yare Navigation, which had been prepared by the bill's solicitors and altered and settled by the Town Clerk. They were of the opinion that as such clauses would answer the purpose of protecting the Navigation, they recommended to the Council that it support the insertion of the clauses in the bill. The Committee also reported that they had met a Mr Rackham, one of the solicitors for the Railway's bill, who had agreed with their suggestion that the Railway Company should pay all expenses to be incurred by the Town Clerk or the Corporation on their behalf in reference to the bill. The Committee also recommended that the Town Clerk should watch the progress of the bill through its different stages and see that the clauses be inserted agreeably to the arrangement between the Committee and the Railway Company. The Town Clerk said that the width of the new channel of the River Yare to be made by the Railway Company was to be the same as the other part of the River – 120 feet opposite Thorpe. They proposed to leave many yards between the new cut and the existing river and thought that 70 feet would be wide enough but after conferring with them agreed that it should be 100 feet. There were to be two bridges and it was proposed that the new cut should be the same width as the river, but it was afterwards agreed that the inside width should be 25 feet, and in case of high water so that it would not overflow it should not be built on solid stone, but on piles 18 inches apart. There was a clause which enacted that if they did not keep the new cut a proper depth, they must pay £10 a day for every day that it remained in an improper state for navigation. Mr C. Darkins asked if there were to be any permanent or swing bridges. The Town Clerk said that under the Yare Navigation's Act, swing bridges were not allowed, but for the purpose of navigation another cut was to be made beyond, so that vessels not capable of passing under the bridges might go round.

There was other opposition to the Yarmouth and Norwich's bill. According to the *Norwich Mercury* of Saturday, 23 April, the committee appointed by parliament to examine the Railway's Bill sat on Monday, 18 April in Room No 8 at 1 o'clock. Messrs Austin, Talbot and Palmer appeared on behalf of the promoters of the Railway; Sergeant Merryweather and Mr Teed opposed it on behalf of Mr John Leathes and Mr Andrews Q C and Mr Hildyard appeared on behalf of the ECR. Mr Austin opened his case by alluding to the vast and growing importance of the city and the town between which the railway was to run and of the importance to increase the facility of communication between the two. He said that there was no opposition to the railway except from Mr Leathes. He said that the ECR had not come to say that the railway should not be built, but rather than instead of the chosen route, which was a cheap and expedient line, to go through high country which would incur greater expenditure and be of uncertain return. He then enlarged on the proceedings relative to the mandamus and pointed at the intention of the ECR to make Colchester their terminus. It could not make the line to Yarmouth and had lost the power of compulsory purchase. On that ground, the supporters of the Yarmouth and Norwich bill had contemplated shutting them out of the inquiry. They had appeared on a technical title for which they had no right. Though they had the parliamentary authority to make the line in five years, they had lost the power of compulsory purchase. Yet the ECR had come forward to oppose them. It was a monstrous thing for the company to do, whose bill had contained all the powers the Yarmouth and Norwich's Bill contained – that the

Yarmouth and Norwich was unnecessary and unfairly laid down to the injury of the landed proprietors. To say that the inhabitants of Yarmouth and Norwich opposed the railway was contrary to the facts and equally so the assertion that the termini were injurious. He then said that the ECR had said that the estimated cost of the line was greatly underrated, but he could not understand how they could ascertain that, and he would prove in evidence that they were mistaken. Those parties were the real opponents of the railway, and they were not in the position of a competing line. Austin then called his witnesses including George Parker Bidder the civil engineer. The hearing went on for several days. On Wednesday, Bidder was cross-examined by Andrews on behalf of the ECR and Sergeant Merryweather for Mr Leathes. On Thursday the whole of the day was occupied in discussing the right of the ECR to appear before the committee, the argument being that the ECR was an existing competing line. Eventually it was decided by the committee that it could. The *Norwich Mercury* of 30 April reported that the committee again sat on Friday, 22 April and the Yarmouth and Norwich Railway was represented by Mr Burke, its parliamentary agent. Hildyard was about to announce that an amicable agreement had been effected between the rival lines when some discussion took place relative to the diversion of the terminus in Norwich. Burke said that they would not be able to come to a conclusion because he thought that the proposition would be destructive to the whole bill and that it would not be doing justice to his clients to consent. Hildyard denied that his clients, the ECR, had any desire to demand what was unreasonable. He denied that the company had abandoned their line, but had every intention of carrying it through as the great difficulties which they had had to hitherto contend with had vanished. Their object, which he understood had been arranged between the engineers of the two companies, was to secure such a construction of the line as it might be made a convenient portion of the plan for making a line from Yarmouth to London. He hoped that the committee would not give the Yarmouth and Norwich

Railway their bill if that company refused to accede to so reasonable a proposition. Burke said that he would readily consent to such an agreement, but the ground of his objection was that his company should not make its railway available to Norwich. The proposed line of his company went to Foundry Bridge, which was reasonable for Norwich, and (Robert) Stephenson had told him that he could easily make a connecting line by branching about a mile. They were willing to do the latter whenever there should be a prospect of the ECR coming to meet the Yarmouth and Norwich Railway, but they would not give up the bulk of the bill by stopping for the ECR a mile from Norwich. The Hon E.T. Yorke said that they must decide on what course to pursue. If they could not agree, the committee would have to go on with the evidence of the two competing lines. Hildyard would not refuse the line to Foundry Bridge but hoped that the line to Carrow Bridge be also made. He required as a guarantee to secure this that the Yarmouth and Norwich Railway should consent to suspend all operations towards the Foundry Bridge until they had constructed the line to Carrow Road. Burke asked if the committee would be satisfied if they (the Yarmouth and Norwich) bound themselves to construct the connecting line when the ECR would be in a position to require it. The chairman said that if there was the slightest chance of the parties coming together, the committee would adjourn. Burke said that he would leave it to the committee to decide on the terms of the arrangement, whilst Hildyard said that all the ECR wanted was that no interested opposition should go against them. He told Yorke that the ECR would permit the Yarmouth and Norwich Railway to be built provided that the connecting line was insured. Burke submitted a clause which he said would meet the case. After a good deal of discussion, it was agreed to adjourn to find an arrangement, which was satisfactorily made. The committee continued its hearings one further day, hearing from other parties' requests for clauses to be inserted in the railway's bill. The committee's report being read, it was ordered to be presented to parliament. The *Norwich Mercury* said that it had since learnt that the ECR had insisted that the Yarmouth and Norwich Railway should not be built further than the road leading to Carrow Bridge until an approach was made to Carrow so that the ECR or other railways might join the Yarmouth and Norwich Railway. The approach to Carrow, it was said, could not be made without a new act. The consequence was that if the Yarmouth and Norwich's Bill was carried through with that clause, its terminus would be at a point below the residence of Nicholas Bacon and the public house – which public house was not stated. According to the *Cambridge Chronicle and Journal* of 7 May, the promoters of the Yarmouth and Norwich Railway had agreed that their railway would not extend further than the east side of Carrow Road until they had secured the sanction of parliament for a branch railway to the station of the ECR on the west side of the river by the Carrow Staithe. The *Ipswich Journal* of 7 May said that the committee on the Railway's Bill had reported to parliament in favour of it and that it would be passed shortly. The *Norfolk Chronicle* of 14 May reported that the Yarmouth and Norwich Railway's Bill had been read a third time in the House of Commons the previous Wednesday and passed by that House. The Railway's Bill then went to the House of Lords. Meanwhile the *Essex Chronicle* of 27 May quoted the *Railway Magazine* as saying that the East Anglian line (Railway) had been sold for £1,500, which if true was a very good system of speculation. There was still opposition to the Yarmouth and Norwich Railway and the *Norfolk Chronicle* of 7 June reported that in consequence of a petition presented against its bill in the House of Lords by Captain King of Thorpe, the Bill was referred to the Committee of the House on Monday, 6. An arrangement was made with Captain King's counsel by which a clause was inserted into the Bill and after a few minutes deliberation, the Committee reported that the preamble was proved. The *Essex Chronicle* of 17 June quoted the *Railway Times* as saying that the Act for the Yarmouth and Norwich Railway was secured. The Railway was to be about 20 miles in length of single line to be worked through the electric telegraph. The *Essex*

Standard of 24 June reported that the previous Saturday the Yarmouth and Norwich Railway's bill had received the Royal Assent.

The *Norfolk Chronicle* of Saturday, 2 July reported that following the passing of the Yarmouth and Norwich's Act, the Directors had met in London the previous Tuesday at which appointments were made and the necessary resolutions were passed to carry into effect the arrangements for the holding of the first general meeting of the proprietors of the railway, which would be announced by advertisement. It was hoped that construction of the railway would start that year.

By the middle of February 1843, agreements had been entered with many of the landowners, for much of the land required for the Norwich and Yarmouth Railway and that much had been acquired. The *Norfolk Chronicle* of the 18th of the month said that when all the land had been acquired, construction would quickly start. The *Ipswich Journal* of 25 February reported that two ships had arrived at Yarmouth with iron for the use of the Railway and that it was hoped that the works would soon commence.

According to George Dow in *The First Railway in Norfolk* (LNER 1947), the contractors for building the line were Messrs Grissell & Peto. Samuel Peto was the Resident Engineer and had his offices at St. Michael-at-Plea, Norwich. In April 1843, work began at Postwick Hall Farm near Thorpe Asylum. The 1,500 men employed made good progress. By October, a ballast train was running between Reedham and Yarmouth.

The *Bury and Norwich Post* of Wednesday, 26 April reported that work had commenced on the construction of the Railway the previous Thursday at Postwick and Reedham. It was expected that in that week 1,100 labourers would be employed and that the work would proceed with all possible despatch. The *Norfolk Chronicle* of 27 May reported that, despite the rain of the previous fortnight, the excavators (as the builders of the railway were called) had been proceeding rapidly with their work on the new channel at Trowse.

At Postwick, the excavators had nearly got across Mr Gillett's land. The embankment had been made within a short distance of the back part of the Asylum. At Reedham, the cuttings and embankments were proceeding rapidly. Temporary rails had been laid down to speed up the work and more were expected daily from Yarmouth. The *Norfolk Chronicle* of 3 June reported that the Railway had succeeded in making agreements with nearly all the landowners along the line of its route. Only three cases were outstanding. The *Norfolk Chronicle* of 17 June carried a detailed report of how the work of building the Railway was proceeding. According to the *Bury and Norwich Post* of 28 June, an engine, tender, etc had been landed at Yarmouth for use in the construction of the Railway. The *Ipswich Journal* of 7 October carried a report on the progress of the Yarmouth and Norwich Railway, including that the engine with the ballasting waggons was running from Reedham to near Yarmouth.

The gauge of the Yarmouth and Norwich Railway was 4ft 8½in – the gauge of railways such as the London and Birmingham, which as mentioned earlier had obtained powers to build a branch line from Blisworth on its main line from the two towns in its name to Peterborough.

The *Norfolk Chronicle* of 21 October reported that there would an extraordinary meeting of the shareholders of the Yarmouth and Norwich Railway to be held at the Royal Hotel Norwich on 4 November to, amongst other things, consider the expediency of applying to parliament for the powers to construct the Carrow Field branch line provided for by the Act of Incorporation or for varying or repealing the provisions of the Act in that respect. Also, of obtaining powers to make another line in lieu thereof and for raising additional capital. At the extraordinary meeting on 4 November, what was proposed was agreed. It was proposed and seconded that the Yarmouth and Norwich Railway enter into an agreement with the proposed Norwich and Brandon Railway to jointly build the Carrow Field branch. The *Norfolk Chronicle* of 11 November carried a notice that it was the intention of the Yarmouth and Norwich Railway to apply to parliament for power to build the Carrow Field branch and to lease or sell the branch railway to the proposed Norwich and Brandon Railway. The *Norfolk Chronicle* of 18 November reported that the works on building the Railway were drawing near to Norwich so as to attract thousands of spectators to gratify their curiosity.

There was still opposition to the Yarmouth and Norwich Railway as the *Norfolk Chronicle* of Saturday, 9 December reported the formation of a committee to protect the interests of those who had property or found employment on the river between Yarmouth and Norwich. The reason was the intention of the Railway to build a bridge over the River Bure at Yarmouth and to take land for the building of a wharf. The *Cambridge General Advertiser* of 3 January 1844 reported that it was the intention of the Yarmouth and Norwich Railway to apply for leave to take the whole of the properties along the North Quay at Yarmouth for wharves, etc. According to the newspaper, the effect of this would be to enable certain capitalists to connect with the line but having interests at variance with the port of Yarmouth to monopolise a vast amount of the import trade of the port to the injury of the port's shipping. The plan to construct the wharves did not materialise, nor did a plan to build a bridge over the River Yare, according to the *Norfolk Chronicle* of 13 January. The same newspaper of 27 January reported that almost all of the permanent way of the Railway was complete and that the previous week Robert Stephenson, the Engineer for the Railway, had inspected the line and expressed his satisfaction with the state of the works. An opening date in April or May was predicted. The proposal to bridge the Bure also met with opposition – from the Commissioners of the Haven of Great Yarmouth at their meeting on 26 January. According to the *Bury and Norwich Post* of 14 February, the Directors, contractor and resident engineer had undertaken a journey over the line by train two days earlier. It said that in the half yearly meeting of the Company on the same day it was stated that the Railway would be open to the public by

1 May. The *Bury and Norwich Post* of 28 February reported that the Directors of the Yarmouth and Norwich Railway had presented their petition to parliament and printed their Bill and that it would then go into committee. The petition was somewhat vague and indefinite in its requirements, but the bill was more explicit, though perhaps not as much as it should have been. It appeared from that that the Company required authority to make a bridge over the Bure or the Yare and to make either of the lines laid down upon their plans. It also seemed in the Company's references that all the land and houses along the North quay in Yarmouth were included as numbered in their plans. It surprised the newspaper that the Company wanted to vest all the land banked from Breydon in it despite an agreement to the contrary. With regards to the Norwich terminus, the bill proceeded in accordance with the plans deposited with the Clerk of the Peace. The same newspaper also said that Mr Cooke, the Patentee of the Electric Telegraph, had been that week superintending the laying down of the 'ingenious invention' along the length of the Railway. According to the *Norfolk Chronicle* of Saturday, 2 March, the bill for amending and enlarging some of the provisions of the Yarmouth and Norwich Railway's Act and to authorise the construction of certain new works went before the Committee on Standing Orders (of the House of Commons) the previous Tuesday, 27 February. Despite an attempt to throw out the bill on the grounds that certain standing orders had not been completed, the Committee voted in favour of it without sending it to the Committee of Appeal of the House. There was opposition to the Railway's proposal to build a bridge across the Bure opposite Lime Kiln Wharf in Yarmouth. The opposition came from Charles Cory, one of the owners of the Yarmouth suspension bridge which had been erected in 1829 and widened in 1832; it was a toll bridge and the Railway Company said that their bridge would be toll free. It was felt that a better location for the new bridge would be opposite Fuller's Hill. The time of the opening of the Railway was drawing near. It seems that people had been in the habit of walking along the

railway line. The *Norwich Mercury* of Saturday, 23 March told people not to walk along it, as they would not only be subject to punishment but also within a few days engines would be running along the line. According to the *Norfolk Chronicle* of Saturday, 6 April the permanent way of the Railway would be laid the whole distance within a week, with the only part remaining unfinished being a short space near the Norwich terminus. The carriages had arrived for first, second and third class passengers, for which the fares would respectively be 3s 6d, 2s 6d and 1s 3d. The termini at both ends were rapidly progressing and would soon be complete. According to the *Norfolk Chronicle* of Saturday, 20 April at a meeting of the Railway's proprietors on the 12th of the month the Chairman of the meeting, Sir Edmund Lacon, said that General Pasley, the Government's Inspector of Railways, had inspected the line that day and said that it could be opened for traffic whenever the Company felt that it was fit to do so. The same newspaper said that the Railway would be open for traffic on Wednesday, 1 May. Trains would leave Norwich at 9 and 11 in the morning and 4 and 7 in the afternoon. They would leave Yarmouth at 8 and 10 in the morning and 3 and 8 in the afternoon. In addition to the earlier mentioned ticket prices, which were for single journeys, return tickets valid on the same day would be 5s first class, 4s second class and 2s third class.

The Yarmouth and Norwich Railway opened for public traffic on 1 May 1844. Prior to the public opening there was the official opening which took place the day before. According to the *Norfolk Chronicle*, the event was marked by great rejoicing and festivity in both Yarmouth and Norwich. On 30 April a special train was run from Norwich to Yarmouth for the Directors of the Railway and their friends. The special train comprising fourteen carriages with one engine at the front and one at the rear left the Norwich terminus between 10:30 and 11 o'clock. On reaching Yarmouth, refreshments provided by Mr Balls of the Victoria Hotel were taken in the booking office. After the passengers had spent some time looking at various sights in Yarmouth, they returned to the station to take the train back to

Norwich for a late luncheon at the Assembly Rooms at which speeches were given. According to the *Suffolk Chronicle* of 3 May, the Railway was open to the public on 1 May and the trains were thronged. The newspapers said of the types of accommodation provided that first class was exceedingly comfortable, but second and third class less so, with the latter simply large boxes without seats or covers and more suited to sheep or calves. In the evening of 1 May, the shareholders of the Railway and their friends held a dinner for the Directors at the Victoria Hotel in Great Yarmouth. The terminus at Norwich Thorpe was only a temporary one and later became, after the opening of the permanent one, the goods station.

The exterior of the original Norwich terminus of the Norwich and Yarmouth from a contemporary drawing. The area seems rather rural as can be evidenced from the windmill in the background. In the background can be made out Norwich cathedral. (Author's collection).

Having the electric telegraph in the form of the Cooke and Wheatstone system, the Railway was the first in Britain to install block signalling, albeit in a primitive form. Besides being for the Railway Company's use, the telegraph was also available for use by the public to send messages for which the company at first charged 4s 6d (later reduced to 2s 6d) including delivery.

On 10 May, the earlier mentioned Norwich and Brandon Railway's Bill received its Royal Assent. The Yarmouth and Norwich Railway Company was having trouble with the owners of the toll bridge in Yarmouth. According to the *Cambridge General Advertiser* of 22 May, because it could not come to an arrangement with the toll bridge's proprietors, the Railway was ferrying passengers by steam boat from the terminus to the North Quay. The newspaper said that it understood on good authority that it would lead to immediate legal action against the Railway Company by the owners of the toll bridge for a direct invasion of their rights. The action was heard at the Vice Chancellor's Court on Saturday, 31 May. The judge refused to restrain the Railway from carrying passengers by boat across the Bure, but that as it had promised to file its affidavit by the following Wednesday it would be sufficient for it to keep a record of the number of passengers crossing the river and abide by any order the Court would make for compensating the proprietors of the suspension bridge. At the hearing on 11 June, it was ruled that both parties had to undertake to go to trial at the next Norfolk Assizes, and that the Railway would keep a record of all passengers, horses and cattle carried by boat and to supply it to the proprietors of the suspension bridge if requested prior to the trial and with a copy of such account previous to the trial and this to be verified by affidavit. The *Norfolk Chronicle* of 22 June said that the Norfolk Assizes would be held on Monday, 22 July and that it was understood that the Railway Company had retained the Attorney General and Mr Fitzroy Kelly for its cause in the case between Cory, the proprietors of the Yarmouth suspension bridge, and it. The *Norwich Mercury* of Saturday, 6 July reported that the form of the issues in the case was settled for trying the question of whether the Railway Company by carrying passengers by steamboat from their station to Great Yarmouth contravened the right of the proprietors of the suspension bridge under its Act of Parliament for building the bridge across the Bure. The case was heard at the Nisi Prius court on Saturday, 3 August. The result was that the Railway Company was to build a new bridge over the Bure at its own expense and that it would pay the expenses of the Act for building the new bridge, the Company and its solicitors to have the conduct of the Act, but Mr Cory was to be the promoter of the Act and at the Company's expense. The Company was to keep the bridge in repair, but the bridge and its approaches were to be Mr Cory's. The Company was to guarantee that the tolls over the new bridge would amount to a clear £600 per annum and that the tolls on both bridges would be the same. Cory was to reduce all the tolls over the new bridge to one half-penny or one penny per day ticket as he pleased. All merchandise that was not travellers' luggage or small parcels that were not charged by weight to and from the railway were to go free over the bridge, including the drivers of horses and carriages. Passenger trains were not to run over the bridge. The Company was not to apply for an act either directly or indirectly to build any bridge except the one mentioned or to take Cory's bridge and deprive of the right of passing to the peninsula from Yarmouth. In the event of not getting a bill the matter was to be referred to Mr Kelly and Mr Serjeant Byles (later Sir John Byles who was a barrister, judge and author of books on law and the economy).

On 18 June the Railway opened its permanent station at Norwich Thorpe.

The *Norfolk Chronicle* of Saturday, 20 July reported that at Great Yarmouth a cutting had been commenced under the bed of the river for the purpose of carrying a gas pipe to the Railway Station, which was expected to be lit up by gas the following week.

It was in August that the first ideas of the Yarmouth and Norwich Railway consolidating, or rather amalgamating, with the as yet

YARMOUTH AND NORWICH. Treasurer. R Till, Guildhall Buildings, London.

Mls.	DOWN TRAINS.	Week Days. 1	2	3	4	Sundays. 1	2	3	Fares. 1st Class	2nd Class	3rd Clas
		a.m.	a.m.	p m.	p.m.	a.m.	p.m.	p.m.	s. d.	s. d.	s. d.
	Norwich	8 45	11 0	*4 0	7 0	8 30	*2 30	7 0	..	..	..
6	Brundall	8 55	11 10	4 10	7 10	8 40	2 40	7 10	1 0	0 9	0 6
8	Buckenham	9 0	11 15	4 15	7 15	8 45	2 45	7 15	1 6	1 0	0 8
10	Cantley..............	9 5	11 20	4 20	7 20	8 50	2 50	7 20	2 0	1 6	0 10
12	Reedham............	9 10	11 25	4 25	7 25	8 55	2 55	7 25	2 6	1 8	1 0
20½	Yarmouth	..	..	..	..	..	..	..	3 6	2 6	1 8
Mls.	UP TRAINS.	1	2	3	4	1	2	3	1st Class	2nd Class	3rd Class
		a.m.	noon.	p.m.	p.m.	a.m.	p.m.	p.m.	s. d.	s. d.	s. d.
	Yarmouth	10 0	12 *0	3 0	8 0	9 30	*6 0	8 0	..	..	..
8	Reedham............	10 10	12 10	3 10	8 10	9 40	6 10	8 10	1 6	1 0	0 8
10	Cantley..............	10 15	12 15	3 15	8 15	9 45	6 15	8 15	2 0	1 6	0 10
12	Buckenham	10 20	12 20	3 20	8 20	9 50	6 20	8 20	2 6	1 8	1 0
14	Brundall	10 25	12 25	3 25	8 25	9 55	6 25	8 25	3 0	2 0	1 2
20½	Norwich	..	..	..	..	..	..	..	3 6	2 6	1 8

* Third class covered carriages by these trains at 1d. per mile.

Omnibuses will run from Beccles to the Reedham station on Mondays, Wednesdays, Saturdays, and Sundays.

Tickets between Yarmouth and Norwich, to go and return the same day, 1st class 5s., 2nd 4s., open carriage 2s.

Monthly tickets may be had on application to the Secretary.

Children in arms free, under ten years of age half price.

Horses and Carriages to and from Norwich and Yarmouth conveyed as follows:—One horse 7s. two horses (one property and in same box) 10s., three horses (one property and in same box) 14s.; Carriages, four wheels 10s., two wheels 7s. Dogs, 1s. each.

The timetable of the Norwich and Yarmouth Railway for July 1845. Note that the timetable does not show the arrival times of the trains at their destination stations. Also details of omnibus connections and the fares for horses, dogs and horse drawn carriages. (Author's collection).

uncompleted Norwich and Brandon Railway were first put forward. The first proposal came from the latter company at a special meeting of the company in Norwich on 15 August called for that purpose and also to consider asking the directors to seek parliamentary authority to build branch lines from Wymondham to East Dereham and near Attleborough to Diss. The Norwich and Yarmouth Railway's half yearly meeting on 30 August was convened for the same purpose. At the meeting it was reported that in addition to passing a resolution declaring the shareholders' approval for the amalgamation of the two Companies from 1 July the following year, powers had been taken to raise £50,000 toward enlarging the terminal stations to take the Norwich and Brandon Railway traffic.

According to the *Norfolk Chronicle* of 21 September, the Norwich terminus of the Railway would shortly be improved by the addition of an elegant colonnade with a tower and a clock.

The *Suffolk Chronicle* of 28 September reported that a meeting of the inhabitants and landowners of Lowestoft would be held in the Town Hall to take into consideration the expediency of forming a railway from Reedham to Lowestoft. According to the *Norfolk Chronicle* of 5 October, the meeting passed a resolution that the building of a railway from Reedham to Lowestoft would be of benefit to the inhabitants and landowners of Lowestoft, by opening immediate communication with Norwich and the important agricultural districts of Norfolk and Suffolk and also with London and the northern and western parts of the country.

According to the *Norfolk Chronicle* of Saturday, 19 October, as from Monday, 21 October, the steam boat from the Railway Station to the Buck Quay at Yarmouth would be discontinued and that the tolls on the suspension bridge would be altered to 1d for foot passengers and that any such person taking a ticket and returning the same day, on giving such ticket to the toll collector, would be allowed to pass free. All merchandise and fish drawn by horses would be allowed to pass free.

The amalgamation of the Yarmouth and Norwich and the Norwich and Brandon railways took a step nearer when, according to the *Norwich Mercury* of Saturday, 16 November, notice was given that an application was to be made to parliament in the ensuing session for an Act for this.

The proposal for building a line from Lowestoft to Reedham took a step further, when according to the *Suffolk Chronicle* of Saturday, 23 November it was intended that an application to parliament for such a railway was going to be made in the next session.

The *Bury and Norwich Post* of 11 December reported that the plans for the extension of the Yarmouth and Norwich Railway by building a bridge over the Bure had been deposited with the Clerk of the Peace for Yarmouth.

The *Norfolk Chronicle* of 18 January 1845 carried a notice of the next General Half Yearly meeting of the shareholders of the Yarmouth and Norwich Railway to be held at the Company's offices at Norwich on Saturday, 1 February. The purpose of the meeting was for: determining of the propriety in conjunction with the Norwich and Brandon Railway to take a lease or otherwise of the proposed Lowestoft Railway and Harbour and Works connected therewith; authorising an application to parliament in the ensuing session in connection with the Norwich and Brandon Railway or otherwise for an extension of the Yarmouth and Norwich Railway into the City of Norwich; and for authorising an application to parliament for powers to carry into effect the agreement made with Mr Cory for the erection of a bridge over the River Bure at Yarmouth.

The *Cambridge General Advertiser* of Wednesday, 29 January reported that a prospectus had just been issued for improving the harbour at Lowestoft and for building a railway from that town to Reedham on the Yarmouth and Norwich Railway. It said that the proposal had the backing of the Yarmouth and Norwich and Norwich and Brandon railways, who intended at their next half yearly meetings their intentions of leasing the undertaking in perpetuity.

The *Norfolk Chronicle* of 8 February carried a report of the Yarmouth and Norwich Railway's General Half Yearly meeting of 1 February at which the aforementioned proposals were approved.

Progress continued towards the amalgamation of the Yarmouth and Norwich Railway with the Norwich and Brandon Railway. The *Norfolk Chronicle* of 15 March reported that a petition was presented to Sub-Committee No 2 of the House of Commons by the former Company for powers to amalgamate it with the Norwich and Brandon Railway and for powers to extend it further into Norwich than it currently was and to build a bridge over the River Bure at Yarmouth. Although the Bill was unopposed because the plans had not been deposited with the Board of Trade until 2 December and neither had the proper deposits of notices, etc been made with the Clerk of the Peace in Norwich; the Sub-Committee decided that the standing orders had not been complied with. According to the same newspaper of 22 March, at the Standing Orders Committee on 17 March that in the case of the Yarmouth and Norwich's Bill the standing orders should be dispensed with and the bill be allowed to proceed. This, according to the newspaper, had been done.

The proposed amalgamation of the Yarmouth and Norwich and Norwich and Brandon railways was not without its opponents. At the meeting of Norwich City Council on 10 April, the Town Clerk read, amongst other things, a petition he had prepared against it. This was adopted.

The *Norfolk Chronicle* of 26 April included a notice of a Special General Meeting of the shareholders of the Yarmouth and Norwich Railway on 27 May to consider the bill for the amalgamation of the Yarmouth and Norwich and Norwich and Brandon railways and authorising the construction of a bridge over the River Bure in Yarmouth and other works in Yarmouth and Norwich in connection with the Railway, as well as a bill for making a railway from Lowestoft to Reedham and improvements to Lowestoft harbour and for altering the line of the Norwich and Brandon Railway and making branches from it to Diss and to East Dereham. They also considered a bill for making a railway from Wells to East Dereham and a bill for making a railway from the Norwich and Brandon Railway near Diss to join the ECR near Colchester. At the meeting, all the motions other than the railway from Diss to Colchester were approved. The reason the latter was not approved was that the bill for it had failed in the standing orders of the House of Commons and was for the time being abandoned.

The mid-1840s saw a few railways in England, Ireland and France try the atmospheric system of traction. This involved using a large metal pipe sealed with an opening flap in which a vacuum was created. Into this went a piston of a traction carriage of a train, the idea being to haul a train along by the vacuum created. The *Bury and Norwich Post* of 7 May carried a report which suggested that the Yarmouth and Norwich Railway might be a suitable candidate for operation by this system. As the atmospheric system was a total disaster, it is fortunate that nothing came of this.

On 2 May 1845, Cory's suspension bridge in Yarmouth collapsed under a load from a crowd who had gathered to watch a circus stunt on the river. Seventy-nine people, mainly children, were killed. An investigation found fault with the design and workmanship of the bridge.

According to the *Norfolk Chronicle* of 31 May, at the Standing Orders Committee of the House of Commons on 27 May, the preamble of the bill for the amalgamation of the Yarmouth and Norwich Railway with the Norwich and Brandon Railway was proved.

The *Suffolk Chronicle* of 7 June reported that the Yarmouth and Norwich and Norwich and Brandon railways had amalgamated.

The *Norfolk Chronicle* of 14 June reported that the Yarmouth and Norwich Railway had reached a satisfactory agreement with the owners of the right of the toll bridge over the River Bure at Yarmouth to build and maintain in 1846 a new bridge which was to be toll free.

Following the amalgamation of the Yarmouth and Norwich Railway with the Norwich and Brandon Railway, the newly combined railway became the Norfolk Railway.

The first mention that we find of the Norwich and Brandon Railway is in the *Norfolk Chronicle* of 2 September 1843 in its report of the half yearly meeting of the Yarmouth and Norwich Railway on 31 August 1843 when Mr S.M. Peto, one of the contractors, strongly advocated the extension of the line to Brandon which would bring it within 40 miles of the ECR at Colchester, the London and Birmingham at Peterborough and the Northern and Eastern at Newport. A shareholder addressing Mr Rackham, one of the directors, said that he must stir up his friends in Norwich to make the line to Brandon. Another shareholder said that the gentlemen of Yarmouth and Norwich should come forward and supply the means. A slightly different account regarding the idea of an extension to Brandon was reported in the *Cambridge General Advertiser* of 6 September. According to that, following Peto's remarks a Mr Reynolds suggested that the Norwich and Yarmouth Railway should make the line to Brandon and then offer it to the Company on lease. This does not seem to make sense. According to the report, Reynolds had told Rackham to stir up his friends in Norwich to make a new Company and let the Yarmouth and Norwich pay that Company a percentage for that line. The Secretary of the Railway Company said that the surveys and plans were already lodged and that if the money was raised, they might go to parliament in the next session. George Bidder said that they had made a survey all the way from Weedon (in Buckinghamshire) to Norwich and that a line would be carried whether they went via Ely or not. He recommended the proprietors to make the line to Brandon via Wymondham and Attleborough as the whole of the London traffic would go that way. It would be 30 miles towards London either way and whoever got there first would get the traffic. If made, there would be a race between the other lines to get to them and the more they raced, the better for their line. According to Rackham, whilst there were many parties who would have nothing to with the line between Norwich and Yarmouth, they would support a line towards London.

The *Norfolk Chronicle* of 23 September 1843 reported that a prospectus had been issued for a Norwich and Brandon Railway to run between those two places – a distance of 30 miles and as mentioned be within 40 miles of the ECR at Colchester, the London and Birmingham at Peterborough and the Northern and Eastern at Newport. Messrs Grisell and Peto, the contractors for the Yarmouth and Norwich Railway, were willing to build the line at a rate of £10,000 per mile. The building of the line would be under the control of George Stephenson and George Bidder, under whose direction surveys and plans had already been made. The capital to be raised was £300,000 in 15,000 shares of £20 each. The line commenced near the terminus of the Yarmouth and Norwich Railway in Norwich.

Things moved quickly. The *Norfolk Chronicle* of 23 September reported that a prospectus had been issued for a Norwich and Brandon Railway to run from Norwich to Brandon – a distance of 30 miles towards London. The capital was £300,000 raised in 15,000 shares of £20 each. According to the same newspaper of 7 October, a meeting was held the previous Saturday of influential promoters of the Railway determined to make an application to parliament to build and maintain a railway from Norwich to Brandon. The reason for

2

Freepost Plus RTKE-RGRJ-KTTX
Pen & Sword Books Ltd
47 Church Street
BARNSLEY
S70 2AS

only going as far as Brandon was, according to the newspaper, that the ECR had resolved to go seek parliamentary approval to build a line from Colchester via Bury St Edmunds to Harling and there to join the Brandon line and the N&ER for an extension of its already authorised line to Newport to Brandon via Cambridge and Ely.

The *Norwich Mercury* of 11 November carried a notice of application to be made to parliament in the ensuing session to make and maintain a railway from Norwich to Brandon. At Norwich, the Railway would join the Yarmouth and Norwich Railway, whilst it was also intended to make a branch line from a place known as Two Mile Bottom near Croxton to Thetford. The *Norfolk Chronicle* of 9 December reported that on the previous Saturday, a meeting of the landowners, agriculturists and merchants of Norfolk had been held in the Shire Hall in Norwich to consider the proposed Norwich and Brandon Railway and that the meeting had voted in favour of the Railway. The *Norwich Mercury* of 16 December carried an advertisement for the Norwich and Brandon Railway. The capital was £380,000 divided into 19,000 shares at £20 each with a deposit of £2. The advertisement carried details of the provisional committee, the engineers, the bankers and the solicitors, as well as places where the prospectus for the company could be obtained. Take up of the shares in the Company was rapid as the same newspaper of 23 December reported that capital for the Company had been subscribed and that no further applications would be accepted. It was proposed and seconded that the Yarmouth and Norwich Railway enter into an agreement with the proposed Norwich and Brandon Railway to jointly build the Carrow Field branch. The *Norfolk Chronicle* of 11 November carried a notice that it was the intention of the Yarmouth and Norwich Railway to apply to parliament for powers to build the Carrow Field branch and to lease or sell the branch railway to the proposed Norwich and Brandon Railway.

The *Norfolk Chronicle* of 24 February 1844 reported that in the House of Commons on Wednesday, 21 February, Edmond Wodehouse had brought up the Report of the Committee on the Norwich and Brandon Railway. The *Bury and Norwich Post* of Wednesday, 28 February reported that the Railway's bill was read a second time in the House of Commons on the preceding Monday and ordered to be committed. It understood that the Standing Orders had not been complied with for a deviation to Thetford instead of passing through Croxton as originally proposed. The *Norfolk Chronicle* of Saturday, 9 March reported that in the House of Commons on the previous Monday, Mr Greenall presented a petition against the Railway. The same newspaper reported on the meeting of Norwich City Council on the previous Tuesday; the Council would not resist the Railway but passed a motion instructing the River Committee to see that the Railway would be of the same gauge as that of the N&ER, with which the Railway would connect at Brandon. The *Bury and Norwich Post* of 13 March reported further petitions against the Railway including one from Norwich City Council. The *Norfolk Chronicle* of 16 March reported that the Railway's bill had gone to the Committee of the House of Commons. The same newspaper of Saturday, 23 March recorded that the previous Monday the Railway's bill was reported and ordered to lie on the table (of the House of Commons) and to be printed. The *Essex Herald* of Wednesday, 26 March said that the report of the Committee on the Railway's bill had already been issued, but that the newspaper would have to defer its publication until the following week. According to the *Bury and Norwich Post* of the following day, the Committee had said that the allegations of the petitioners of the Railway's bill were satisfactorily proved. The *Norfolk Chronicle* of 30 March said that the report of the Railway's bill was further considered for the introduction of an amendment which was to do with bridges in Norwich. According to the *Essex Herald* of 2 April, the Norwich and Brandon Railway bill was read the third time and passed in the House of Commons on Friday, 29 March. The *Norfolk Chronicle* of 20 April reported that the Norwich and Brandon Railway bill had passed the standing orders of the House of Lords. According to the *Essex Herald* of Tuesday, 14 May, the Norwich and

Brandon Railway bill received its Royal Assent the previous Friday. The *Bury and Norwich Post* of Wednesday, 15 May reported that works on the building of the railway were expected to commence the following week at Ketteringham. The *Norfolk Chronicle* of 1 June carried a notice that the First General Meeting of the proprietors of the Railway would be held on 14 June at the company's offices in London. The *Bury and Norwich Post* of Wednesday, 12 June stated that works on constructing the Railway had commenced the previous Thursday. The *Essex Standard* of Friday, 21 June carried a report of the meeting of the proprietors of the Norwich and Brandon Railway on 14 June. At the meeting, the report of the Directors said that the Railway's Act had received the Royal Assent, the contract for building the Railway had been taken by Messrs Grissell and Peto and that nearly all of the land had been purchased. Work on constructing the Railway had commenced and there was reason to believe that the whole line (including a double line of rails as recommended by parliament) would be completed and opened to the public the following summer. The Report was unanimously adopted. It was stated that the ECR was determined to lay a double line of railway from Cambridge to Brandon and on altering the gauge of their line throughout so that through carriages could be run from London to Norwich. According to the *Norwich Mercury* of 22 June, the works on the Railway had recently commenced near Wymondham and that the line had been staked out as far as Attleborough. The *Norfolk Chronicle* of 6 July reported that works were proceeding rapidly between Wymondham and Attleborough and that three miles of rails had been laid at Brandon. The *Norfolk Chronicle* of 17 August reported that the work of building the Railway was in full progress. On 15 August, there was a meeting of the shareholders of the Company for the purpose of considering amalgamating with the Yarmouth and Norwich Railway. The argument put forward for doing so was that in order to be represented and respected by the big railways such as the ECR, given the Railway's size, it was politic that it should join with the

Yarmouth and Norwich Railway because, if it did not, it would not be able to maintain a proper independence or command traffic so great as would necessarily follow the connection with the ECR. The proposal was accepted. The same meeting also considered the expediency of authorising the Directors to apply to parliament in the next session for powers to build branch lines from Wymondham to East Dereham and Attleborough to Diss. This proposal was also accepted. The *Norfolk Chronicle* of 31 August said that the Norwich terminus of the Norwich and Brandon was in the course of erection. The *Cambridge General Advertiser* of 11 September recorded that nine ships with timber for Messrs Grissel and Peto had been unloading at Lynn and that more were expected.

The proposal for a line from Attleborough to Diss met with opposition. At a meeting of the landowners and inhabitants of Diss and the neighbourhood in that town on 27 September, a resolution was passed opposing the line and in favour of a direct line from Ipswich to Norwich by 69 to 14 votes. There was also a rival scheme to the branch to East Dereham. The *Norwich Mercury* of 5 October carried a prospectus for an East Dereham and Norwich Railway to run direct between the two towns.

The failure of the Norwich and Brandon Railway not to directly serve the important town of Thetford, but merely serving it by a branch line, caused it to apply for powers to make a deviation of its line so as to directly serve that town. The *Norfolk Chronicle* of 19 October 1844 carried a report of a meeting held in the town of 12 October attended by G.P. Bidder, the engineer of the Railway, who tried unsuccessfully to persuade the inhabitants to support the original intention of the Railway to go via Croxton. The meeting voted in favour of a pledge made by the Company to serve the town directly.

Work was progressing on building the Norwich and Brandon Railway. The *Chelmsford Chronicle* of 25 October reported that 4,000 men were employed on the Railway, of whom 2,700 were labourers and excavators. In the neighbourhood of Eccles and Attleborough, the greatest activity was observable and workmen were employed night and day in building the bridges in that vicinity.

The *Cambridge Chronicle and Journal* of 9 November reported that the Norwich and Brandon Railway would be opened the following May.

The *Norfolk Chronicle* of 16 November carried a report that it was proposed that an application be made to parliament for an Act to amalgamate the Norwich and Brandon and Yarmouth and Norwich railways.

The East Dereham and Norwich Railway meanwhile had got to the point where, according to the *Norfolk Chronicle* of 23 November, it had decided to apply to parliament for an Act to build and maintain its railway.

The *Bury and Norwich Post* of 4 December carried a report of a dinner given by the farmers along the line of the Norwich and Brandon Railway for Samuel Peto. The farmers were in favour of the Railway as it would enable them to sell their cattle to the Midlands and other districts which they had not previously been able to do.

As mentioned in the previous chapter, the *Norfolk Chronicle* of 14 December reported that work on the railway from Norwich to Brandon and thence through to Ely, Cambridge, Newport and Bishop's Stortford was in so forward a state that the whole line from London to Norwich would be open by the middle of the next summer. If the predictions of Samuel Peto were correct, Norwich would be only 4¼ hours from London. At this time, the fastest stage coach from London to Norwich and vice versa took 11 hours.

The *Norfolk Chronicle* of 18 January 1845 carried an announcement of a meeting of the proprietors of the Norwich and Brandon Railway to be held on 5 February for determining the propriety of taking a lease with the Yarmouth and Norwich Railway or otherwise of the proposed Lowestoft Railway and Harbour and works connected therewith and for authorising in conjunction with the Yarmouth and Norwich Railway or otherwise an application to parliament for an extension of the Railway into the City of Norwich. At the meeting, the directors reported the progress of constructing the Railway since the last general meeting was such as to justify the expectation that the Railway would be open in the ensuing summer. Near Thetford, works had been suspended in consequence of it having been determined to make the railway through Thetford rather than serve it by a branch line as originally intended. There was every reason to believe that the whole line would be traversed by locomotives in the following month. Arrangements had been made with the contractors building the railway from Bishop's Stortford to Brandon for it to be opened at the same time. At the same meeting, the shareholders authorised the directors to go to parliament to seek powers to build branches from Wymondham to East Dereham and Attleborough to Diss and gave their executive power for the Railway in conjunction with the Yarmouth and Norwich Railway to lease an intended branch to Lowestoft, embracing the purchase of the harbour and to take the necessary powers to extend the terminus of the Railway into the heart of Norwich. The *Norfolk News* of 22 February reported that the deviation had passed the standing orders committee of the House of Commons. The *Norfolk Chronicle* of 1 March reported that the deviation had been staked out. The *Cambridge General Advertiser* of 19 March reported that work on the deviation was progressing as fast as the weather would allow. Norwich City Council was not in favour of the Norwich and Brandon Railway's proposed branch line from Wymondham to East Dereham. It preferred the East Dereham and Norwich Railway. At a meeting of the Council on 15 February, a motion was passed opposing the former's bill for the promotion of the branch line and a Committee was set up to watch the proceedings of the Railway Company's Bill in parliament and to cause the Council's petition to be presented and prosecuted. Indirectly, this meant that the Council was opposing the branch line from Attleborough to Diss, although not specified at the meeting. The opposition to both branches by the City Council was confirmed by a report of its meeting of 10 April in the *Norfolk Chronicle* of 12 April. The previous month, the *Norfolk News* of 18 January had reported that it was expected that the line from Attleborough to Diss would be open at the same time that the line from Norwich to Brandon was opened. The view of the Board of Trade was that it was against this proposed line. The *Norfolk Chronicle* of 25 January reported that memoranda had been signed at Diss in favour of, amongst other lines, that from Attleborough to that town. The *Norfolk Chronicle* of 1 March reported that in parliament on 26 February the petition for the Norwich and Brandon Railway's Deviation and Diss and Dereham branches bill was reported and the bill ordered to be brought in by Messrs Wodehouse and Burroughes. The same newspaper of 8 March carried a report of the Railway Department of the Board of Trade dated 4 March. The main point of this report was that the Board did approve of the route from London to Norwich via the Northern and Eastern and Norwich and Brandon railways, but preferred the alternative route proposed via the ECR and as yet unbuilt EUR. The same newspaper of 15 March reported that a petition would be presented to parliament by the Yarmouth and Norwich Railway for the Norwich and Brandon and Yarmouth and Norwich railways to amalgamate. According to the same edition of the newspaper, the Norwich and Brandon had agreed with the concurrence of the N&ER to rent the proposed London and Norwich Direct Railway. This railway, which was never built, was planned to run from Elsenham on the N&ER to Norwich via Henham, Debden, Radwinter, Hempstead, Bumpstead, Kedinglington, Wickhambrook, Bury St Edmunds, Fornham, Ingham, Barnham to Thetford. The *Norfolk News* of 22 March expanded this a little further, saying that, in addition, the Norwich and Brandon Railway had taken a lease in perpetuity of the N&ER line between Ely and Brandon. The *Chelmsford Chronicle* of 2 May reported that there would be a special meeting of the Norwich and Brandon Railway proprietors on 20 May for the purpose of considering the drafts of the bills before parliament for altering the line of the Railway (Thetford Deviation), and making branches to Diss and East Dereham and also for amalgamating the Norwich and

Brandon Railway with the Yarmouth and Norwich Railway, making a railway from the Yarmouth and Norwich Railway to Lowestoft, a railway from Wells to East Dereham and a railway from Diss to join the ECR near Colchester. According to the *Norfolk Chronicle* of 24 May, whilst the meeting approved the first five there is no mention of the last two. According to the *Ipswich Journal* of the same day, the Chairman had said that the Committee would decide whether they would throw out the Diss and Colchester branch. It is not specified which committee is involved, but presumably it means the Railway Committee of the House of Commons examining the bill. According to the *Norfolk News* of 14 June, the Railway Committee of the House of Commons siting on 10 June had said that the case made out by the promoters of the Diss and Attleborough branch had not been proven. The Committee said that it did not prefer the East Dereham and Norwich Railway to the East Dereham and Wymondham branch. The outcome was that the Railway Committee was in favour of the Railway's branch to East Dereham and against its branch to Diss.

According to the *Norfolk Chronicle* of 21 June, an engine with a train of bricks was running daily on the Norwich and Brandon Railway. The *Bury and Norwich Post* of 25 June said that the Railway had advertised the opening of their line (in conjunction with the N&ER) to London on 1 July. Unfortunately, they had not completed all their works at the Norwich end. A bridge over the Wensum on the south of the Carrow bridge had not been completed. A station had been built at Trowse about a mile from the city on the south side of the river and it was intended that trains should start from that station. It was a full half mile from the Yarmouth and Norwich Railway station and also from the proposed Norwich and Brandon Railway station. Until the bridge was completed, there would be no connection between the two railways.

On 30 June 1845, the Yarmouth and Norwich and Norwich and Brandon railways amalgamated to form the Norfolk Railway. Meanwhile, the opening of the line from Norwich to Brandon did not take place on 1 July. The *Bury and Norwich Post* of 2 July carried an advertisement that it would be open on 9 July. The bill for the two proposed branch lines of the Norwich and Brandon Railway was reported to the House of Commons by the Railways Committee. The Committee struck out the branch to Diss but approved the branch to East Dereham. Confidence in the opening of the railway from Norwich to Brandon and connection to London on 9 July was shown by the *Ipswich Journal* of 5 July, which published a summary timetable of the proposed service – three trains a day in each direction; the traffic to be conveyed was passengers and light goods. There is no mention of ordinary goods traffic.

The opening did not take place. The *Cambridge General Advertiser* of 9 July carried an advertisement that, owing to unavoidable circumstances, the opening had been postponed for a few days. That was not the only problem. The *Norfolk News* of 12 July reported that a petition from Norwich against the proposed Wymondham and East Dereham branch had received 11,000 signatures! The *Norfolk Chronicle* of the same day carried a report of four meetings held in Norwich, Swaffham and Yarmouth against the branch.

It was all to no avail; the *Ipswich Journal* of 19 July reported that the bill for the branch had received its third reading in the House of Lords and would be included in the next batch of bills to receive the Royal Assent. According to the *Journal*, the line was not favourably regarded at Norwich, Yarmouth and Lynn which preferred the direct Norwich and Dereham Railway. However, the *Norfolk Chronicle* of the same day stated an agreement had been reached between the two rivals and opposition to the branch had been withdrawn.

The proposed branch to Diss did not fare so well. The *Norfolk Chronicle* of 5 July reported that the House of Commons Committee examining the branch line from Wymondham to Dereham had struck out all reference to 'a branch line to the town of Diss'.

The opening of the line from Norwich to Brandon took a step nearer, when, according to the *Norfolk Chronicle* of 26 July, the railway and its associated connecting line to London would be open on 30 July.

The line duly opened on the day in question. On 29 July, an inspection of the entire line from London to Norwich was undertaken by the directors of the Norfolk Railway and the ECR, which had taken over the working of the N&ER. The *Norfolk Chronicle* of 2 August carried a special supplement on the opening of the Norfolk Railway. It is clear from an announcement in the same newspaper of 26 July that in addition to passenger traffic, goods traffic would be carried.

When the line from London opened it was prevented from going to the Thorpe station of the former Yarmouth and Norwich Railway because the swing bridge over the River Wensum was not complete. With the completion of the swing bridge in December 1845, through services into Thorpe station from London began.

On 2 March 1846 the section of the ECR between Ely and Brandon was taken over by the Norfolk Railway.

On 7 December 1846, the section of line from Wymondham to Dereham was opened for the conveyance of goods and coal. The opening for passengers had to wait until 15 February 1847. On the opening day for passengers, a luncheon was given for any distinguished persons travelling that day at the Norfolk Hotel in Norwich at half past one.

Chapter 4

The Eastern Union Railway to the End of 1846

The EUR came about from the failure of the ECR to build its line beyond Colchester.

One of the earliest references to the EUR, albeit an indirect one, is in the *Suffolk Chronicle* of Saturday, 29 July 1843, in a notice of a forthcoming meeting to be held in Ipswich Town Hall at 12 o'clock on Tuesday, 8 August:

> Such parties as are desirous of promoting the extension of the ECR from Colchester to Norwich by way of Ipswich, with branches to Bury St Edmunds and Harwich Harbour at which plans, sections and estimates which have been submitted by Mr Wm Tierney Clark and Mr P. Bruff will be submitted'.

The civil engineer William Tierney Clark was a specialist in the design and construction of bridges, especially suspension bridges, in which he was a pioneer. Peter Schuyler Bruff, also a civil engineer, is best known for founding the seaside resort town of Clacton.

The *Ipswich Journal* of the same day reported that it understood that a meeting of several influential parties was held in the town the previous day, with the Mayor in the chair, and the plans, sections and estimates for the extension of the ECR from Colchester to Norwich by way of Ipswich, with branches to Bury St Edmunds and Harwich Harbour, were unanimously approved.

The first actual mention of the EUR appears to be in a report in the *Chelmsford Chronicle* of Friday, 11 August 1843 which carried the report of the engineers of the provisional committee of the EUR dated 24 July. The engineers said that they had surveyed the route of a railway from Colchester to Norwich of a highly favourable character while rejecting the ECR parliamentary route as being too expensive and that instead of crossing the main valleys of the country at right angles as intended, it was proposed to follow them as far as possible and adhere to the natural contours of the country. It was proposed to build branches to Bury St Edmunds and to Harwich Harbour on the Suffolk side of the Stour Estuary. The report was signed by W. Tierney Clark, Engineer, and Peter Bruff, Assistant Engineer.

The *Ipswich Journal* of 12 August carried a full report of the meeting held in Ipswich Town Hall on 8 August. At the meeting, Tierney Clark was not present. According to Hugh Moffatt in *East Anglia's First Railways* (Terrance Dalton 1987) Bruff had approached Tierney Clark as he was a better and more well known engineer. Bruff told the meeting that he and Tierney Clark had considered every aspect and the cost of the projected EUR with a double track main line and single track branch lines would be less than £16,000 per mile including stations, land and rolling stock. The report was adopted, and a committee was appointed to carry the project forward. At the meeting the following resolutions were passed.

Firstly, that the formation of the ECR as far as Colchester had been of great advantage to Ipswich and district and that the extension of the Railway to Norwich by way of Ipswich with branches to Harwich Harbour and Bury St Edmunds would be of great private and public convenience.

Secondly, that the plans, sections and estimates prepared by Messrs Tierney Clark and Bruff and submitted to the meeting appeared to have been prepared with much skill, care and judgement.

Thirdly, that it appeared to the meeting that the undertaking would be remunerative to the parties promoting it and that it would be especially advantageous to the interests of the shareholders of the ECR and that the concurrence and cooperation of the Directors of that Company were earnestly solicited.

Fourthly, that a provisional committee be formed for taking the necessary measures for advancing the undertaking as they might see fit.

Fifthly, that a fund be established for discharging the preliminary expenses to be thereafter incurred.

Sixthly, that those resolutions be advertised in the Ipswich, Colchester, Norwich and Bury St Edmunds newspapers, the *Railway Times*, the *Railway Magazine* and the *Mining Journal* and that copies be sent to the Members of Parliament and boroughs of Essex, Suffolk and Norfolk requesting their support and finally that thanks be given to the Mayor of Ipswich for calling the meeting and the High Sheriff of Suffolk for attending it.

The *Essex Herald* of Tuesday, 5 September reported that the Committee that had recently been appointed at the public meeting was energetically employed in adopting measures for the furtherance of the project. An eminent engineer had been employed to resurvey the proposed line and report thereon.

The next public meeting about the EUR was held in Ipswich Town hall on Tuesday, 10 October for the purpose of receiving the report of the provisional committee appointed at the previous public meeting and for the purpose of taking the necessary measures for the advancement of the undertaking. The meeting was chaired by the Mayor of Ipswich, C. Josselyn Esq, and the minutes of the previous meeting were read by John Chevalier Cobbold, who had acted as Honorary Secretary to the Committee and who had recorded the earlier meeting.

At the meeting the committee reported that it had submitted the scheme to the engineer Joseph Locke for his comments. Locke approved, but there was a slight conflict of interests as he was at the time concerned with the Harwich Railway, the first four miles of which would coincide with the Eastern Union's line, so he suggested that the proposed branch line from Holbrook to Shotley – the line proposed by Tierney Clark and Bruff – should be abandoned. Of the boroughs, only Ipswich accepted. According to the report of the Committee, a letter was sent by the Mayor of Ipswich to the Board of Directors of the ECR annexing the resolutions passed at the meeting of 8 August and requesting that they nominate any gentleman from their number to be added to the Provisional Committee. The answer received was that the communication would be laid before the next monthly meeting of the Board of Directors. Subsequently the Directors of the ECR were to refuse the invitation to nominate a Director to the Provisional Committee and they added that a line of railway from Colchester through or near Hadleigh and Bury St Edmunds (to Thetford) with a branch to Ipswich would best unite and promote all interests and hoped that they, the ECR, would have the support and assistance of the Ipswich interests.

At the meeting, it was resolved that the Railway should pass through or near Ipswich – there is no mention of Norwich, suggesting that Ipswich would be the first objective of the Railway. The contemplated junction with the Birmingham and Midland Counties railways leading to the west and north of England should be by means of a line from Scole or Diss through Thetford or Brandon to join the Peterborough Railway. This would be of great advantage to the district because it would open a channel of communication from the eastern part of the country to the midland, western and northern parts, which would be a huge improvement.

The *Ipswich Journal* of Saturday, 21 October reported that at the General Meeting of the ECR on 12 October, the Directors had decided not to oppose the EUR's line to Ipswich.

The same paper a week later reported that the line of country from Colchester to Ipswich that had been selected for the EUR had been staked out and a flag-staff on Stoke Hills, at Ipswich, showed the direction of the tunnel there. At a meeting of the ECR on 25 October, allusion was made to the EUR and it was regarded favourably by some of the proprietors. The newspaper said that it was not likely that an undertaking which promised to be of great benefit to the ECR would be opposed in the House of Commons without remonstrance by an influential body of proprietors and that it would at least be assented to by that Company. It was high time that a prospectus (of the EUR) was made generally public and its scheme more widely diffused. The newspaper said that it was happy to report that Locke's line to Harwich had been approved at a public meeting in that town. The concurrent interests of the two lines would present such a moral force as would bear down on the ECR, if any was intended. As a proposed branch railway to Hadleigh had also been marked out, the newspaper still saw sufficient reason for the EUR to be 'up and doing'.

The *Essex Standard* of Friday, 10 November reported that a meeting had been held in Ipswich the previous Saturday, at which the Town Council agreed to make a liberal grant from the Corporation Funds to counteract the ECR's proposed line from Colchester to Thetford, putting Ipswich on a branch line.

As mentioned previously, the proposed ECR line via Hadleigh and Bury was naturally of concern to the embryonic Eastern Union. The *Bury and Norwich Post* of Wednesday, 15 November reported that the Provisional Committee of the Railway had held a meeting in Ipswich on 'Saturday week' at which a motion was passed which was deprecatory of the Hadleigh and Bury line as injurious to the trade of Ipswich and that it was the duty of the Town Council and its inhabitants to prevent the line being built. At the meeting it was resolved to apply for powers to build the Railway as far as Ipswich. The same newspaper reported that the previous Thursday, the Ipswich Dock Commissioners held a special meeting at which a motion was passed opposing the carrying through in parliament of any railway which would in their opinion have the effect of diminishing the returns of the Dock Commissioners.

At the end of November 1843, movement was made towards getting an Act to permit the construction of the Railway from Colchester to Ipswich. The *Ipswich Journal* of Saturday, 25 November carried an announcement that an application was to be made to Parliament in the ensuing session for such an Act.

According to the *Ipswich Journal* of 2 December, the reason for the EUR deciding only to apply for powers to build as far as Ipswich was the lateness of the season and the propriety of awaiting the result of the proposed application of the Norwich and Brandon Railway. The same newspaper said that the plans and books of reference for the EUR had been deposited with the Clerks of the Peace of the respective counties.

The *Essex Standard* of Friday, 22 December reported that on Wednesday, 13 December there had been a meeting held in Bury St Edmunds in support of the proposed ECR line from Colchester to Norwich through Bury St Edmunds. The *Ipswich Journal* of 30 December reported the ECR had abandoned its proposed railway from Colchester to Norwich via Bury St Edmunds with a branch to Ipswich.

It was in January 1844 that John Chevalier Cobbold became Chairman of the EUR. Cobbold was a leading townsman of Ipswich and a member of a highly respected Suffolk family.

Following its introduction to Parliament, the Eastern Union's Bill received its second reading in the Commons on 29 March. On 10 June, the Company's bill was read a third time in the Commons and passed by that House, receiving the Royal Assent on 19 July.

On 1 August there was a meeting held at Ipswich Town Hall for the purpose of hearing a report from the provisional committee which had been set up at the meeting held on 8 August the previous year. The Committee said that overtures should be made to Bury St Edmunds and Norwich to support the extension of the EUR to those places. A motion in favour of the Committee's proposal was passed by the meeting.

The Directors of the ECR at the Company's General Meeting on 8 August reported that they had deemed it their duty to oppose the Eastern Union's bill unless that Company had agreed to stop their line at the point where it would intersect the proposed Harwich line agreed by the ECR to be leased to the Eastern Union at a point 4 miles from Colchester. All the Eastern Union had agreed to was to start their line 2½ miles from Colchester. This stretch of line to be built by the ECR and to be common to both companies.

By the middle of October, work had started on building the railway from Colchester to Ipswich. The *Norfolk Chronicle* of Saturday, 12 October said that work had commenced 'Tuesday week' i.e., 1 October. According to the *Ipswich Journal* of 19 October, excavations had commenced on the hill at Brantham and work extended over a distance of 2 miles. The *Journal* had been informed that work would commence the following week, the week 20 to 26 October, on the Essex side of the Stour. Meanwhile a provisional committee had been formed under the chairmanship of John Cobbold to raise money to extend the line from Ipswich to Norwich. The engineer for the building of the line was Joseph Locke.

During the middle to latter part of November 1844, an announcement appeared in various local newspapers that the EUR intended to make an application to parliament in the ensuing session for an Act to construct a railway from Ipswich to Norwich. The Norwich terminus would not be that of the Yarmouth and Norwich and Norwich and Brandon railways but a separate one at Victoria Gardens.

At the end of December 1844 at the Chelmsford Quarter Sessions on 31 December, Mr Ryland told the magistrates that he had been asked by the EUR to apply to the magistrates under the company's Act to appoint a competent engineer to act as an inspector of the works near Colchester. He said that the ECR had contemplated carrying their line from Colchester to Ipswich but had abandoned it and 'would not go an inch beyond Colchester'. What was decided was that the ECR would construct three miles beyond Colchester and the Eastern Union was to be dovetailed into it. The magistrates agreed and after consulting appointed James Walker, the government engineer, as inspector. Other candidates were Brunel of the Great Western and Cubitt of the London and South Western Railway.

By May 1845, good progress had been made in the building of the line between Ardleigh and Ipswich and at Bentley a length of the track had been laid. Between Ardleigh and Colchester things were in a less satisfactory state. Prior to its opening to Colchester, the ECR had purchased land beyond Colchester as far as Ardleigh and John Braithwaite, the ECR engineer, had surveyed a route for a railway called the Colchester and Harwich Railway which used this land. The ECR had, having abandoned work on constructing the line beyond Colchester, now restarted work. What happened was that on 22 September 1845 an agreement was reached between the two companies that the Eastern Union should complete the work for a sum to be agreed between Joseph Locke for the Eastern Union and Robert Stephenson for the ECR with Isambard Kingdom Brunel acting as umpire.

The *Suffolk Chronicle* of 11 October reported that the line would be opened on 1 May the following year.

The location of the station in Ipswich was of concern to the inhabitants of the town. It was near the ancient house in Stoke called New Place but known as Haxall's Farm and was regarded as rather inconvenient for the town. The Friar's Bridge was considered to be the best location for a station. A meeting was held in the Town Hall on Monday, 22 December. The result was that a committee was formed to confer with the directors of the EUR and the Corporation of Ipswich and to adopt such proceedings with reference to the approaches to the town as would be most advantageous to the town and to the public generally.

At the beginning of 1846, the engineers of the Railway, reporting to the Directors, stated that everything would be ready for the railway to be opened at the end of May and that the work on the ECR section of the projected line about 2½ miles beyond Colchester was progressing more rapidly. It would appear that the Eastern Union actually did the work on this latter section and compensated the ECR as provided for in the Act of incorporation of the Eastern Union. To enable this to be done legally, an Act dated 26 June 1846 was obtained.

By the latter part of May, the time was approaching when the EUR would be ready for inspection by the Board of Trade. The *Suffolk*

Chronicle of Saturday, 23 May reported that General Pasley, the Inspector of Railways, was expected to inspect the line the following Tuesday. A trip had been made over the entire length of the line on Tuesday, 5 May by a number of people at the instigation of Mr Olgivie, the agent for Messrs Brassey and Mackenzie, the contractors.

The *Essex Standard* of 29 May reported that the date of opening of the Railway had not been officially announced, but that 11 June was the probable date. The date might have been earlier had not the engagements of General Pasley prevented him from making his inspection. It was expected that, following the inspection, the line would be open to goods immediately and to passengers on the following Monday.

On Tuesday, 2 June, General Pasley finally made his inspection of the Railway. However, even before the inspection, goods traffic had already started on the previous day. This seems rather irregular. As the tunnel had not been completed, the station at Ipswich was not on the site of the present one, but rather a temporary one south of the tunnel. Following the inspection and approval being given, the official opening took place on Thursday, 11 June, followed by the opening to public traffic on Monday, 15 June. On the day of the official opening, all the shops and workplaces were closed and the day was a general holiday. At 10.30am a special train hauled by two locomotives and consisting of twelve carriages and a truck carrying a band, left Ipswich conveying invited guests. At the mouth of the tunnel, the junction of the extension north and at Bentley, triumphal arches had been erected. Stops were made at Bentley, where the Chairman of the Company, John Chevalier Cobbold, joined the train, Manningtree, Lawford Mills, where water was taken on, and Ardleigh. When the train reached Colchester, it was greeted by George Hudson, the Chairman of the ECR, and others who had travelled down from London by a special train of six carriages. The two trains were then joined together and reached Ipswich hauled by two locomotives. After a lunch, some of the party went for a steamer trip down the Orwell to Harwich. At 5pm, about 200 people sat down to a banquet in the Assembly Room. At the same time, 270 of the workers involved in building the railway were entertained by the contractors at Manningtree, whilst at Ipswich there were dinners for the Company's staff and for the sub-contractors. The navvies involved in building the tunnel at Ipswich for the extension north were given a meal at the Railroad Tavern at Stoke Hill, which, according to Hugh Moffat in *East Anglia's Railways* (Terrance Dalton 1987), appears to have been a house temporarily converted to a public house. On the day of the opening to public traffic, 450 passengers traversed the line.

The EUR had a desire to develop the sources of traffic which they anticipated over their line in conjunction with the ECR. They anticipated regular communication could be established with the continent from Harwich and arranged with the Orwell Steam Navigation Company to run an excursion from Ipswich and Harwich to Rotterdam and back on the steam ship *Orwell.* According to the *Essex Standard* of 26 June, a special train left Shoreditch station at half-past five in the morning on 17 June carrying directors

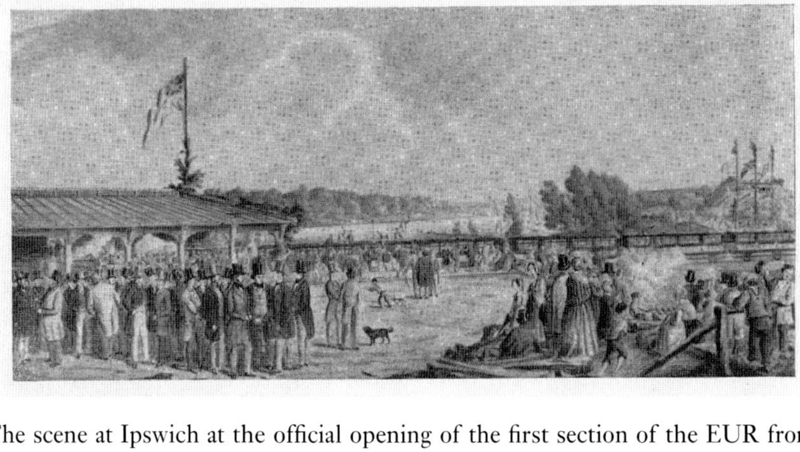

The scene at Ipswich at the official opening of the first section of the EUR from Colchester to Ipswich on Thursday, 11 June 1846. The official opening of the railway was followed by the opening to the public on Monday, 15 June 1846, thus connecting Ipswich to London by railway. (Author's collection).

and other gentlemen and reached Ipswich at twenty past seven. Here they joined other gentlemen connected with the railways and embarked on the *Orwell* steamer lying alongside the quay. At twenty-five minutes past seven the steamer set off. Obviously, a quick embarkation. The steamer was off Harwich at twenty minutes past eight, where it paused for a few minutes before heading off for Rotterdam. Rotterdam was reached at a quarter to nine in the evening, the journey having taken 15¼ hours. The party stayed overnight in the Hotel de Pays Bas. The following morning, the party left Rotterdam at half past ten in the morning and reached Ipswich at half past ten in the evening, where the party dined on board the *Orwell*. Those going to London left Ipswich by special train at eleven o'clock and reached Shoreditch station at one o'clock in the morning of 19 June. The *Essex Standard* said that the experiment proved that when the railway reached Harwich and effective steamers were in service between Harwich and Rotterdam, a traveller would be able to leave London at six o'clock in the morning and be in The Hague at six o'clock in the evening and that letters from Holland would be able to reach London on the same day they were written in time for being posted all over the world. What was not mentioned was that the railway in Holland had not yet reached Rotterdam.

At Colchester, the EUR at first shared the facilities with the ECR. At Ipswich the original terminus was in Croft Street, but this was regarded as temporary.

Even prior to the EUR having obtained its Act, there were various proposals to connect Bury St Edmunds to the railway network. As soon as the Eastern Union had obtained its Act in July 1844, surveys were made for extending the line to Bury St Edmunds and also to Norwich. The *Chelmsford Chronicle* of 23 August reported that it had surveyed an extension of its line to Norwich and a branch to Bury St Edmunds. According to the *Bury and Norwich Post* of Wednesday, 11 September, the survey of the line from Ipswich to Norwich having been completed, plans would be laid before the Board of Trade the

The exterior of Ipswich station as it was originally built. Ipswich was the headquarters of the EUR and according to *Bradshaw's Railway Guide* for March 1850, J.C. Cobbold was the Chairman, J.F. Saunders, Secretary, P. Bruff, Engineer and Manager and J.H. Sollas, Goods Superintendent. (Author's collection).

following week. The survey of the branch to Bury St Edmunds was nearly completed. On the western side of Bury St Edmunds, the ECR had given notice of its intention to construct a railway to that town from Cambridge. The *Suffolk Chronicle* of Saturday, 16 November gave notice of the EUR's intention to apply to parliament in the ensuing session for powers to construct and maintain a railway from Ipswich to Bury St Edmunds. Meanwhile, according to the *Lynn Advertiser* of Saturday, 23 November, the EUR announced its intention to apply to parliament in the ensuing session for powers to construct and maintain a railway from Ipswich to Norwich. According to the *Bury and Norwich Post* of 4 December, the following plans for the EUR had been deposited with the Clerk of the Peace for Suffolk – Ipswich to Norwich and Ipswich to Bury St Edmunds. According to the *Essex Standard* of 13 December, application had been made to parliament for lines from Ipswich to Norwich via Stowmarket and Diss and Stowmarket to Bury St Edmunds. The same newspaper also mentioned an application to parliament by the ECR to build a line from Cambridge to Bury St Edmunds via Newmarket.

The Eastern Union's proposed line to Bury St Edmunds did not go through without opposition. For example, the *Bury and Norwich Post* of Wednesday, 15 January 1845 carried reports of there being forty-one objectors to the line, although the newspaper is not specific regarding the scheme to which they objected. Probably the London and Norwich Direct Railway through Bury St Edmunds and Thetford. According to the same newspaper of Wednesday, 29 January, the Railway Board of the Board of Trade had decided in favour of the Eastern Union's line over the London and Norwich Direct promoted in 1844.

In March 1845, the ECR suffered a setback in its intention to reach Bury St Edmunds from Cambridge when the Board of Trade rejected the proposal, according to the *Ipswich Journal* of 29 March. The *Norfolk Chronicle* of the same date reported on petitions for the Eastern Union and Bury St Edmunds Railway (No2) and the Eastern Union and Norwich (No2) being amongst other bills which were referred to the Select Committee for Private Bills of the House of Commons. Of the two bills, that for the line to Norwich was rejected on technical grounds, but that for the line to Bury St Edmunds was approved, according to the *Norfolk Chronicle* of 26 April. Despite the rejection of the bill for the line to Norwich, the EUR was not put off and according to the *Norfolk Chronicle* of 3 May intended to proceed in the next session of parliament.

It is in July 1845 that there is the first mention of the Ipswich and Bury St Edmunds Railway (I&BR). The *Ipswich Journal* of 5 July reported that the Board of Trade had approved the Bill of the Ipswich and Bury Railway. According to the same newspaper of Saturday, 26 July, on the previous Monday the Bill for the I&BR had received the Royal Assent. According to the *Suffolk Chronicle* of the same day, the works for the Railway (which the *Chronicle* called the Bury and Ipswich Railway) were all contracted for and the contractor would be in Bury in a few days to make arrangements for commencing operations. The *Ipswich Journal* of 2 August carried a report of the breaking of the first ground for the extension. The newspaper said that the I&BR left the existing line from Colchester to Ipswich at a place called Halifax Junction, which was just south of the tunnel.

According to the *Norfolk Chronicle* of 9 August and the *Bury and the Norwich Post* of Wednesday, 27 August, the Act authorising the extension was incorporated under the title of the I&BR. The part sanctioned (26 miles) contained 15 miles of the extension to Norwich. The Directors of the EUR would apply to parliament in the next session for powers to construct the remaining 30 miles to Norwich.

Although the I&BR was an independent company at least in name, six of the Eastern Unions's directors had seats on the Board including John Cobbold, who was Chairman of both boards. The latter railway was to all intents and purposes an extension of the former railway.

Work on acquiring land for the I&BR started as soon as it became apparent that the Bill for the Railway would be passed and work on constructing the line commenced within a few days of the passing of the Company's Act. According to the *Ipswich Journal* of Saturday, 2 August, work had commenced the previous day, when excavators commenced work on one of the shafts from the summit of Stoke Hill towards the proposed tunnel. At one o'clock, the official ceremony for the start of the construction took place. The Mayor of Ipswich, William Rodwell Esq, commenced operations by loading a wheelbarrow and removing it to the intended extremity slope. He was followed by a further eleven men with wheelbarrows. These were prominent local people and directors of the EUR and the I&BR railways. The whole ceremony was attended by a number of people connected with or associated with the Railway or the town of Ipswich. The Ipswich station would be at the foot of the hill, in, according to the newspaper, a field planted with turnips, and a bridge would be made across the river and roads.

The *Suffolk Chronicle* of 11 October reported that the perpendicular shafts on the summit of the hill at Stoke for the use of the intended tunnelling were well lined with masonry and were as well and rapidly sunk as necessity demanded. The tunnel would be commenced with all possible dispatch. The line would be opened on 1 October the following year.

During the construction of the I&BR to Ipswich, the fossilized remains of a mammoth were found in the immediate vicinity of Ipswich as reported by the *Essex Herald* of 21 October 1845.

By the middle of January 1846, the building of the tunnel through Stoke Hill was proceeding rapidly. Preparations were also being made for the erection of a temporary station in a field near the Stoke Meeting House.

According to Hugh Moffat in *East Anglia's First Railway*, consideration was given in constructing the tunnel to be adapted for the broad gauge, 7ft ¼in of the GWR. Why this is puzzling is that the ECR and the Northern Eastern railways had been converted to the gauge of 4ft 8½in used by the majority of the railways of England, Scotland and Wales. In building the tunnel at Ipswich, problems were encountered with drainage. When this was solved, another problem arose in that the wells supplying water to nearby houses dried up. The Company was liable for a penalty of £5 a day for this, but somehow they managed to avoid paying it. In 1847, they got around to providing a well and a pump for the poor of the parish. The tunnel was finally completed in September 1847 and on 19 September, fifty guests attended the ceremonial insertion of the last four bricks in the lining of it.

Meanwhile, the construction of the rest of the Railway progressed so that by the end of November 1846, the line through to Bury was ready for opening. However, even out of the tunnel the construction of the line was not without difficulties. Along the valley of the River Gipping at Stowmarket, the line was and is carried on a low embankment. According to Moffat, in the last week of May the work there had shown a slight tendency to subside, but on 1 June the navvies found that several yards of the embankment had almost disappeared. The problem continued throughout the summer, and it was not until September that the decision was taken to float the embankment on a raft of faggots and brushwood as George Stephenson had done at

Chat Moss on the Liverpool and Manchester Railway. The bog at Stowmarket though was, at 80ft deep, twice that of Chat Moss.

On 26 November 1846, the first trial run from Ipswich to Bury St Edmunds took place, comprising a locomotive and five carriages. The train stopped at Claydon, Needham, Haughley, Elmswell and Thurston and reached Bury nearly two hours after leaving Ipswich and stopped at a temporary station on the Ipswich side of the bridge over the Northgate Road, which was as far as the Company's Act allowed the construction of the line. Following the successful trip, the line was opened to goods traffic on 30 November. On 15 December, the line was inspected by Captain Coddington of the Board of Trade. Following the inspection, it was expected that the line would open for passenger traffic on 21 December, but it was not until the afternoon of 23 December that permission to open the line to passengers was given. At four o'clock the following morning, a special train with notices to all stations left Ipswich and at ten past nine the first passenger train left Ipswich for Bury St Edmunds. This was a rather nice Christmas present for the people of Bury St Edmunds. The *Chelmsford Chronicle* of Christmas Day reported that the previous day the railway had opened to passengers as authority to do so had been received. The *Ipswich Journal* of 26 December also carried a report of the opening.

At Ipswich, trains coming from the south going north had to reverse out of the station before proceeding onwards and trains coming from the north going south had to reverse in to the station before proceeding onwards. This was not very satisfactory and according to D.I. Gordon in the *Regional History of the Railways of Great Britain Volume 5 – the Eastern Counties Railway* (David and Charles 1968), the EUR made an undertaking with the Corporation of Ipswich in 1846 that the permanent station in the town was to be on the line of the I&BR. Moffat says that designs for a joint permanent station at Ipswich for both the Eastern Union and I&BR were invited in early 1846. There were nineteen entries received and the winning design

The ornate exterior of Stowmarket station. The line through Stowmarket to Bury St Edmunds was opened to goods traffic on 30 November 1846 and to passenger traffic on 24 December 1846, thus giving the inhabitants of those towns a very nice Christmas present that year. (Author's collection).

was that of Sancton Wood. Because of severe financial restrictions, the building of the station was not started for another twelve years.

Even before the I&BR was completed there was further expansion in the air. In the *Morning Chronicle* of Tuesday, 2 December 1845 and quoted in the *Morning Post* the following day, was a list of projected railway lines that had been deposited with the Board of Trade in compliance with the Standing Orders of the House of Commons. In total there were 573 lines. Of these, the I&BR's Norwich extension was number 142. Following its passage through parliament, it received its Royal Assent on 27 July 1846.

The next step to the enlargement of the Eastern Union was the Norwich extension. The Act for this work was obtained by the Ipswich & Bury before it amalgamated with its more powerful partner and provided for a capital of £550,000 with authority to raise a further sum of £183,333 by loan or mortgage. A clause in the Act provided for the purchase of this line and the remainder of the Ipswich & Bury by the Eastern Union, and as this Act was drafted and given Royal Assent before the former began to function, it is quite certain that the Eastern Union Directors contemplated acquiring the Ipswich & Bury at an early date. At the Norwich end, a branch line was to be made at Trowse to form a connection with the ECR. The latter company, when taking over the Norfolk Railway, accepted its obligations, one of which was that in the event of the government railway department deciding that the level crossing at Trowse station was unsuitable, a bridge should be built. As the additional traffic arising from the Ipswich & Bury line might cause such a decision to be made, a clause was inserted in the Ipswich & Bury bill at the instigation of the Eastern Counties, compelling the former to contribute to the cost.

In 1841, railway speculator John Attwood was elected as one of the Members of Parliament for Harwich and one of his promises was that if he was successful, he would advance the sum of £20,000 for a railway to the town. Having got elected he did not immediately make good his promise. Prior to its opening to Colchester, the ECR had purchased land beyond Colchester as far as Ardleigh and John Braithwaite, the ECR engineer, had surveyed a route for a railway called the Colchester and HR which used this land. In early 1843, when the Eastern Counties' line to Colchester was about to be opened, the Mayor of Harwich convened a meeting to remind Attwood of his promise. A deputation met Attwood, who now had to act. Being reluctant to stake his political future on Braithwaite's estimates of the cost of a scheme which was backed by some of his opponents in Harwich, he turned to Joseph Locke and the result was the Harwich Railway and Pier, which followed a more northerly course from Ardleigh than Brathwaite's. Both schemes were rejected by parliament on the grounds that there was not thought to be sufficient traffic. According to Moffat, Attwood was so confident of the success of his scheme that he had ordered the rails for it! Following the failure of his scheme, he persuaded the backers of the Colchester and Harwich scheme to join forces with him and Braithwaite prepared a new HR and Pier scheme which used part of Locke's design. Locke had now become the engineer in chief of the EUR and under his guidance Peter Bruff surveyed a branch from Manningtree to Harwich. In the parliamentary session of 1844-5, both John Attwood's line to the town supported by the ECR and the EUR's branch to the town along with schemes by William Hosking and R.B. Mosse were submitted. All failed to pass Standing Orders. In the following year, the two main contenders repeated their attempts. This time Attwood's scheme was called the Harwich and Eastern Counties Junction Railway but the ECR did not support him. By an agreement of September 1845, the ECR undertook to abandon their own proposal for a direct line from Colchester to Harwich and to support the Eastern Union's new branch from Manningree. On its completion they would work it and be given running powers over the Eastern Union from Colchester to Manningtree. However, the Bills for both the proposed lines were not passed in that session.

Chapter 5

The Eastern Counties Railway from August 1845 to December 1850

We left the ECR having just extended to Brandon to join the Norfolk Railway. Probably the most important thing that happened between the beginning of August and the end of December 1845 was that George Hudson was appointed Chairman of the Railway on 13 October. Hudson has been described as many things, but he was in fact merely a product of his age – he was known as the Railway King because of the number of railways he was concerned in, but the story does not have a happy ending.

Prior to Hudson becoming Chairman of the ECR, he acquired control of a number of lines in the North East and the Midlands. Those in the former eventually became part of the North Eastern Railway (NER) and in the latter became the Midland Railway.

As mentioned previously, it is in November 1844 that we first find mention of George Hudson, who the following year would become Chairman. The *Norfolk Chronicle* of 23 November reported that the proposed project for a Cambridge and Lincoln railway had been taken up by the ECR and that Hudson had consented to join it. Six ECR directors had been placed on the committee of the Cambridge and Lincoln. The other Company involved was the MR. It was possible that two or three Hudson directors would join him in the management.

By the latter part of 1845, the ECR was not in a particularly happy financial position. Hudson at this time was enjoying a rather glowing reputation and was the man to have as Chairman if a railway wanted to improve its financial position. Hudson, however, had his own agenda. At this time the only way to get from London to the north of England, including York, was from Euston station by what later became the London and North Western Railway and the MR, which latter Hudson controlled. Hudson wanted an independent route – controlled by him. There was at this time the stirrings of what materialised as the Great Northern Railway (GNR), in which Hudson had no financial or controlling interest. The ECR had obtained powers to build a line from Ely to Peterborough and the MR had obtained powers to build a line from Syston to Peterborough. By this route, Hudson hoped to have an alternative route to York and the north controlled by him. The fact that it was very circuitous was of no relevance to Hudson. The GNR received its Act of authorisation on 26 June 1846.

On being appointed Chairman of the ECR, one of Hudson's first actions was to appoint David Waddington as his deputy chairman. Waddington was born in 1810 in Manchester, the son of an iron founder. It is not known when they first met.

Unfortunately, Hudson's methods were not as straight as they might appear at first glance. He decided the levels of the dividends to be paid to shareholders and then left it to Waddington to doctor the traffic accounts to make them appear legally earned. In this way, Waddington also siphoned off £8,000 of the ECR's money into a parliamentary slush fund. This strained relations between him and Hudson.

In 1848 things started to go wrong for Hudson. A pamphlet entitled *The bubble of the age or The fallacy of railway investment, Railway Accounts and Railway dividends* alleged that the dividends that were paid by Hudson's companies were paid out of capital rather than out of revenue. In February 1849, he was attacked by MR shareholder and Liverpool shipowner J.H. Brankner over his fight with the GNR. This was then exacerbated by Hudson's agreement with the Great Northern to allow them to use the Burton Salmon route of the York and North Midland Railway (which later became part of the NER). Many felt that Hudson had effectively sold them out.

In order to keep some of his companies afloat, Hudson had been borrowing money at a high interest rate. A payment of £400,000 had to be made in 1849; many of these companies were left in a difficult position with falling revenues, an economic depression and little scope for future shareholder dividends.

The shareholders who had praised Hudson for their huge profits now turned against him. At a an MR meeting on 15 February 1849 there were demands for an official enquiry; Hudson threatened to resign and the call was dropped. Five days later, Horatio Love and Robert Prance, shareholders in the York, Newcastle and Berwick Railway, revealed that shares had been sold far in excess of their actual value; Hudson was the beneficiary.

The following week, the ECR held its AGM; Hudson was not there. Furious shareholders demanded action from Vice Chairman David Waddington, who blamed Hudson for the shortfall in their dividends. Two enquiries were now set up and Hudson resigned.

In April, it was revealed that Hudson had to repay £30,000 over the shares scandal. In early May, Francis Charteris MP began a further enquiry into the bribery of MPs. Hudson was MP for Sunderland and addressed parliament, but the damage was done. And the net of enquiries ensnared William Cash, who had himself set up a committee to investigate Hudson's malpractice. Cash was involved in double-dealing himself.

George Hudson's days were over, and he was succeeded as Chairman of the ECR by Edward Betts, partner of Samuel Peto. Betts held the chair until 1851.

Hudson was not a bad man; he was just a product of his time and who could blame him for what he did? He was no worse than others, but had the misfortune to get found out; he died on 14 December 1871 aged 71.

During the period covered by this chapter, further extensions of the ECR took place. The Eastern Counties and Thames Junction Railway had obtained its Act on 4 July 1844. Under the Act, the ECR was given powers to purchase the ECR and Thames Junction Railway. On the south bank of the Thames was the military and market town of Woolwich in Kent. By an accident of history, there was a very small part of Woolwich on the north bank of the Thames. This was North Woolwich and was also a part of Kent. The town was not served by any railways. The nearest railway station was Greenwich on the London and Greenwich Railway, which was leased by the South Eastern Railway in 1845. In that same year, the South Eastern Railway obtained an Act to extend the London and Greenwich Railway to Gravesend via Woolwich and Dartford. On the north bank of the Thames, an extension of the Eastern Counties and Thames Junction Railway to North Woolwich seemed an attractive proposition to its directors and so, having met no opposition, the Railway obtained an Act for the extension on 21 July 1845. The building of the Eastern Counties and Thames Junction Railway to Thames Wharf was delayed by flooding of Plaistow Marsh and of other land east of Bow Creek. The line eventually opened to Thames Wharf for goods traffic on 29 April 1846 as a single track. Whilst the preparations for the extension to North Woolwich were going ahead, the ECR and Thames Junction Railway obtained powers to build a branch across the River Lea to the East India Dock Company's pepper warehouses and also a quarter of a mile long curve at Stratford pointing in the direction of London. In 1847, whilst the extension to North Woolwich was under construction, the ECR bought the Eastern Counties and Thames Junction Railway. The extension to North Woolwich opened on 14 June, together with a second track on the original section and the new curve at Stratford. At the 21st general meeting of the ECR on 9 February 1847, the engineer had reported that the double line of the Stratford and Thames Junction Railway would be ready for opening in the course of a few days.

On the ECR proper, the working of the section of line from Ely to Brandon was taken over by the Norfolk Railway on 2 March 1846.

On the line from Ely to Peterborough: at the 18th general meeting of the Railway on 28 August 1845 the engineer reported that 'The earth-work is well advanced between Peterborough and Whittlesea, and the permanent way materials nearly all delivered for the entire length from Ely to Peterborough'.

On 14 January 1847, the ECR opened its line from Ely to Peterborough. The new line provided an alternative route to London to that provided by the London and North Western Railway via Northampton. On 7 August 1850, the GNR opened its direct line through Peterborough to London.

The GNR would become a threat to the ECR as we shall see later. The GNR wanted to reach Cambridge and even before it had opened its first section made an agreement with the Royston and Hitchin Railway, which had been projected as the Cambridge and Oxford railway, but its Bill had been cut down in the House of Lords. The railway received its Act on 16 July 1846. In 1848, the ECR obtained powers to build a railway from Cambridge to Bedford, but it failed to build the line. The GNR wanted at all costs to keep the ECR out of its territory and was concerned that the latter Company could seize control of the Royston and Hitchin Railway, which would give it another penetrating line into GNR territory in addition to the Ely to Peterborough line. On 14 August 1848, the Royston and Hitchin Railway obtained an Act to extend its line from Royston to Shepreth, joining the proposed Cambridge to Bedford branch there. If the ECR failed to construct its Cambridge to Bedford line in a reasonable time, the Royston and Hitchin Railway would have the power to build the line itself. The construction of the Royston and Hitchin Railway was not difficult or expensive, and the 12¾ miles from Hitchin junction to Royston was opened on 21 October 1850 and was worked by the GNR. Meanwhile, the ECR was compelled by a condition in its Act to build a line from Cambridge to Bedford to open its line to Shepreth, which it did on 1 August 1851. It did not physically connect with the Royston and Hitchin Railway.

During the latter part of 1846 or the early part of 1847, the Hertford branch was doubled, except for the line through Ware station, which for some reason remained single track. At the 20th general meeting of the Company on 6 August 1846, Directors reported that a double line was about to be laid from the Broxbourne Junction to Hertford. At the next meeting on 9 February 1847, the engineer reported that the double line of the Hertford Branch had been completed at a cost of £1,500 under the estimate.

1847 saw further expansion of the ECR when it opened a branch line from March on the Ely to Peterborough line to Wisbech on 3 May.

The *Cambridge Journal and Chronicle* of 8 May reported:

> WISBECH. Opening of the Railway. On Monday, the line of the ECR between Wisbech and March was opened for traffic, and the first passenger train conveyed the respected Mayor of this borough, William Stevens Esq, Mr. Alderman Leach, and other members of the corporation to London, to continue their duties before a committee of the House of Commons on the several railways affecting this town. The shops were closed, and the day throughout was a holiday. Nearly 600 persons availed themselves the opportunity of visiting Cambridge afforded by the Company's excursion trains. The children of the National Schools and the children in the Union were treated with a trip to Ely. The occasion drew an immense concourse; and it is probable that had not the weather been so unfavourable, a greater number of people would have been assembled than had ever been seen in the town before. The arrangements of the station appear to be very complete and under the judicious superintendence of our fellow townsman, Mr. Charles Exley, the station-master, everything went off in good style.

On 17 August, the ECR opened another branch line; this time to St Ives from Chesterton Junction. Here it met with the East Anglian Railway (EAR), which is the subject of the next chapter.

In Essex two branches from Witham between Chelmsford and Colchester to Maldon and Braintree were opened. These had been promoted locally in 1845 as a single railway by the Maldon, Witham and Braintree Railway which had received its act on 18 June 1846. Construction of the railway started in March 1847. Whilst all this was going on, the ECR purchased the Maldon, Witham and Braintree Railway. It was originally intended that the Railway would cross over the ECR at Witham with connections to the latter Railway, but the latter ECR redesigned the layout at Witham to become two separate branches. The terminal station at Maldon was rather grander than that at Braintree. This was because David Waddington, the Deputy Chairman of the ECR, was standing for election as a Conservative for Maldon in the General Election of 1847. The rather grandiose station was clearly an inducement to the electors of Maldon to vote for him. During the election campaign, Waddington contrived to have a large number of men who were eligible to vote taken into the nominal payroll of the railway for the sum of one guinea (21s) a week. This 'workforce' was employed regardless of their age, of their calling or their capacity for work. It would seem that they did little if any work on the railway. The inhabitants of Maldon called these men 'Waddington's Guinea Pigs'. Waddington was duly elected to Parliament. The employment of the 'Guinea Pigs' ceased the Tuesday after the election. A report published after the following General Election which took place in 1852, at which Waddington was standing for Harwich, was quite damning in its belated assessment of the 1847 election. The two branch lines, which were double track, were opened for goods traffic on 15 August 1848. Following the opening to goods traffic, in one week in September 1848 goods trains carried 300 tons of coal and 350 tons of other freight. On 30 September, the Board of Trade Railway Department Inspector, Captain George Wynne, Royal Engineers, inspected the railway and declared it fit for opening for passenger traffic, which event duly took place on 2 October. The first passenger train left Maldon carrying a number of merchants bound for the

London markets. The first train to arrive at Braintree was welcomed by a crowd of hundreds. The *Chelmsford Chronicle* of 6 October reported:

> INSPECTION AND OPENING OF THE MALDON, WITHAM, & BRAINTREE LINE. This branch of the Eastern Counties Railway, which has been traversed for some weeks by goods trains, was on Monday opened for passenger traffic, after inspection by Captain Wynn and other officers from the Railway Board of Commissioners on Saturday last, who, we understand, expressed their satisfaction at the general appearance of the permanent way, and the manner in which the comfort and convenience of the public were studied in all the arrangements which had been made. This is an important link in the railway communication of this county, connecting, as it does, the inland town of Braintree with the port of Maldon and giving its inhabitants the advantages which rapid transit invariably affords, in addition to the reduction of about 5s. per ton in the price of coals, which have hitherto been carted from Maldon at an expense of 8s. per ton. The opening of the line had caused considerable interest amongst the inhabitants of the parishes through which it passed, and every bridge or spot from which a view of the train could be obtained was crowded with spectators. The first train from Maldon to Braintree carried a goodly company of merchants and others, but it was reserved for the down train from London, in connection with which the directors had issued tickets from Chelmsford and Hatfield, at reduced fares, to carry into Braintree the principal company of the morning. On reaching the Witham station, eight carriages were detached from the main train, and started for Braintree crowded with passengers, to enjoy the pleasures of the fair.

Although the railway was built, at Maldon work had been started on a dock adjacent to the railway, but it was never completed.

The ornate frontage of Maldon (East) station in 1848 as the terminus of a branch line from Witham. The reason for the design was to induce the electors of Maldon to vote for David Waddington, one of the ECR's directors, at a forthcoming general election. (Author).

In Middlesex, following local pressure, an Enfield, Edmonton and Eastern Counties Railway was promoted in 1845 and in 1846 an Enfield and Edmonton Railway. The latter was successful and asked the ECR to take over the Company and build the line from Angel Road station, which was then named Water Lane, on the Cambridge line via Edmonton to Enfield. Work started on the line in 1848 and it was opened on 1 March 1849 without 'formal or public demonstrations'. The *Evening Standard* of 2 March reported:

> 'Opening of the Edmonton and Enfield Branch — Yesterday the branch line leading from the Edmonton station of the ECR to Edmonton and Enfield, which is a distance of nearly three miles, was opened for the conveyance of passengers to and from the

metropolis. The fares were raised to Edmonton and Enfield: 2d. the single ticket, and 3d. the return ticket'.

Most journeys involved a change at Water Lane, but there were a few through trains. Shortly after the opening, a 2-2-0 rail motor named *Enfield* was employed on the line. *Enfield* was a 2-2-0 well tank locomotive and a 36-seat 4-compartment 4-wheeled carriage seating 42 passengers on one frame. It was built by W.B. Adams at Fairfield Works, Bow. It was normally attached to a 9 ton 116 seat carriage and used for the through journeys between Enfield and London. Despite being more economical on fuel than a normal locomotive, it was not a consistent success, and the locomotive was detached from its carriage and converted into a 2-2-2 well tank.

During the rest of 1849 and all of 1850 there were not any more openings by the ECR, the next opening by the Company being the aforementioned line to Shepreth on 1 August 1851.

One of the problems that railways entering London faced in the early days was getting their passengers into the centre of London. Of all the railways, only the L&BR's terminus at Fenchurch Street approached the City of London. Some were worse than others, the Great Western's at Paddington and the London and South Western's original terminus at Nine Elms being the furthest away from the City, as was the terminus constructed by the South Eastern at Bricklayers Arms. The Shoreditch terminus of the ECR and the Northern and Eastern was relatively near to the City of London.

In 1846, the ECR approached the Metropolitan Railway Commissioners, who had been appointed in April of that year to investigate the various railway projects, whose termini were proposed to be within, or in the immediate vicinity of, the metropolis. Their report was published at the end of June that year. There were three proposals. The first one was to extend the ECR line half a mile from Shoreditch to Finsbury Square. The second one was for a line branching off the ECR line at Bearbinder's Lane and running via Cambridge Heath, Haggerstone and Moorfields to Fore Street (Barbican). The third one was to run from the Northern and Eastern line at Tottenham via Islington and City Road to Farringdon Street. Nothing came of the proposals as they were not supported by the Commissioners.

In 1847, the ECR had opened 196 miles of line, and according to the Chairman, George Hudson, had in the space of six months carried nearly one million passengers, giving a weekly income of £12,554. On 12 July 1846, Shoreditch station was renamed Bishopsgate with the intention of drawing more City workers by naming it after the major thoroughfare in the heart of the financial district. In 1847, the Railway Company obtained an Act to redevelop Bishopsgate and Stratford stations. The contract for the work at Bishopsgate was awarded to Messrs Piper and was for a new viaduct, bridges, truss bridges, station development including an arrival platform, a turntable, a traverser, a house for engine drivers, a ticket platform and the fitting up of stables and other various works. The total cost of the contract was £11,001 1s 6d. According to Richard Bradley, writing in *Great Eastern Journal No 167* in July 2016, the work was completed in either late August or early September 1847.

1850 saw the first travelling post office on the ECR when a 'Sorting Tender' first ran in both directions on Saturday/Sunday nights between Ipswich and Shoreditch. That year also saw a 'Sorting Tender' in use on some nights between Cambridge and Shoreditch.

In August 1850 there was a strike of drivers and firemen on the ECR. It arose from the conditions imposed on the men by the new Locomotive Superintendent of the railway, John Viret Gooch, the brother of Daniel Gooch of the GWR. Gooch had taken up his post on 22 July, having been the Locomotive Superintendent of the London and South Western Railway from 1841 to 1850. Gooch's brief was to reduce working costs but he had a good incentive. He would receive 2½ per cent of any savings made. Gooch did not have to prove how he was making the savings, he would just tell the accountant what he had saved and receive his payment. The main target of his costs were the engine drivers and firemen because they received 7s 6d and 4s 0d per day respectively, agreed by the directors. He would sack them and then offer them their own jobs back at a lower rate, and fine them by deducting money from their wages for various things which could not be held to be their fault such as late running or mechanical failure. This took place within a few days of taking up his post. Following a meeting between a deputation of men and one of the Directors, Mr Ellis, on 12 August, 178 drivers, firemen and fitters handed in their notices, sick of the injustices and financial penalties being inflicted on them and in the hope that Gooch would be forced to resign. The board backed Gooch and the 178 men were blacklisted from future railway employment, with replacement staff being recruited from other railway companies. At first, train services were erratic. However, the strikers did not go back to work and the railway continued to work with the new men and eventually train services returned to normal.

Chapter 6

The East Anglian Railway to the End of 1849

The EAR was formed on 22 July 1847 by the amalgamation of three smaller railways, the Lynn and Ely (L&ER), the Lynn and Dereham Railway (L&DR) and the Ely and Huntingdon (E&HR).

Of the three constituent companies, the first to receive its Act was the Lynn and Ely Railway (L&ER). The idea of the railway went back to early 1844, although the earliest reference I can find to it is in the *Cambridge General Advertiser* of 10 April 1844, which reported that 'This undertaking progresses most favourably; the proposed line has been carefully inspected by Mr Rastrick, the engineer, who in every respect confirms the opinion entertained by the projectors of its eligibility in regard to purchase of land and total absence of difficulties in construction'.

The next mention in the press of the L&ER comes in October 1844, when in an advertisement for the proposed L&DR in the *Cambridge Chronicle and Journal* of 26 October, the proposed Railway was intended to commence at the King's Lynn terminus of the proposed L&ER. The next mention is in the *Norfolk News* of 4 January 1845, which says that the disputed point of the terminus had definitely been settled and also mentions the extension of the line to Wisbech. Information on the line was somewhat scarce. The L&ER obtained its Act on 30 June 1845. It opened its first section from Lynn to Downham Market on 27 October 1846. Downham Market was at this point not connected to the rest of the railway network. The next extension was in January 1847 when the line was extended to Denver Road, later Denver. It was not until 26 October 1847 that connection to the rest of the railway system was made with the extension to Ely North Junction, thus completing a direct line of railway from London to Lynn. In building the railway, the Company ran into serious financial difficulties over the crossings of the Great and Little Ouse rivers because of the insistence of the river commissioners on there being adequate bridge clearance. These were not the only expensive works. The heavy embankments between the bridges and those raising the line to them at each end consumed not only money, but also time, as a foundation of eighteen feet of sand and gravel was necessary to support them on the marshy Fenland soil. The Wisbech branch, which diverged from the main line at Watlington Junction, 11 chains south of Watlington station, was opened in January 1848. The line ran through a perfectly level country. The line was built with E&HR funds. George Hudson, the Chairman of the ECR, insisted that its construction would have to be a condition of any lease of the East Anglian Railway's (EAR) line by the ECR; thus, should the L&ER be forced to close, the ECR would still have access to Lynn from its March to Wisbech line. This was to prevent the GNR using the EAR's lines to enter Norfolk, if negotiations with the ECR broke down – which they did.

The earliest mention of the L&DR in the press is in the earlier mentioned advertisement of 26 October 1844 in the *Cambridge Chronicle and Journal*. The next mention is in the *Lynn Advertiser* of 16 November 1844, in a notice advising of the intention of the Railway's promoters to apply to parliament in the ensuing session for an Act to make and maintain a Railway from Lynn to Dereham. The following year, the Company received its Act on 21 July. The Railway opened to Narborough on 27 October 1847, the same day that the L&ER opened to Downham Market. The Railway was extended to Swaffham on 10 August 1847, to Sporle (a temporary station about two miles east of Swaffham) on 26 October 1847 and to Dereham on 11 September 1848.

When the L&ER and the L&DR simultaneously opened their first sections on 27 October 1846, the first timetable of the two railways was advertised in the local press, according to D.I. Gordon in *A Regional History of the Railways of Great Britain: Volume 5 – The Eastern Counties* (David and Charles 1968) as EARs even though the official amalgamation did not come until the following year.

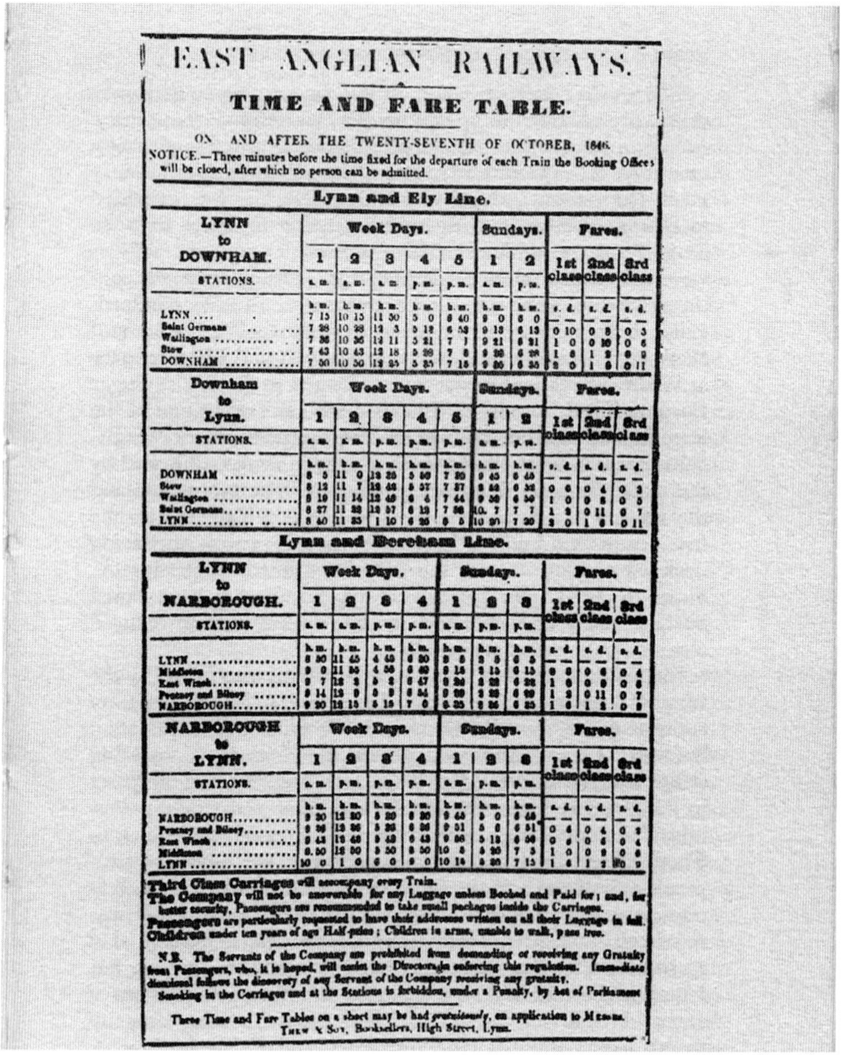

EAST ANGLIAN RAILWAYS.

TIME AND FARE TABLE.

ON AND AFTER THE TWENTY-SEVENTH OF OCTOBER, 1846.

NOTICE.—Three minutes before the time fixed for the departure of each Train the Booking Offices will be closed, after which no person can be admitted.

Lynn and Ely Line.

LYNN to DOWNHAM.	Week Days.					Sundays.		Fares.		
	1	2	3	4	5	1	2	1st class	2nd class	3rd class
STATIONS.	a.m.	a.m.	a.m.	p.m.	p.m.	a.m.	p.m.			
	h. m.	h. m.	h. m.	h. m.	h. m.	h. m.	h. m.	s. d.	s. d.	s. d.
LYNN	7 15	10 15	11 30	5 0	6 40	9 0	6 0	—	—	—
Saint Germans	7 28	10 28	12 3	5 12	6 53	9 13	6 13	0 10	0 8	0 3
Watlington	7 36	10 36	12 11	5 21	7 1	9 21	6 21	1 0	0 10	0 5
Stow	7 43	10 43	12 18	5 28	7 8	9 28	6 28	1 8	1 2	0 9
DOWNHAM	7 50	10 50	12 25	5 35	7 15	9 35	6 35	2 0	1 6	0 11

Downham to Lynn.	Week Days.					Sundays.		Fares.		
	1	2	3	4	5	1	2	1st class	2nd class	3rd class
STATIONS.	a.m.	a.m.	p.m.	p.m.	p.m.	a.m.	p.m.			
	h. m.	h. m.	h. m.	h. m.	h. m.	h. m.	h. m.	s. d.	s. d.	s. d.
DOWNHAM	8 5	11 0	12 35	5 50	7 30	9 45	6 45	—	—	—
Stow	8 12	11 7	12 42	5 57	7 37	9 52	6 52	0 6	0 4	0 3
Watlington	8 19	11 14	12 49	6 4	7 44	9 59	6 59	1 0	0 8	0 5
Saint Germans	8 27	11 22	12 57	6 12	7 52	10 7	7 7	1 3	0 11	0 7
LYNN	8 40	11 35	1 10	6 25	8 5	10 20	7 20	2 0	1 6	0 11

Lynn and Dereham Line.

LYNN to NARBOROUGH.	Week Days.				Sundays.			Fares.		
	1	2	3	4	1	2	3	1st class	2nd class	3rd class
STATIONS.	a.m.	a.m.	p.m.	p.m.	a.m.	p.m.	p.m.			
	h. m.	h. m.	h. m.	h. m.	h. m.	h. m.	h. m.	s. d.	s. d.	s. d.
LYNN	8 30	11 45	4 40	6 30	9 5	3 5	6 5	—	—	—
Middleton	9 0	11 55	4 55	6 40	9 15	3 15	6 15	0 8	0 6	0 4
East Winch	9 7	12 3	5 2	6 47	9 22	3 22	6 22	1 0	0 9	0 6
Pentney and Bilney	9 14	12 9	5 9	6 54	9 29	3 29	6 29	1 3	0 11	0 7
NARBOROUGH	9 20	12 15	5 15	7 0	9 35	3 35	6 35	1 6	1 2	0 9

NARBOROUGH to LYNN.	Week Days.				Sundays.			Fares.		
	1	2	3	4	1	2	3	1st class	2nd class	3rd class
STATIONS.	a.m.	p.m.	p.m.	p.m.	a.m.	p.m.	p.m.			
	h. m.	h. m.	h. m.	h. m.	h. m.	h. m.	h. m.	s. d.	s. d.	s. d.
NARBOROUGH	9 30	12 30	5 30	8 30	9 45	5 0	6 45	—	—	—
Pentney and Bilney	9 36	12 36	5 36	8 36	9 51	5 6	6 51	0 4	0 4	0 2
East Winch	9 43	12 43	5 43	8 43	9 58	5 13	6 58	0 9	0 6	0 4
Middleton	9 50	12 50	5 50	8 50	10 5	5 20	7 5	1 0	0 9	0 6
LYNN	10 0	1 0	6 0	9 0	10 15	5 30	7 15	1 6	1 2	0 9

Third Class Carriages will accompany every Train.
The Company will not be answerable for any Luggage unless Booked and Paid for; and, for better security, Passengers are recommended to take small packages inside the Carriages.
Passengers are particularly requested to have their addresses written on all their Luggage in full.
Children under ten years of age Half-price; Children in arms, unable to walk, pass free.

N.B. The Servants of the Company are prohibited from demanding or receiving any Gratuity from Passengers, who, it is hoped, will assist the Directors in enforcing this regulation. Immediate dismissal follows the discovery of any Servant of the Company receiving any gratuity.

Smoking in the Carriages and at the Stations is forbidden, under a Penalty, by Act of Parliament.

These Time and Fare Tables on a sheet may be had *gratuitously*, on application to Messrs. Thew & Son, Booksellers, High Street, Lynn.

The timetable for the opening of the ELR and LDR on 27 October 1846. Although separate companies, the two railways were marketing themselves jointly. The formal amalgamation took place on 27 July 1847. (Author's collection).

The E&HR was projected to form a line between the two towns. The Act authorising the construction of the Railway was obtained in June 1845. The line was opened from St Ives to Huntingdon on 17 August 1847 on the same day as the Cambridge (Chesterton Junction) and St Ives line of the ECR opened. The original Huntingdon terminus was situated at Godmanchester. Because the line was isolated from the rest of the East Anglian system it was, under agreement, worked by the ECR from the date of opening. It was, however, a financial failure and the original service of six trains a day each was gradually cut down, until in November 1849, there was only one train a day each way, and no staff maintained at Godmanchester; tickets being issued by the guard.

The section of the E&HR between Needingworth Junction and Ely was not proceeded with at the time owing to the inability of the company to raise the necessary capital. In fact, after obtaining the Act nothing further was done as to constructing the line until July 1849, when a further Act was obtained by the EAR (in which the E&HR had become merged) extending the time limit for the completion of the railway. At the half yearly meeting of the EAR, on 23 August of that year, when the report of the directors and the accounts for the past year were submitted, the report specially referred to the Act recently obtained in parliament for making the line from Ely to St. Ives, and authorised the conversion of the bond debt into share capital and the raising of £80,726 for paying the liabilities of the company by the issue of preference shares at 7 per cent. The statement of revenue for the half· year ending 30 June exhibited a diminished amount of receipts over the previous half-year. The extended powers obtained under the Act of 1849 having been allowed to lapse owing to the financial depression and other causes, no further steps were taken to promote the construction of the line for a period of fifteen years, when a new company, called the Ely, Haddenham and Sutton Railway Company, obtained an Act, dated 23 June 1864, authorising them to make a line from the GER at a point 1 mile 2 chains south of Ely station to Sutton, a distance of 6 miles 45 chains. This line was opened for traffic on

6 April 1866. A further period of ten years elapsed before the next extension took place, when on 7 April 1876, the Ely, Haddenham and Sutton Railway obtained an extension Act authorising them to extend their line to Needingworth Junction, on the St. Ives and March line of the GER, and at the same time to change the name of the railway to the Ely and St. Ives Railway. This extension was opened for traffic on May 10 1878, and at the same time was leased to the GER, who in 1898 purchased the line outright.

Chapter 7

The Norfolk Railway and the Eastern Counties Railway to the End of 1850

The Norfolk Railway's branch line from Wymondham to Dereham opened to goods traffic on 7 December 1846 and to passenger traffic on 15 February 1847.

1847 saw a further extension of the Norfolk Railway, when a line was opened from a junction near Reedham on the Yarmouth line to Lowestoft for goods on 3 May and passengers on 1 July. The line to Lowestoft was owned by the Lowestoft Railway and Harbour Company, which had been promoted in 1844 to build a railway from Lowestoft to Reedham and to purchase the Norwich and Lowestoft Navigation and Lowestoft Harbour and to improve the harbour. The Norwich and Lowestoft Navigation had been promoted in 1826 to provide a connection between the two towns using existing and new waterways. It obtained its Act in 1827 and was opened in 1833. Announcements about the promotion of the new Company appeared in various local newspapers in November 1844. The Chairman and promotor of the Company was Sir Samuel Morton Peto, an English entrepreneur, civil engineer and railway developer, and, for more than twenty years, a Member of Parliament. The new Company obtained its Act of incorporation on 30 June 1845. Even before the Railway had been built, we find a mention of the Norfolk Railway wanting to lease the new Company. For example, the *Norfolk News* of 9 August carried a notice of a meeting of the Norfolk Railway on 22 August, at which one of the purposes was to consider authorising its Directors to make arrangements for leasing the Lowestoft Company. According to the report of the Directors of the Norfolk Railway reported in the *Bury and Norwich Post* of 27 August, the proprietors (shareholders) of the Lowestoft Company had authorised the lease of it to the Norfolk Company. Although it isn't clear from reports when it was done, it must have been at the First Ordinary Meeting of the Company following its incorporation. The *Norfolk Chronicle* of 22 November reported that the Norfolk Railway had given notice of its intention in the ensuing session of parliament to introduce a bill to enable it to purchase or rent the Lowestoft Railway and Harbour Company.

By the latter part of January 1846, work on constructing the Lowestoft railway had commenced. According to the *Norfolk News* of 24 January, forty to fifty acres of land in Lowestoft had been purchased and a cutting had been dug.

At a General Meeting of the Lowestoft Company on 28 February, it was reported that all the land required for the Railway had been purchased and that half of the earthworks had been completed.

The *Norfolk News* of 16 May reported that about 350 men were employed in building both the Railway and works at the Harbour at Lowestoft. The Act enabling the Norfolk Railway to lease the Lowestoft Railway and Harbour Company was passed on 3 July 1846. It also took over the Norwich and Lowestoft Navigation which had been owned by Peto since 1844 and over which the Railway had to provide swing bridges at Reedham and Somerleyton.

The line to Lowestoft was opened for goods traffic on 3 May 1847, followed on 1 July by the opening to passenger traffic with much celebration. People flocked to Lowestoft station to witness the departure of the first train from the station and the first train into the station. The station was separated from the town on the clifftop by about half a mile of green fields and farmland at first, although a new turnpike road linked it to Lowestoft. When the harbour was built in 1847 development in the area really took off and a more substantial station building was added to the original two platforms that were originally provided, in 1855. In 1847, $1\frac{1}{4}$ miles of railway was added at the Yarmouth end from Vauxhall station to the fish market.

In 1847 there was a possibility that the Norfolk Railway would be amalgamated with the EUR. The proposed amalgamation arose from the Norfolk Railway's opposition in 1845 to the I&BR and the extension of the Eastern Union to Norwich. The Norfolk Railway proposed in opposition a Spooner Row and Stowmarket Railway and undertook to lease, if they were authorised, the Thetford, Bury and Newmarket and the Ipswich, Norwich and Yarmouth railways. The three schemes failed. As we know, the other two schemes succeeded. On 1 January 1847, the EUR and the I&BR started working as one and were formally amalgamated on 9 July of that year, which was subject to the approval of details by the Railway Commissioners. In March 1844, the EUR directors had decided that the Company should amalgamate with the Eastern Union Extension Railway, which had become the I&BR, and even the Norwich and Brandon Railway if suitable terms could be arranged and the shareholders' consent obtained. In February 1847, the Directors of the Eastern Union and the Norfolk railways agreed that the amalgamation of the two companies should take place with the Norfolk shareholders receiving a guaranteed seven and a half per cent on their shareholdings. After the proposals were briefly outlined to shareholders of the two Companies at their respective half yearly meetings, it was decided not to vote on the question until the EUR and the I&BR were fully amalgamated. The Norfolk Railway shareholders were told that it was best to accept the seven and a half per cent. The Railway Commissioners withheld their certificate for over a year. During this time, the shareholders of the EUR and the I&BR had time to think over the state of the Norfolk Railway, whose capital debt was higher than that of the I&BR. In July 1847, an influential group of Ipswich and Bury shareholders met in York and resolved to oppose the purchase or lease of the Norfolk Railway. On 25 October, a special meeting of the I&BR was called to consider both the proposed takeover of the Norfolk Railway, but also the general financial state of their own railway. After much debate, the proposed takeover of the Norfolk Railway was rejected by forty-three votes to five.

The failure of the EUR to acquire the Norfolk Railway gave the ECR, which also wanted to acquire the Norfolk, the opportunity to open negotiations with it. Despite some opposition, an agreement was concluded with the ECR on 2 May 1848 and six days later the ECR took possession of the whole of the Norfolk Railway lines, works and rolling stock. It dismissed the staff and replaced them with its own officials. Fares and rates on the Norfolk Railway were revised and brought into line with those in force on other parts of the ECR system. This was all done without the approval of parliament. Pending parliament's approval, it was agreed inter alia that the ECR would keep up the Norfolk rolling stock to the same state of efficiency as it was at the time it took over the working of the Norfolk. If by May 1855 the amalgamation of the two companies had not been sanctioned by parliament, the Norfolk Company could repurchase from the ECR the rolling stock at the same price that it would now pay for it. The working agreement was duly ratified by parliament. An attempt by the two companies to amalgamate in 1849 was thrown out by the House of Lords, despite being approved by the ECR shareholders.

The ECR now operated the Norfolk Railway, which reduced the latter Company's activity to simply being an owner of the line but not having any hand in its operation. Although the Norfolk Railway now had only financial matters to concern it, these proved extremely troublesome due to haphazard financial control and accounting during its active lifetime. On 4 July 1850, the ECR finally completed the purchase of the Norfolk Railway.

Whilst all this was going on, the Norfolk Railway promoted a bill to extend its line from Dereham to Fakenham, Wells and Blakeney. According to the *Sun* of 14 August 1846, at the half yearly general meeting of the Company the previous day, the Secretary said that the previous day the Company had been successful in obtaining a bill for this line. The next mention of the railway is in the *Norfolk Chronicle* of 2 September 1848, when it was reported that the works of the Dereham and Fakenham Railway were to be vigorously prosecuted and that the contractors were advertising for 500 men. According to the same newspaper of 24 February 1849, works in building the Dereham and Fakenham railway were proceeding with great activity. The following month, the same newspaper of 24 March reported the opening to Fakenham for passengers and goods on 20 March. The proposal to construct a line beyond Fakenham to Wells and Blakeney had been abandoned.

Chapter 8

London and Blackwall Railway to the End of 1850

The idea of building a railway to serve Blackwall goes back to the mid-1830s. The earliest reference seems to be a notice in the *Chelmsford Chronicle* of 18 January 1833 that:

> The usual notice required in such cases has been affixed to the doors of the Middlesex Session-house, of an intention to apply to Parliament during the ensuing session to form a railroad from the Commercial Road, Limehouse to the river Thames at East Ham, opposite to Woolwich; and also a carriage road to run parallel, or nearly so, with the railway.

There were two rival schemes. There was the Commercial Railway. According to the *Public Ledger and Daily Advertiser* of 8 October 1835, a meeting had been held at the Mansion House in the City of London on 30 September to connect the City to the East and West India Docks and the Thames at Blackwall and that a provisional committee had been formed for the purpose of putting the scheme into effect. The engineers Sir John Rennie and James Walker had been authorised to consider how to put the scheme into effect. The same newspaper of 14 November, apart from confirming Sir John Rennie as engineer, said that the Provisional Committee, having been informed that the undertaking had been abandoned, thought it their duty to contradict any such report and to the contrary state that the surveys were nearly completed, the schedules were in progress and all the preliminaries required by parliament were in a great state of forwardness. The *Evening Standard* of 3 December carried a notice to the effect that the Commercial Railway by the original south line to Blackwall and the East and West India Docks needed capital of £600,000 shares at £50 each and with a £2 deposit. Shareholders were requested to exchange the Bankers' Receipts for Scrip Certificates and to execute the Parliamentary Contract and Subscribers' Agreement at the offices of the solicitors – Messrs Stokes, Hollingsworth and Tyerman at 24 Cateaton Street.

There was also the L&BR. The *Chelmsford Chronicle* of Friday, 11 September 1835 carried an advertisement about the L&BR with branches to the East and West India Docks and the Steam Navigation Depot Company. According to the notice, the survey, plan and estimate were under the direction of George Stephenson Esq of Liverpool, the famous George Stephenson of *Rocket* fame. The capital of the company was £400,000, divided into 8,000 shares of £50 each. The object of the company was firstly to reduce the cost of carrying goods from the East and West India Docks by a half of the cost of that appertaining at the time, secondly to reduce the cost and time of conveying passengers to the East and West India Docks and thirdly by building a 'steam depot' for the accommodation of steam vessels and steam passengers by the construction of floating piers at or near Blackwall for conveying horses, carriages, passengers and luggage to and from steamers at any stage of the tide. This Company had grand ideas of being part of a railway to Southend and Hole Haven (Thames Haven) as the *Essex Standard* of 1 January 1836 carried an advertisement for a Southend and Hole Haven Railway which was to be a continuation of the L&BR.

Clearly the promotion of the London and Blackwall Company was successful as the *Norwich Mercury* of 31 October quotes the closing price for shares in the company at six and a half. The *Suffolk Chronicle* of 7 November, in a table of railway speculations, gives for the L&BR 12,000 shares at £50 each and capital of £600,000. But the same figures applied to the Commercial Railway.

The principal difference between the two schemes was that the L&BR ran north of the Commercial Road whilst the Commercial Railway ran south of it. Inevitably there was opposition to any railway, particularly from the owners of stage coaches and omnibuses plying the Commercial Road to Blackwall and the owners of properties effected by the building of the railway which could include the demolition of such properties.

What happened was not clear cut. Both companies in their advertisements in the press put the merits of their railway being the best. By the end of April or very early May of 1836, the two companies had decided to bury the hatchet and according to *The Times* of 7 May had, it was said, formed a 'junction' and agreed together in obtaining an Act of Parliament. According to, amongst other newspapers, the *Globe* of 17 May 1836, the *Public Ledger and Daily Advertiser* of 18 May and the *Morning Advertiser* of the same day, at the suggestion of the Parliamentary Committee that was examining both bills that all future proceedings as far as the competing companies were concerned should be confined to enabling the Parliamentary Committee to decide which was the better; the line to be adopted should be the one recommended by the committee; the subscribers to both lines should become equally interested in the one that was chosen and the shares should be reduced from £50 to £25; the committee of the line fixed should exist as at that time with the addition of four members from the committee of the rejected line to be selected by the latter company; the committee so constituted to have the power of selecting their engineer, surveyor, solicitors, bankers, etc, as already provided for by deed of settlement; each company to bear its own expenses up to the decision of the Parliamentary Committee being obtained when the deposit of shares was to be equalised and a joint deed of settlement to be executed; and advertisements to be inserted in all the metropolitan daily newspapers informing the subscribers to both companies of the arrangement and calling on any who might object to it to give in their dissent on or before 21 May so that they might have their deposits returned less their proportion of the expenses incurred up to the latter day. The notice was signed by John Warmington, the Secretary to both Railways. The Parliamentary Committee reported in favour of the Commercial Railway. Now the newspapers reported a change of name. The *London Courier and Evening Gazette* of 30 June reported that the previous day the London and Blackwall Commercial Railway Bill had received its third reading in the House of Commons and was passed. According to the *Morning Advertiser* of 29 July, the Railway's bill received its Royal Assent in the House of Lords the previous day. By the end of October, it was simply called the London and Blackwall Railway.

Moves now started to construct the Railway. The *Evening Standard* of 2 November reported that the Blackwall Railway Company was in treaty with the East India (Trading Company) Directors for the purchase of East India House to be used as a depot for the Railway Company.

As originally authorised the L&BR was to run from the Minories to Blackwall, but in early 1837 it decided to apply to parliament for a line west from the Minories to Leadenhall Street in the City of London. The *Hertford Mercury and Reformer* of 7 February said 'from the Minories to East India House in Leadenhall Street'. As with the original proposal to build the Railway, there was opposition to the proposed extension. Despite this, the Act for the extension received the Royal Assent on 25 July. The new western terminus was the first railway station in the City of London. This was Fenchurch Street station. This was the Act which changed the name of the Railway to the L&BR.

It was in May 1838 that the idea of the N&ER abandoning its original authorised terminus in Islington and Tottenham and instead building a line from the latter place to join the L&BR came up. As mentioned, the N&ER instead made a junction with the ECR at Stratford.

Building the Railway made some people money. To give an example from the *Norfolk Chronicle* of Saturday, 26 January 1839; the previous Tuesday in the Sheriff's Court, Mr King, a boat builder in the Commercial Road in London, received the sum of £400 in compensation from the Railway for the loss of trade and the expense of removal to which he would be put in consequence of the Railway requiring part of his premises. By late November, work on constructing the Railway was in full swing. However, it hit a hurdle as, according to the *Chelmsford Chronicle* of Friday, 22 November, an injunction was granted in the Vice Chancellor's Court on the previous Monday to restrain it from excavating near the premises of Mr Warburton in the Minories, the work endangering the lives of the inmates. Mr Warburton's premises were not specified.

Work had progressed sufficiently that on Friday, 4 July 1840 the Railway was formally opened from the Minories to Blackwall. The occasion was marked by the directors making an experimental trip. The opening to the public took place on the following Monday. Just prior to the opening, a number of newspapers carried details of the opening date and of the service to be provided. For example, the *Morning Advertiser* of 30 June said that the trains would run every fifteen minutes between 8 o'clock in the morning and 10 o'clock in the evening. Trains would start simultaneously from Limehouse, Poplar and the other intermediate stations. Fares would be 6d first class and 3d second class. There were no third class carriages according to the newspaper. Whishaw's *Railways of Great Britain and Ireland* (1842) said that there was one such carriage. The *Morning Chronicle* of 6 July, amongst other newspapers, carried an account of the official opening.

When built, the Railway had adopted a gauge of five feet like the ECR and N&ER. This was at the instigation of William Cubitt who had been appointed engineer of the Railway. The reason for his appointment was that the Company wanted someone who was not associated with the original proposals. The reason for the 5ft gauge was that Cubitt said that it would be more convenient whenever much business was required to be done at a great speed. It was also not intended to connect the Railway with any other railway. As we have seen, the N&ER had been interested in connecting with the L&BR and that that Railway was being built to the gauge of 5ft.

At that time, the Port of London was rather full of sailing ships despite the advent of steam ships and consequently there was a real danger of sparks from steam locomotives setting fire to the sails. The only alternatives to steam haulage were horse haulage and cable haulage. Horse haulage would not have been any more than a stage coach or an omnibus on rails and was not really much faster than the vehicles using the road. Cable haulage offered greater speed. The account of the official opening described how the railway worked. There were two marine compound steam engines at either end of the line which hauled the ropes, of which there were two, one going in a loop from the Minories to Blackwall and the other in the reverse direction. Each carriage on the Railway had at each end of it a device for gripping the rope. At the start of the working day, a train of seven carriages would be lined up at each terminus and a single carriage at each individual station. To communicate between the stations there was an electric telegraph. When all the carriages had gripped the rope, the signal was communicated to the respective winding engines and the signal to start would be given. The carriages from the intermediate stations would travel towards their respective termini followed by the main trains which would deposit the majority of their carriages at their respective termini. When the trains were about twenty yards short of their first station, the guard on the last carriage would remove the pin of the coupling connecting it to the next carriage and release the gripping device on the rope. The carriage would then glide along its respective platform where the guard would stop it with his handbrake. This procedure was repeated all the way along the line until the trains reached their terminal stations. The procedure was then repeated in the reverse direction. The disadvantage of the system as compared to using steam or horse haulage was that in order to get from one intermediate station to the next station it was necessary to travel via the respective termini.

The machinery to work the cable proved rather noisy and the *Essex Standard* of Friday, 31 July reported that the inhabitants of the parish of St George's in the East had met the previous Thursday and decided to indict the Blackwall Railway for nuisance if it did not adopt a means to prevent the machinery making so much noise.

Rope haulage, like locomotive haulage, had its hazards and the *Chelmsford Chronicle* of Friday, 4 December reported that the previous Friday, George Walton, the foreman of a gang of navvies employed on the Blackwall Railway, was killed near West India Dock station. At about 12 o'clock, Walton was at work on the line and in a stooping position when the Up Blackwall train was approaching. He was struck on the head by the lamp iron of the first carriage which knocked him down between the rails under the rope and the other carriage passed over him.

On 2 August 1841, the Railway was opened from the Minories to the new western terminus at Fenchurch Street. When the extension was opened, trains for the station were released from the rope on entering the Minories station and continued under their own momentum to the terminus. Departing trains from Fenchurch Street had sometimes to be pushed by station staff until they started to roll down the 1 in 150 incline to the winding house where they would be connected to the rope.

When the extension to Fenchurch Street was opened, trains were not allowed to run into the station on a Sunday, but they were from 5 June 1842. There was, and as far as I know had been from the initial opening of the Railway, a cessation of the service between 10.45am and 1pm on Sundays as these were deemed the hours of church service.

In mid to late October 1841 there was a severe storm. According to *The Times* of 19 October this resulted in the Railway being flooded at the Blackwall end on the previous day and trains discontinued from 4 o'clock onwards. Services recommenced the following morning.

Sometimes the rope broke. For example, according to the *Essex Herald* of 12 October 1841 this happened to the Blackwall direction rope shortly after 2 o'clock on 10 October at about a quarter of a mile from the Minories station and caused trains to be delayed. When this happened, the London rope was stopped until the other rope was mended. There were clearly points on the line as the report says that after a delay of half an hour the train was drawn along the other line to Blackwall station.

In late 1842 there was a proposal which ultimately proved unsuccessful by the Thames Haven Railway mentioned earlier in connection with the ECR. The proposal was that instead of building a line from Romford on the ECR to Thames Haven, to build a line to the L&BR through West and East Ham, Barking, the Ockendons, Orsett (with a branch to Tilbury Fort) to Thames Haven.

Whilst the Railway's principal traffic was passengers, including those taking excursion steamers from Blackwall, in 1842 the Railway started carrying goods traffic. I have not been able to find the exact date of the start of goods traffic. According to the *Morning Advertiser* of 5 January 1843, the Company would carry heavy and light goods (with the exception of woods) from the East and West India Docks to a warehouse the Company had in Crutched Friars Street. According to Jim Connor in *Stepney's Own Railway* (2nd edition Connor and Butler 1987), the structure was only temporary and was very primitive. There was a siding in which seven carriages could stand and a platform about 25 feet wide for receiving goods. The platform had three traps, of which one had a crane for lowering goods onto carts in the street below. The other two traps had connecting chutes for sliding merchandise in bags or bales down to an intermediate store. On the lower storey there were more cranes. There was a similar establishment beside the line at West India Docks and at Poplar a goods hoist was installed. According to Jim Connor the method by which the railway was operated was little suited for the conveyance of goods traffic and the meagre service was abandoned after a few years.

Because the number of passengers did not reach the total number that the Company had anticipated, to attempt to boost the flagging

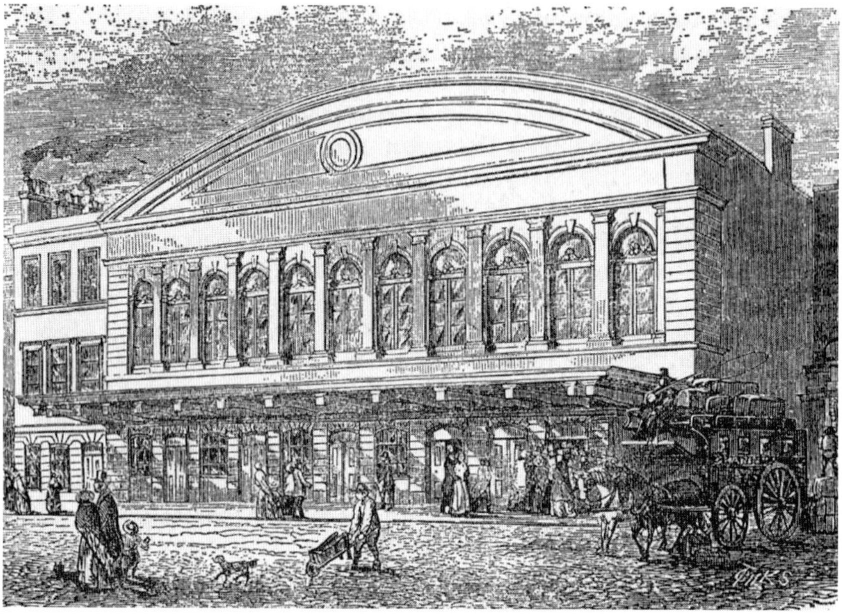

The exterior of Fenchurch Street station in 1857. Fenchurch Street station was the first, and for a time, the only terminus station in London that was within the boundary of the City of London. The station was first opened in 1841, but was rebuilt in the form shown in 1854. (Author's collection).

A drawing showing the exterior of West India Dock station on the L&BR in the days when that railway was still of 5 foot gauge and was worked by cable haulage. Note the presence of a rival omnibus and two hansom cabs. Note also the overall roof of the station. (Author's collection).

receipts a new station was opened at Cannon Street Road between the Minories and Shadwell on 21 August 1842. This, sadly, did little to improve the financial state of the Company and in that same August the Board of Directors announced that there would not be a dividend paid to the shareholders for the previous six months.

Despite more and more ships beginning to use Brunswick Wharf, attracted by the facilities offered by the Railway, the anticipated increase in the number of people using the Railway did not materialise. A regular sailing to Antwerp and Rotterdam, which had just been started by the Batavia Line, resulted in the Company running special boat trains from Fenchurch Street. Passenger numbers still continued to decline and on 12 September 1842 the Company raised the price of the fares, but because this proved so unpopular, the fares from the intermediate stations reverted to their old rates from 3 November.

Part of the Railway's problem was competition from horse buses that were operating along the Commercial Road. These had had the advantage over the Railway in that a passenger could get on at one stop and get off at the next stop, whereas on the railway a long detour via one of the terminal stations was necessary. This made the bus journeys quicker overall, despite the railway being able to travel faster.

On 28 February 1843, there was a reduction in the prices of the fares. These were to the pre-12 September level for passengers travelling from Fenchurch Street to Blackwall and reductions to fares between the intermediate stations. This did attract more passengers overall – even if traffic to and from the intermediate stations failed to improve.

By 1844 the Company was beginning to regret having decided to use cable haulage to operate the railway. According to the Company report of February 1844, there had been six breakages of the cable in the space of six months. The Directors for a time thought of converting the Railway to the atmospheric system because this had an advantage over cable haulage as trains could stop at individual stations. In February

1844 were no railways using atmospheric traction in operation. The first one to do so was the Dublin and Kingstown in Ireland which started operation on 29 March that year. However, the idea of using atmospheric traction was rejected.

Following the conversion of the gauge of the ECR and N&ERs from 5ft to 4ft 8½in, the L&BR was left as the sole railway using the 5ft gauge.

In January 1845, at a Special General Meeting of the Company's shareholders, authorisation was obtained from them to apply to parliament to build a line from Stepney to Bow on the ECR and then to use that Company's line to Stratford and then to build a line from there to Epping via Wanstead, Woodford, Chigwell, Loughton and Abridge. Although the London and Blackwall offered to allow the ECR to run some trains to Fenchurch Street, the latter Company objected. In the end, an agreement was reached that the London and Blackwall would only build the line from Stepney to Bow and that the ECR would have the sole right to the Epping scheme. Powers for the London and Blackwall to build the line to Bow were obtained in 1845. The new line was called the London and Blackwall Extension Railway. Under the terms of the Act, the L&BR was given the power to purchase the new Company, which it did in 1846. Additionally, Acts were also obtained in 1845 and 1846 to convert the Railway to the gauge of 4ft 8½in and to replace rope haulage with steam locomotive haulage.

Conversion of the gauge and the conversion to steam locomotive operation took place in early 1849. On 14 February, steam locomotives began operating a reduced service over the Down or North Line. On the same day, the Extension Line to the ECR was opened for goods traffic. It had originally been intended to open it during the previous October, but it was delayed because a bridge over the Commercial Road was unfinished. The bridge was completed by January 1849. A further delay then occurred whilst the proposal to use steam locomotives on the original line was approved by the Commission of Woods and Forests.

To comply with safety regulations, the entire section of the line beside the Regents Canal Basin had to be covered with a light iron roof to lessen the danger of any wooden ship being set on fire by a stray spark from one of the locomotives. When all that work had been done, the line was pronounced safe and ready for operation by locomotives. On 2 April, the Extension Line to the ECR was opened for passengers. The connecting station at the junction with the ECR was named Victoria Park and Bow and whilst *Bradshaw's Guide* for March 1850 shows a service of two trains an hour on the line from Fenchurch Street and Stepney, the ECR was rather less frequent. Between Stepney and Victoria Park and Bow there was a station officially called Bow and Bromley, but contemporary documents also refer to it as Old Ford. Run round facilities were provided at that station and trains only ran through to Victoria Park and Bow if there was a chance that an ECR train might stop there to pick up its passengers. Although there was a physical junction at Bow it remained unused for a few years and at one point was severed for a time by the ECR in a fit of aggression, the ECR refusing to have any Fenchurch Street line trains over its lines. Services on the branch were originally worked by detaching or attaching a portion of a Blackwall line train at Stepney but following a collision whilst attaching some vehicles to a Fenchurch Street bound service a shuttle service was introduced, later to be superseded by the aforementioned through service. The antagonism caused by the ECR to the L&BR came to a head after the former refused to refer matters in dispute to arbitration and the directors of the L&BR were forced to seek parliamentary assistance. They obtained an Act passed in 1850 which forced the ECR to provide the necessary connecting services and to allow through bookings between their stations and those on the L&BR.

From 22 June 1849, non-stop trains on the original line were introduced to connect with certain sailings from Brunswick Wharf and covered the three and a half miles from Fenchurch Street to Blackwall in five minutes.

Whilst the stationary winding engines were sold at the end of May 1849, the carriages were converted to the 4ft 8½in gauge. To work the line with locomotives, six small well tank locomotives of the 2-2-2 wheel arrangement were acquired from the firm of Messrs Jones and Potts. A 2-2-2 wheel arrangement means that the locomotive has two non-driving wheels at the front, then two driving wheels and two non-driving wheels at the back, a well tank locomotive being one that carried its fuel, such as coke, in a bunker on it as opposed to a separate tender and the same in regard to its water in a tank under the fuel bunker at the back. Additionally, a further two tank locomotives of the same wheel arrangement were acquired from the Hatcham Iron works of George England and Company. Following the change to steam locomotive operation, there were a couple of closures. Cannon Street Road closed in either November or December 1849, whilst the Minories was temporarily closed between 15 February and 9 September 1849.

Additional traffic came to the L&BR in September 1850 when the East & West India Docks & Birmingham Junction Railway (E&WID&BJR) started running from Islington to Fenchurch Street

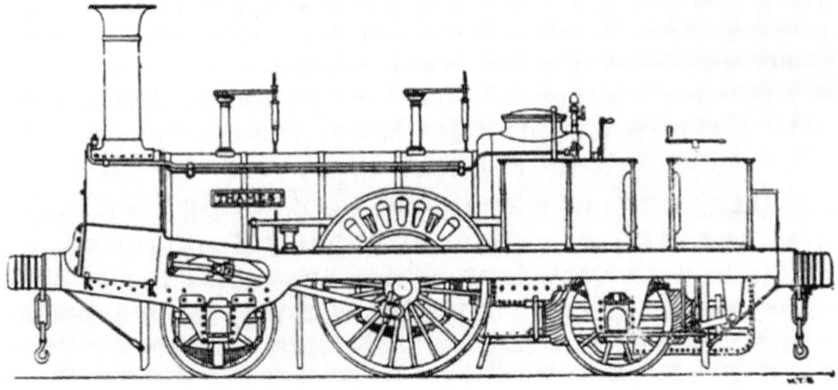

A drawing of L&BR 2-2-2 tank locomotive No 6 *Thames* that was built by Jones and Potts in 1848. The locomotive was a well tank locomotive carrying its water in a tank under the rear coal bunker. The last member of the class was withdrawn in 1882. (Author's collection).

via a connection at Bow, which is not to be confused with the junction with the ECR at Victoria Park and Bow. The E&WID&BJR had been promoted in 1845 to build a railway to connect the London & North Western Railway to the docks at Blackwall. It obtained its Act on 20 August 1846. On 7 December the Railway extended its line to Camden Town. The E&WID&BJR later changed its name to the North London Railway.

Chapter 9

The Newmarket and Chesterford Railway

At this point in our story, we turn to the Newmarket Railway or, as it was originally called, the Newmarket and Chesterford Railway. In some ways this can be held to be one of the more tragic railways in railway history, as part of it was closed as early as October 1851.

The Railway was conceived in the late summer/early autumn of 1845 for the purpose of constructing a railway from Newmarket to Great Chesterford on the ECR's Cambridge and Brandon main line, with a branch line to Cambridge. At Newmarket the station would be on the south side of the town, clear of the racecourse and training ground. The total length of the Railway including the branch would be about twenty-four miles. A notice announcing this intention first appeared in the *Cambridge Independent Press* of 6 September 1845. The engineers of the proposed Railway Company were Robert Stephenson and John Braithwaite. By the middle of October, the Railway had changed its name from the Newmarket Railway to the Newmarket and Chesterford Railway, according to the *Chelmsford Chronicle* of 6 October.

Support for the Railway came from the Jockey Club, as, according to the *Cambridge Independent Press* of 25 October 1845, at a meeting of the Club held at Newmarket on 14 October the members and stewards inspected the plans of the Railway and gave it their support. The reason for the support from the Jockey Club was that it would enable members of parliament who were members of the Club to superintend a race during the afternoon and run back to London for the same night's debate. Other support for the Railway came from local landowners. Opposition came from Cambridge, which would be bypassed by the main line of the Railway, and the ECR. One suspects that one reason being that apart from the Newmarket being a rival company, by bypassing Cambridge it would provide a shorter route to Newmarket than would be by any line through Cambridge, should the ECR decide to build such a line.

Given the support that the Railway had from Members of Parliament, it had an easy passage through parliament and received its Act on 16 July 1846. The Act contained a number of interesting clauses relating to Cambridge and to the University. These included giving officers of the University of Cambridge the right to have access to the stations to search for any member of the University and forbidding the company to carry any member of the University under the rank of MA, Bachelor of Civil Law or Medicine, whom the proper University authorities might prohibit, and a further provision compelling the company to employ special constables who were subject to the University authorities to superintend, manage, and control the workmen engaged in works within three miles of the town of Cambridge. It was also made unlawful for the company to take up or set down passengers at the Cambridge railway station or within three miles thereof between the hours of 10am and 3pm on Sundays, under pain of a penalty of £5 per person payable to Addenbrooke's Hospital or other charity nominated under the Seal of the University. The authorised share capital was £350,000 in 14,000 shares of £25 each, with borrowing powers of £ 116,666 13s. 4d.

Following the passing of the Company's Act, no time was lost in getting on with the work of construction.

The contractor for building the Railway was Thomas Jackson. The turning of the first sod took place on 30 September at Dullingham by 10-year-old Christopher William Jeaffreson, who was the heir to the late General Jeaffreson, the eldest son of W. Piggott Esq.

In 1847, the Company drew up plans for extensions to Bury St Edmunds, to Thetford and to Ely. The Act for these received its

Royal Assent on 11 June 1847. Of the extensions, only that to Bury St Edmunds was ever completed. By the same Act, the Railway changed its name back to the Newmarket Railway.

The extension to Thetford would, if it had been constructed, have provided a through route from London via Newmarket to Norwich, $5^3/_4$ miles shorter than the existing route via Ely, giving the Newmarket Railway a connection with the Norfolk Railway which ran from Brandon to Norwich and Yarmouth. The fact is, though, through traffic would still have been dependent on the ECR between London and Chesterford. It was at this point that the Newmarket Railway became a pawn in a complicated game between the ECR and the Norfolk Railway. At a meeting on 14 August 1846, the Chairman of the Newmarket Railway reported that negotiations had been pending with the Norfolk Railway for the latter leasing the line, as it was at present with the proposed extension to Thetford, at 6 per cent on the total outlay and half the profits, and that upon a meeting to settle the contract with the Norfolk negotiations were broken off, as the Norfolk announced for the first time that it did not have the power to enter into any agreement without the sanction of the Eastern Counties. In November 1846 the ECR was going to take a lease of the Newmarket Railway on the completion of the main line and the Cambridge branch on a five per cent basis of its capital. The directors of the company were delighted with the bargain that they thought that they had made, and they issued a glowing report to their shareholders in which they congratulated themselves on their success. Things then took a different turn. When the meeting to sanction the arrangement was held on 11 November 1846, the Chairman was not present and a quarter of an hour's indulgence had to be asked for him because he was attending a deputation to the Eastern Counties.

When he did arrive he had to announce, after listening to the Secretary's reading of the report of the board which had been circulated to the shareholders, that just before the meeting, the board had received an intimation from the ECR that the report was not in accordance with the spirit of the agreement. Because the parties were not in agreement with each other as to what the agreement meant, the Solicitor to the Company advised that parliament would never sanction and enforce the agreement. It seems that as a reprisal to this breaking off of negotiations by the ECR that the Newmarket's proprietors authorised, on 10 August 1847, a line from Chesterford to Royston, which would have given the GNR (whose main line was then in the course of construction), in conjunction with the Newmarket Railway, entirely independent access to the heart of the ECR by connections with the Norfolk Railway at Thetford and the EUR at Bury. Even at this very early stage of its life, the Great Northern was looking to expand into East Anglia.

Construction of the main line was now proceeding well. The *Cambridge Independent Press* of Saturday, 1 January 1848 carried a notice that the directors of the Newmarket had determined to open the railway between Chesterford and Newmarket for goods traffic on Monday, 3 January 1848. The *Norfolk Chronicle* of the same date said that the railway would open for passenger traffic on 3 January. All that happened was the main line was opened on 3 January 1848 for goods traffic. The opening of the main line for passenger traffic took place on 3 April.

At the time of opening, the Railway owned six locomotives, eighty-one carriages (twenty-six 1st class, twenty-five 2nd and thirty 3rd class), twenty-two horse boxes, seven luggage vans and eighteen carriage trucks.

There were four intermediate stations, namely, Bourne Bridge, Balsham Road, Six Mile Bottom (originally called Westley) and Dullingham. On 12 May, just over a month after opening to passengers, an accident occurred which could have had terrible consequences. Whilst the engine of the 3.30pm ex-Newmarket train was detached at Dullingham and shunted into a siding to pick up some luggage vans, the engineless train ran away along four miles of down gradient from Dullingham to Newmarket and, gathering speed as it went, dashed into Newmarket station. It is extraordinary that no serious injury was caused to any of the naturally alarmed passengers.

Returning to the financial problems of the Newmarket, in February further but unsuccessful negotiations took place with the ECR to lease or amalgamate with the Newmarket. Following this failure, the Newmarket approached the Norfolk which agreed to transfer the proposed Newmarket to Thetford line to them. Before an agreement was reached with the Norfolk, the ECR approached the Newmarket with a new proposal. On 27 March, an agreement was made allowing the ECR to take over the management of the Newmarket. As a result of this, the Newmarket deferred its agreement with the Norfolk and abandoned its own scheme to extend its own main line south to Royston to connect with the Great Northern. As part of the agreement, the ECR would provide funds to liquidate the liabilities of the Newmarket and complete the Cambridge branch, which the Newmarket did not have any capital to complete. Newmarket shareholders would receive a guaranteed dividend of three per cent for a minimum of two years. The agreement took effect on 2 October 1848. Meanwhile, on 8 May 1848 the ECR had taken over the working of the Norfolk. The agreement for the ECR to take over the management of the Newmarket still had to be agreed by the ECR shareholders. Things now got caught up in the fall of the Chairman of the Eastern Counties, George Hudson. By October 1848 it was doubtful whether the disgruntled ECR shareholders would approve the agreement with the Newmarket. At the Eastern Counties' Annual General Meeting on 28 February 1849 Hudson and his Directors decided not to put the agreement before the shareholders and within a short time he was forced to resign and the agreement with the Newmarket was scuppered.

At this point, skulduggery crept in. Following the scuppering of the agreement the Newmarket was then indeed left high and dry. The ECR proceeded with the double treatment of simultaneously starving and bleeding the Newmarket line. The ECR sought to charge 1/5d a mile for locomotive power, while on the London and South Western

Railway the cost was only 9d and on the London, Brighton and South Coast Railway the cost was 8½d. In addition, the ECR also charged the Newmarket £600 a year for the management of the line. The Chairman of the Newmarket had no scruples in calling it 'the mismanagement of the line'. The result of this was that the three months working of the Newmarket by the ECR to 4 January 1849 showed a gross profit to the Newmarket Company of only £704. Out of this it had to pay bond interest of £2,000, a problem that was rendered all the more difficult because the ECR held on to even the small balance on the grounds of alleged other claims. Additionally, the Newmarket had to defray out of capital the cost of maintaining the permanent way and stations. The directors considered resuming possession of their line, and of making arrangements with Thomas Jackson, the contractor who built it, to work it.

On 22 March 1849, a committee was set up to look into the Company's affairs. The committee was chaired by Cecil Fane, a Commissioner in Bankruptcy. He was of the opinion that the only way to save the company was to construct the Cambridge branch. In view of what happened later, one has a suspicion that the ECR may have had a hand in the appointment of Fane as chairman of the committee.

LONDON AND NEWMARKET, via Eastern Counties Station, Shoreditch.

Mils.	Stations between London and Chesterfield, page 26.	Week Days. 1 2 3 gov.	mail.	1 & 2 clss.	1 cls exp	Sundys. 1 2 3 class.	1 2 3 gov.
		mrn	morn	aft.	aft.	morn	aft.
—	**London** (Shoreditch St.) d	6 * 0	11*30	5 * 0	6 * 0	7 * 0	1*30
—	Chesterford .... arr	8 48	1 15	7 10	7 35	9 17	4 16
	Chesterford .... dep	9 0	1 20	7 40	7 40	9 25	6 50
5¼	Bourne Bridge	9 15	1 34	7 55	7 55	9 39	7 5
9½	Balsham Road............	9 24	1 46	8 8	8 8	9 51	7 14
12½	Six Mile Bottom..........	9 33	1 54	8 17	8 17	9 59	7 23
14½	Dullingham...............	9 40	2 0	8 24	8 24	10 5	7 30
18	**Newmarket** ......arr	9 55	2 10	8 40	8 40	10 15	7 45

For trains from Chesterfield, Cambridge, Peterbro', Ely, and Norwich, p. 26	Week Days. 1 & 2 exp	1 2 3 gov.	1 & 2 gov.	Sundys. 1 2 3 class.	1 2 3 gov.
	mrn	morn	aft.	morn	aft.
Newmarket ...... dep	8 * 0	10 10	5*45	8*20	3*20
Dullingham..............	8 8	10 20	6 0	8 30	3 29
Six Mile Bottom..........	8 13	10 25	6 8	8 35	3 34
Balsham Road	8 23	10 36	6 28	8 47	3 45
Bourne Bridge	8 31	10 46	6 43	8 58	3 55
Chesterford .... arr	8 45	11 5	7 5	9 13	4 10
Chesterford .... dep	9 18	11 12	8 29	10 26	6 48
Londn (Shoredtch. Sta) ar	11 0	1 35	10 40	1 15	9 40

Fares. London to Newmarket, 15s., 11s., 7s., and 5s. 5½d.
* In connexion at Chesterford with trains to and from Cambridge, St. Ives, Huntingdon, Ely, Brandon, Peterbro', &c.

The timetable of the Newmarket and Chesterford Railway from *Bradshaw's Railway Guide* for March 1850. The inhabitants of the places near Bourne Bridge and Balsham Road must surely have been outraged when the section between Chesterford and Six Mile Bottom was closed. (Author's collection).

The original and somewhat ornate terminal station of the Newmarket and Chesterford Railway at Newmarket. The station was somewhat inconveniently situated for passengers but survived for use by passengers until it was replaced by the present through station in 1902. (Author's collection).

In the end, nothing was achieved and following a final futile appeal to the ECR for justice, the directors were forced to close the line without even consulting the shareholders. According to the *Norfolk Chronicle* of 29 June 1850, the directors of the Railway had issued a public notice that it would cease carrying passengers and goods from 30 June. Working expenses for a long period had been exceeding receipts and negotiations with the ECR and other parties proving unsuccessful were believed to be the reason for the closing of the line. In the *Cambridge Independent Press*, the Newmarket Railway announced their intention to close their branch from Chesterford and that coaches would run in connection with the trains at Cambridge.

Kenneth Brown, in his history of the Railway published in the *Railway Magazine* in November and December 1941, says:

> The Newmarket Company was now in a parlous position. It was in pawn under debentures issued to Mr. Jackson for the company's unpaid obligations to him as contractor and to other debenture holders. No doubt the policy of starving and bleeding the line adopted by the ECR was deliberately intended to enable that Company to buy up the concern when the debentures fell due.

All the Newmarket's locomotives and rolling stock had to go to the ECR under what the company's directors called 'an equitable arrangement', but which, according to Brown, looks uncommonly like a case of the ECR astutely taking the rolling stock in payment of what otherwise might prove a bad debt.

The position of the company was that the Chesterford line was closed and the Cambridge branch was uncompleted. The Company had no money to complete the Cambridge branch except for an uncalled £2 per share on the shares, which it might be very difficult to collect from disillusioned and disgruntled shareholders. The Company's other creditors were pressing, and it was involved in a Chancery suit. It was at this point that Cecil Fane came and took control. In this I again suspect the hand of the Eastern Counties. As mentioned, Fane had already been Chairman of the committee appointed on 22 March 1849 to go into the affairs of the Company, and the report of the Committee was handed in on 14 May 1849. The report had urged the immediate pressing on with the Cambridge branch as the Company's one hope of salvation. For a time, he had also been a Director of the Company and had resigned owing to his dissatisfaction with the management of its affairs. When at the meeting of 27 July 1850 the Company's directors came forward and told the story of their defeatist policy of closing the line on the previous 30 June without even having called the shareholders together on the matter, Fane rose in his wrath and tore the board to shreds. He showed that if running the line would probably entail a loss, keeping it shut would mean a larger loss; he criticised the mistake of making as the pivot of the line Chesterford, a small village, and not Cambridge, a large town; and denounced in no measured terms the bungling of the various negotiations with the Norfolk and the ECRs and the tactless handling by the directors of the contractor and debenture holder. Whilst Chesterford might have been a small village, it was larger than Marks Tey which was the junction of the Colchester, Stour Valley and Halstead Railway which had opened to Sudbury on 2 July 1849. In 1848, the population of (Great) Chesterford was 917, whereas that of Marks Tey was only 397. As I say, I suspect the hand of the ECR in this.

At the meeting in question, the shareholders by a large majority cast out the existing Chairman, Lord George Manners, and his board and replaced them with Fane as Chairman and a new board of directors. The result was that on 9 September 1850 the line reopened using locomotives and rolling stock borrowed from the Eastern Counties. The Secretary of the Company, Mr G.W. Brown, became the Manager and, due to his efforts, revenue increased and expenses decreased.

Fane came to an arrangement with Jackson, the contractor, to re-adjust his 1846 contract prices which had been made during the railway boom and write £26,000 off his bill, and to reduce his debenture interest from 5 per cent to 3½ per cent. He also induced other debenture holders to reduce their interest. He even got the carriage builder and engine builder to reduce their accounts, when they must surely have been rather exasperated that the Company had sold the rolling stock to the ECR before it had been fully paid for. According to Brown, Fane stirred up the defaulting shareholders in arrears two years with their calls and got in the calls on 3,000 shares and forfeited 2,000 shares. He also settled the Chancery suit on the basis of the other side paying the costs and buying for £500 a piece of land the company did not want. Fane also made an arrangement with the ECR to accommodate (when opened) the Cambridge branch at Cambridge station and so avoid the expense of a separate station and staff there, and also secured certain advantageous traffic arrangements and – last but not least – an undertaking embodied in an agreement dated 28 May 1851, that in any year after the opening of the Cambridge branch in which the revenue was insufficient to pay a dividend of 3 per cent on the Newmarket Company's capital of £350,000, the ECR would make it good up to a sum not exceeding £5,000 in any one year. This agreement was confirmed by the ECR and Newmarket Railways Arrangements Act, 1852.

In addition, Fane got Jackson to agree to complete the line to Cambridge for a sum not exceeding £9,000, on being furnished with a certain quantity of rails and sleepers which the company would have at its disposal. This last phrase covered a most ingenious move on Fane's part. The original main line from Chesterford to Newmarket was laid with double lines. A single line was ample for the traffic, so Fane had one set of rails and sleepers (barring presumably necessary passing places) pulled up from Chesterford to the junction with the Cambridge branch and so had some eleven miles of rails with sleepers to pave the branch to Cambridge and leave some £7,000 worth of rails over.

The urgent desire of the energetic Fane to get the Cambridge branch open as soon as possible was met with annoying technical difficulties as to the junction with the ECR at Cambridge. In the parliamentary plans, the curve at the junction was shown as one of a radius of 20 chains but it was found necessary from unavoidable circumstances to alter the curve to one of 8 chains. For this, the consent of the Commissioners of Railways was required and was applied for in July 1851. As, however, the Company's compulsory powers of acquiring land had expired, the Commissioners refused to approve the deviation without the consents of the owners and occupiers of the land affected. This plunged Fane into despair as, in order to save time, he wanted to get the deviation approved first and the consents of the landowners afterwards. On

30 July 1851, Fane wrote to Captain Simmons, RE, of the Railway Commissioners' Office, asking permission to do what he wanted. The Commissioners refused Fane's request and the latter was compelled to concede to the Commissioners' request.

On 29 September, the Inspector Engineer of the Commissioners, following his inspection of the line, reported that the connecting line at Cambridge was not laid. Fane was still waiting for the Commissioners' consent to that new curve, the fencing near the junction at Six Mile Bottom was far from complete, that at one of the stations no platform had yet been laid, and that the permanent way was as yet in a very rough state and required a good deal of adjustment. The Commissioners declared the opening of the line must be postponed for a month. Fane, however, was not to be outdone and, according to Brown, 'succeeded even in infusing some of his abounding energy into a Civil Service Department'. On 7 October, he secured both the Commissioners' approval of the new curve and the passing of the line by the Inspecting Engineer, the fencing and junction having been completed, and on 8 October the formal consent to the line being opened for public traffic, which took place the following day, 9 October. Immediately the Cambridge line was opened the Chesterford line was closed to all traffic. The *Bury and Norwich Post* on 8 October 1851 announced that the Cambridge branch of the Newmarket railway would open for general traffic on 9 October and that the line between Six Mile Bottom and Chesterford would be closed 'for the present'. The *Cambridge Independent Press* of 11 October had the same announcement but in the past tense. The ECR had got its way and Cambridge was satisfied. Following the opening of the Cambridge line, the Company's fortunes improved and it was taken out of bankruptcy and by the end of February 1852 had even declared a dividend.

Although the Company had said that the section between Six Mile Bottom and Chesterford was suspended as opposed to closed and despite calls for it to be reopened, such as one at Bury St Edmunds in 1852, it is clear that the company had no intention of doing so.

The *Bury and Norwich Post* of 3 August 1853 reported:

> THE CHESTERFORD RAILWAY Now that the Eastern Counties Company and the Newmarket Company have come to an amicable agreement, several workmen are busily engaged in taking up the branch between Newmarket and Chesterford. Sleepers are raised, platforms dismantled, trams translated, chairs relieved of their heavy burden, and the telegraph lines alone are left to look down and mourn over the desolate that knows them no more. The plough, the drill and the harrow, which a few years ago were so unceremoniously vanished then from the spot, will again resume their profitable function.

In 1852, the ECR obtained an Act authorising it to purchase the Newmarket at any time which it did on 30 March 1854. Meanwhile, construction of the extension from Newmarket to Bury St Edmunds started and was completed by the end of March 1854. Opening to all traffic took place on 1 April that year. The section of line to Chesterford was not officially abandoned until after the passing of the Abandonment Act of 1858.

Chapter 10

The East Anglian Railway from the End of 1849 to the End of 1851

The Great Northern Railway was interested in extending into Norfolk and creating a route from the north to Cambridge. It was also interested in reaching Cambridge from London, but that is not relevant at this point. In 1849, an agreement had been entered into between the Great Northern and ECRs whereby the former secured running powers from Peterborough to Wisbech in return for abandoning their powers to construct a line from Stamford via Peterborough to Wisbech, which it had inherited from the Boston, Stamford and Birmingham Railway which it had absorbed.

During 1851, the EAR was very nearly absorbed by the GNR, instead of which, however, it afterwards became an integral part of the GER. In the year in question, the GNR entered into an agreement to work the EAR, but this was afterwards objected to by the GNR shareholders on two grounds: first, that it had been entered into without their authority; and second, that it involved a guarantee of £15,000 per annum, and that three guarantees which had previously been entered into by the railway had all turned out to be very unprofitable bargains. There was also another objection, that of inaccessibility. The EAR lay practically and wholly within the ECR territory and the only point at which the GNR could get in touch with the smaller line was at Wisbech.

In February 1851, the officers of the Great Northern inspected the EAR and its rolling stock and on 16 May a traffic agreement was signed. The Great Northern was to have at least forty per cent of the receipts and to maintain the plant and the lines. The East Anglian agreed to make permanent bridges on the Wisbech branch and to complete a junction with the Great Northern at Huntingdon. The Great Northern had to advance the East Anglian £3,500 for works and £1,109 for land. The three-quarter mile long line was inspected by the Board of Trade on 27 September, but the opening was postponed for a month as the Inspecting Officer was not satisfied with the signalling arrangements. The line was double track until it reached Great Northern property at Huntingdon, where the two lines converged to form Godmanchester Junction, with the Great Northern Up line 13 chains south of the station facing in the direction of London. Without a further application to the Board of Trade, the line was bought into use on 29 October.

The Great Northern resolved to commence working the local traffic of the East Anglian from 25 May and general traffic from 1 July. I assume this to be 1851 as John Wrottesley in Volume 1 of his history of the GNR published in 1979 does not make the year clear, but it seems the most logical. Accordingly, the Great Northern gave notice to the ECR under the 1849 agreement. The ECR accepted the notice and promised the Great Northern the co-operation of its officers. The Eastern Counties must have viewed the Great Northern's designs on reaching Cambridge with some apprehension, as it notified the Great Northern's General Manager (Seymour Clarke) of its intention to single the line from St Ives to Cambridge.

The new arrangements were not put into operation until 10 July. When the first Great Northern train intending to travel to Lynn reached Wisbech ECR junction, it found the junction points blocked against it by vehicles chained to the rails. A train coming from the other direction from Lynn faced the same obstacle. The ECR officials asserted that the Great Northern had no running powers over the short stretch of line between its station at Wisbech and the terminus of the EAR. Wentworth Clarke, the Manager of the East Anglian, was prepared for something of that nature and had omnibuses ready to convey passengers between the two Wisbech stations which were about half a mile apart. This arrangement was not conducive to the development of traffic. As traffic could not be satisfactorily maintained whilst the junction remained blocked, the dispute was referred to the Railway Commissioners. The ECR maintained that the East Anglian had departed from the authorised line and that it had no right to join it where the line did, that in granting running powers to the Great Northern it expected the latter to work its trains into its (the Eastern Counties) station at Wisbech and not to a junction outside. And that, anyway, the connecting powers did not cover the connecting line to the East Anglian station; and that that had been provided to give the East Anglian a route to its isolated section at St Ives. Had the connection not been approved by the Inspecting Officer, the Commissioners would probably have ordered the removal of the obstruction. But it had not and when it was, they washed their hands of the matter. The Great Northern then applied to the Court of Chancery for an injunction to compel the ECR to keep to the 1849 agreement and remove the obstruction. Confident in its case, the Great Northern provided temporary accommodation at St Ives and contemplated building its own station at Wisbech, whilst the East Anglian prepared plans for a permanent station at St Ives. Although Vice Chancellor Turner of the Court of Chancery was disposed to find that the ECR was bound under the agreement to allow the Great Northern to use the connecting line, in the end he decided against the latter on the grounds that the agreement was really a lease and was invalid without the sanction of parliament and refused an injunction. As a result, there were further Great Northern-East Anglian negotiations with the latter proposing that the former would pay money for the plant instead of paying an annuity as stipulated in the agreement. Under the new terms, the Great Northern was to buy the plant at a valuation of £52,000. The bridges and the works were to be paid out of that sale and bonds were to be given for the balance. An Act would be sought to grant a working contract to the Great Northern for twenty-five years, which were to be substantially on the terms of the previous contract including a specified guarantee of £15,000 per annum. During the interim the Great Northern would work the line.

Almost immediately the East Anglian used the draft agreement to bargain with the Eastern Counties. In a sharply worded letter to the East Anglian solicitor, Baxter, one of the Great Northern's solicitors informed the former that the Great Northern did not intend to bid against the Eastern Counties, nor would it allow the terms to stand over and that the plant would be handed over as soon as the East Anglian settled its accounts with the Great Northern. On 25 November, arrangements were made to transfer the working of the line back to the East Anglian. In early December, the plant was restored to the East Anglian. Meanwhile, as a result of negotiations between the two larger railways, an arrangement was entered into whereby the ECR took over from 1 January 1852 the working of the EAR and became responsible for the guarantee. Under this new arrangement, the ECR took over the East Anglian's properties and rolling stock at a valuation and the payment so obtained was used to replace the timber bridges over the Ouse and Middle Drain and to pay off the East Anglian's creditors. It was also agreed that the East Anglian's net revenue should not be less than £17,000 per annum.

Chapter 11

The Eastern Union and its Associated Railways from 1847 to 1853

This chapter will include what may be termed subsidiary, or related companies, the Eastern Union and Hadleigh Junction Railway (EU&HJR) and the Colchester, Stour Valley, Sudbury and Halstead Railway as well as the beginning of the Waveney Valley Railway, the EUR's proposal for a branch to Woodbridge and a branch to Harwich, the independent Scole Railway and the Ipswich and Stowmarket Navigation.

A new station, albeit incomplete at the time of opening, was opened at Bury St Edmunds in November 1847.

Cecil J. Allen in *The Great Eastern Railway* (Fourth Edition 1967 Ian Allan) says that the relations between the EUR and the I&BR were so intimate that it was no surprise that a decision was reached, no more

A rather nice view of the original Bury St Edmunds station. The frontage of the station is still substantially the same today and is a rather attractive building. From the almost total lack of people in the photograph, one must assume that the photograph is a posed one. (Author's collection).

than a week after the opening of the latter Railway, that the two railways should be worked as one. The arrangement began on 1 January 1847 and full amalgamation followed, ratified by an Act of Parliament dated 9 July of that year. According to the *Ipswich Journal* of Saturday, 12 December 1846, a meeting of the shareholders of the Ipswich and Bury St Edmunds Railway had been held at its offices in Ipswich on the previous Tuesday for the purposes of considering and confirming an arrangement for amalgamating that Company and the EUR into one Company. On the same day and at the same place, a meeting of the shareholders of the EUR was held for the same purposes.

The Ipswich and Stowmarket Navigation had been formed by an Act of Parliament in 1789 for the purpose of making the River Gipping navigable between Ipswich and Stowmarket. The Navigation opened in 1793 and was 17 miles long and had 15 locks. In 1844, the Trustees of the Navigation, learning that the EUR planned an extension of its Railway, negotiated with the Railway Company to lease the Navigation in the hope that it would help the Railway Company by removing one source of opposition to their plans. They submitted a firm proposal for the lease on 8 February 1845, to which the Railway Company agreed, and the shareholders sanctioned the action soon afterwards. The Trustees engaged a parliamentary agent to handle the details, who realised that unfortunately the original Act of Parliament, dating from 1790, expressly prohibited the Trustees from leasing the Navigation. By September of that year the two sides had agreed that each of them would seek to obtain powers to overturn the clause in the Act of 1790. The Railway Company would pay £1,070 per year for the first 21 years, and £850 per year for the second 21 years. The Trustees sought an Act of Parliament to authorise this, which contained a clause requiring the Railway Company to maintain the navigation. The House of Lords were not convinced that the clause was strong enough, and amended it to ensure that the Railway Company had to maintain it 'in as good a state and condition as the same shall be at the time of passing of the Act'. With this amendment in place, the Act was passed on 26 June 1846. Following the opening of the Railway to Bury St Edmunds through Stowmarket in 1846, the Navigation suffered a serious decline in traffic.

The Victoria Station Hotel in Colchester had been constructed by Samuel Morton Peto for the sum of £15,000 and had been designed by Lewis Cubitt, who later designed King's Cross station in London. The hotel opened in 1846, but it was not a success and according to D.I. Gordon, by 1850 it had been converted into an asylum.

As mentioned previously, the Act for the extension of the line from Haughley Junction to Norwich was obtained by the I&BR before it was amalgamated with the EUR. According to H.F. Hilton in *The EUR 1846 to 1862* (LNER 1946), the Act authorising the construction of the line provided for a capital of £550,000 with authority to raise a further sum of £183,333 by loan or mortgage. A clause within it provided for the purchase of this line and the remainder of the I&BR by the EUR. As the Act was drafted and given Royal Assent before the I&BR began to function, it is quite certain that the EUR Directors contemplated acquiring the I&BR at an early date. At the Norwich end of the line, a branch line was to be made at Trowse to form a connection with the ECR. The ECR, when it took over the Norfolk Railway, accepted its obligations, one of which was that in the event of the government's Railway Department deciding that the level crossing at Trowse station was unsuitable, a bridge should be built. As the additional traffic arising from the I&BR line might cause such a decision to be made, a clause was inserted, at the instigation of the ECR, in the I&BR bill compelling the former to contribute to the cost of the bridge.

According to Hilton, construction of the line to Norwich started on 25 February 1847 at Norwich:

> The Chairman of the Company and the Mayor of Norwich between them dug and wheeled away the first earth to be moved. The people of Norwich, although having taken part in the ceremonies of opening two other railways, were ready to do full justice to this event as they looked for a shortening of the distance by railway to London with the completion of the Norwich extension. The day was fine and with flags flying from the churches and other conspicuous buildings, a great number of people assembled on Mr. Cyrus Gillett's farm at Lakenham overlooking the River Tas.

Construction work also started at the other end of the line between Stowmarket and Haughley stations. It was originally intended also to provide a junction facing in the direction of Bury St Edmunds as well as one facing in the direction of Ipswich, but this was never completed.

As work on the line from Ipswich to Bury was completed, men and plant transferred to the Norwich line. By July 1847, 1,200 men and 150 horses were engaged in the work on constructing the line. Thrandeston Marsh was a problem for the contractor, John Douglas; problems which were solved by floating the bank on a raft of faggots and brushwood. Even so, the bank continued to sink until a vast amount of material had been absorbed and the surrounding ground heaved up. This was the time of recession after the Railway Mania and in October most of the work was suspended. Work did not resume until early in 1848 and by the end of May there were about 450 men engaged on the work of constructing the line. Public goods services began to Finningham on 7 June 1848.

The summer of 1848 was a wet one and work slowed. By the middle of January 1849, track of some sort had reached Diss and on 19 January a contractor's locomotive reached that town. The event was witnessed by crowds of people. On 28 May, a single line was opened for goods traffic to Mellis and Diss. On 11 June, the service was extended to Burston and within a short time a second line was completed, and passenger traffic began between Haughley Junction and Burston. When the Burston section was finished, a new station named Haughley Junction was opened where the Norwich line connected with the Bury St Edmunds line, and the old Haughley station which was situated about one mile nearer Bury was closed. According to Hilton, a notification appeared in the *Ipswich Journal* which read 'On and from Monday, July 7th the Haughley Station will be closed, and business will be transferred to Haughley Junction. Squire Martin, Supt'. Pending the completion of the line beyond Burston, passengers wishing to travel further were conveyed by road vehicles.

At Lakenham on the approach to Norwich, although the foundation stone for the viaduct there had been laid on 30 August 1847, work had only proceeded at a slow pace. The scaffolding stood for so long that the rope lashings and staging round one of the piers collapsed and injured four men. By February 1849, construction of the viaduct was only up to springing height, the point where the arch leaves its support. It was only in June of that year that the Markshall cutting was completed, at which time the permanent way hardly extended north of Burston other than an isolated length on the north side of the viaduct to Peafield. By the beginning of October, a double line of permanent way extended from Haughley to Flordon and a single line as far as Swainsthorpe. The skew bridge at Dunston carrying the Norwich to Scole road over the railway was complete and the Lakenham viaduct was nearly complete with the embankments on each side almost closed. It was not until November 1849 that the line was completed to Norwich. The Eastern Union terminus at Norwich was at Victoria Gardens, formerly known as Ranelagh Gardens.

The official opening to Norwich was somewhat premature so that that it could be celebrated during the mayoralty of Samuel Bignold. Only a single line had been laid down from Burston to accommodate the special traffic for the event. Samuel Bignold, who was one of Norwich's prominent and progressive citizens, had for some time given much practical assistance to railway construction and on the fusion of the

Lakenham viaduct on the EUR just south of Norwich. The line from Ipswich to Norwich was not completed until November 1849, thus completing the shorter route from London to Norwich, but initially a change of companies was involved at Colchester which caused problems. (Author's collection).

EUR and I&BR had joined the board of the combined companies. The Directors held their opening ceremony on 7 November 1849 when a long train left Norwich at 11.30 decorated with flowers and carrying passengers who had been supplied with special tickets and others who, having paid the fare to Burston, were allowed to travel to that point, although they had 'often ridiculed the railway and made sport of the losses of the projectors'. Another train left Ipswich at noon and carried a large number of people as guests of the Directors, from Ipswich and from Colchester. It was planned for both trains to reach Stowmarket at about the same time, but the one from Norwich did not arrive until 1.30 and during the meantime the travellers from Ipswich had taken their luncheon. When the Norwich contingent got there, their appetites had sharpened and the rooms at the station 'set out with well-laden tables presented an envious and bustling scene, and everyone was anxious to obtain something edible and potable'. According to Hilton, 'Amidst good natured confusion one of the company, regardless of etiquette, snatched up half a pigeon pie' to share with a friend. Another with 'woe begotten countenance received a leg of partridge' while others 'in good humour put into practice the theory of growing fat on laughter'. Hilton goes on to say that:

> After long and frantic blowing of the engines' whistles, the company at last got settled in the united trains of some twenty carriages of various types hauled by two locomotives named *City of Norwich* and *Ipswich*. Short stoppages were made at some of the stations en route, including one at Diss for the engines to take water and for the Directors to receive the ovations of the inhabitants. Most of the stations were decorated with the usual arches, flags were flying and church bells ringing.

A train of coal from the Port of Ipswich was standing on an adjoining line at Diss as a reminder that the railway was living up to its intention to benefit the community and for its own traffic advertisement. This seems to have been somewhat symbolic as the actual opening of the line for goods traffic did not take place for nearly another month. At Norwich, the station building had been adapted from a building known as the Pantheon which had been a feature of the gardens and had been used for circuses and other entertainment. According to Hilton, 'The visitors were met at the "rotunda" terminus by the civic authorities who, accompanied by the band of the 16th Lancers, formed a procession through the streets, lined by enthusiastic spectators, to St. Andrews Hall, where a sumptuous dinner was provided'. An advertisement in the *Norfolk Chronicle* of 3 November was as follows, 'Eastern Union Railway Opening to the Victoria Station, Norwich, November 7th 1849'. The weather on the day of the official opening was typically English – wet. Goods traffic began on 3 December followed by the opening to passenger traffic on 10 December. The new route to Norwich from London was 12½ miles shorter than the existing route via Cambridge and Ely. The connecting line between the two railways at Norwich (Trowse Upper to Lower Junctions) did not open until 8 September 1851.

The Colchester, Stour Valley, Sudbury and Halstead Railway obtained its Act on 26 June 1846. This Railway was in three sections as authorised, of which only two were built by the Company. The first, which commenced at a junction with the ECR at Marks Tey, continued 11¾ miles to Sudbury. There were two intermediate stations, at Chappel and Wakes Colne and Bures. At Marks Tey, the Stour Valley platform was on the curve at the back of the ECR Down platform and the other curve proposed leading towards London was not constructed. At Chappel, there was a viaduct over the valley of the small River Colne of 30 arches, each of 30ft. span and 75ft. in height. At Chappel and Wakes Colne there was to be a branch line of 6 miles in length to Halstead, which was never built by the Company. The other line that was authorised to be built was from the Eastern Union station at Colchester to The Hythe where the riverside quay of the Borough of Colchester accommodated sea-going ships. Both this line and the Marks Tey-Sudbury line were opened for traffic on 2 July 1849 with little ceremony and it is recorded that the passengers by the Directors' train walked aimlessly about Sudbury until lunch was ready. Only the Marks Tey to Sudbury line had a passenger service, the line to The Hythe at Colchester being only for goods traffic. The ECR gave the EUR running powers over the section of its line from Marks Tey to Colchester. The ECR unsuccessfully promoted its own rival line to Bures and the Stour Valley commencing at Lexden.

On 8 June 1847, the Company obtained three acts, one was to build an extension from Sudbury via Long Melford to Clare with a branch from Long Melford to Lavenham, one was to build a further extension from Lavenham to Bury St Edmunds and the third authorised the company to lease itself to the I&BR.

By the Eastern Union Railway Arrangements Act 1852, it was provided that from 1 July 1852 the sum of £9, 500 per annum should

Chappel Viaduct adjoining Chappell and Wakes Colne station on the line from Marks Tey to Sudbury was, and is, the longest viaduct in the Eastern Counties. The viaduct has thirty arches, each of 30ft span and 75ft in height. The Sudbury branch was opened to traffic on 2 July 1849. (Juliet Brown).

be paid to the Colchester, Stour Valley, Sudbury and Halstead Railway for the rent of their line instead of the fluctuating amount previously agreed.

The failure of the railway to construct the branch to Halstead led Halstead to consider and eventually build its own railway which became the Colne Valley and Halstead Railway (CV&HR).

Another railway company was the Eastern Union and Hadleigh Junction Railway (EU&HJR) which obtained its Act on 18 June 1846. It was authorised to build a line from near Bentley station, between Manningtree and Ipswich, to Hadleigh. It commenced with two junctions with the Eastern Union near Bentley, one leading towards Colchester and the other towards Ipswich. There is some debate as to what use was made of the Ipswich facing junction. This short branch,

7¼ miles in length, was apparently managed by the same officers as the Eastern Union although built as an independent Company. The Chairman of the Company was J.C. Cobbold and two Directors also had seats on the Boards of the EUR and I&BR. The capital was £75,000. The line was opened on 21 August 1847 with an opening ceremony. According to Hugh Moffat in *East Anglia's First Railways* (Terence Dalton 1987), before the line had been completed the Company's Engineer, Peter Bruff, prepared a scheme for extending the line to Lavenham, but this was abandoned, partly no doubt for financial reasons, partly because he considered it advisable to pass the track under Station Road at Hadleigh, which would have meant altering the levels of the work in hand. According to Peter Paye in *The Hadleigh Branch* (Oakwood Press, 2006), the Directors of the Company were keen to extend the line to Lavenham, so they put in hand the necessary measures to secure parliamentary authorisation. The EUR was encouraging the Colchester, Stour Valley, Sudbury and Halstead Railway (S&HR) at this point, as it had just received its authorising Act to extend to Lavenham. The Lavenham extension would conflict with the strategic objectives of the EUR, and they asked the EU&HJR to defer their proposal. At first the local company declined to do so, but they were later persuaded to relent.

Even before the EU&HJR had obtained its Act, a lease of it to the EUR was agreed in October 1845. The Act authorising amalgamation of the EU&HJR with the EUR was passed in the following session of parliament, on 8 June 1847.

On 10 June 1846, Cornelius Welton, who was a land agent and surveyor from Wickham Market, produced a plan for a line from Ipswich to Woodbridge via Ashbock and Clopton with a branch from the latter to Framlingham. He felt sure the scheme would be opposed in Woodbridge, where a more direct line was wanted. A Woodbridge committee was set up to explore ways and means of getting a railway. In November 1846, the EUR and the I&BR both deposited bills with parliament for two alternative Woodbridge branches. The plans of the two rival schemes were drawn up by Peter Bruff, who was the engineer of both Railways. The I&BR's Bill received the Royal Assent on 9 July 1847 authorising £200,000 in new shares in addition to the usual borrowing powers. The state of the money market prevented a start being made, although some land was acquired before the Company's powers lapsed in 1850.

In 1847, the EUR's bill for a line from Manningtree to Harwich received the approval of the Railway Commissioners and an Act authorising its construction was obtained on 27 July 1847 that authorised the EUR to raise capital of £200,000 and to lease the line to the ECR on completion. Due to lack of funds work had to be postponed, but a token start was made at Manningtree in October 1848. Cobbold, the chairman of the EUR, and his Directors agreed with their opposite numbers on the ECR to lease the line to the latter Company for 999 years at an annual rent of 4½ per cent with a division of any profits above that figure. The powers to build the line expired but were revived by another Act in 1850. The ECR decided that 4½ per cent was too optimistic and another agreement in 1851 lowered the rent to 4 per cent. Eventually, the capital was raised to build the line by lowering the dividend on some 6 per cent preference stock that was about to be issued to 4 per cent and guaranteeing that the accounts for the Harwich branch would be kept separated from the rest of the Company's business. This was in the EUR's Act of 1852. In 1851, the people of Harwich had grown tired of waiting for the railway to provide them with a pier and obtained an Act to carry out various improvements including a pier and quay from the Shipyard to King's Head Street. Work commenced on 2 June 1852 and the pier was opened in July 1853. At the beginning of January 1853, work began in earnest on constructing the Harwich branch. The first train traversed the line on 29 July 1853 carrying a large party of navvies with the engineer Peter Bruff and his assistant Francis Leonard and

The original Harwich station which was opened in 1854. Observe the two four wheeled carriages at the platform, which I would suggest were third class as they do not appear to have any glass in them. Note also the open wagon with its rounded ends. (Author's collection).

constructors' representatives. About 2 miles from Harwich the train stopped to pick up a band from Harwich. Major Wynne of the Board of Trade inspected the line on 4 August, and it was opened for traffic on 15 August.

The Waveney Valley Railway Company was promoted in 1850 with its advertised intention being to introduce a Bill in parliament to build a railway from Tivetshall on the Norwich line via Bungay to Beccles and from Bungay to Halesworth and from Bungay to the Lowestoft Railway at Raveningham. The rather ambitious hopes had to be pruned and the Act obtained on 3 July 1851 only authorised the construction from Tivetshall to Bungay. The Act authorised the making of working arrangements for the working of the line with the EUR and another obtained in 1853 sanctioned the extension of the line to Beccles. Investing members of the public declined to take up shares and the story of the Company was a story of Acts to extend the time for completing the line.

The Scole Railway opened in 1850, the brainchild of William Betts, who owned Frenze Hall and estates. As a substantial landowner, he had plans to create a market garden and the Scole Railway's main reason for being built was so that he could get his produce to the London markets in good time. The Railway's total length was only 7 miles up to the point where it reached the main lines of the EUR and had some sidings near the Great Barn on the Frenze Estate to allow for the produce, once sorted and packed, to be loaded onto the trains. The Railway started from behind the Jolly Porter inn at Diss. To make the line even more profitable, Betts created two large brickfields, also connected to his railway, which increased the long-term value of his estate as well as providing the raw material for the construction of workers' cottages. When Betts died in 1885 the Railway closed.

When the EUR opened its line to Norwich, which as indicated earlier was shorter than that owned wholly by the ECR, its ownership of the new route was 51 per cent compared to the ECR's 49 per cent. The ECR, prior to the opening of the new shorter route, was clearly aware that the new route would attract travellers from its route and raised rates on the Colchester line by 18 per cent for passengers and 10 per cent for goods. According to Moffat, the *Suffolk Chronicle* protested that the 2nd class fare from Ipswich to London would be 13s – a 30 per cent increase in just over 3 years. The *Norwich Mercury* complained that passengers joining London bound trains at Colchester were charged less than through travellers from the EUR. The *Ipswich Journal* said that the 2nd class fare from Norwich to Colchester was 8/2d, but from there to London 10s but the ECR compelled the EUR to charge 21s in order to make up the difference of 2/10d. The charges between Stowmarket and Norwich were eccentric. From Flordon to Norwich – a distance of 6.5 miles – the charge was 2/6d, but in the opposite direction the charge was only 11d. To give another example of what went on, many cheap excursions were run by the ECR, one of which conveyed 1,000 passengers in 52 carriages to London and back at fares of 1s for adults and 6d for children. Later, in the Down direction, the fares became even more odd. There were artificially low fares to Norwich subsidised with higher fares to intermediate stations as the EUR strove to compete with the ECR and its longer route. And then there was a court case in May 1853 of a Mr Frere who was a JP of Roydon Hall near Diss and was convicted at Colchester Magistrates' Court of travelling on the railway without paying the proper fare. Frere had bought a 2nd class ticket from Colchester to Norwich costing 5s but alighted at Diss where the fare from Colchester to Diss was 7s. Frere appealed to the Quarter Sessions, where the case was adjudged to be so important that it was referred to the High Court, which set aside the fine of 10s imposed by Colchester Magistrates. Whilst counsel for the EUR argued that Frere had obtained his ticket by false pretences, the court decided that a passenger was entitled to alight at any intermediate station unless there were specific byelaws to the contrary. By that time, the EUR had been taken over by the ECR and the matter was a dead letter. Long before that, the EUR had been striving to achieve some sort of agreement with the ECR on the whole question of the Norwich traffic and in theory an accord had been reached. On 27 February 1850, the two companies concluded a formal agreement to pool and divide the receipts from all London to Norwich traffic on both routes – 75 per cent to the ECR as they owned about that amount of the combined mileage and 25 per cent to the EUR. Things did not work according to plan. For example, according to the *Ipswich Journal,* on one Monday passengers at Shoreditch station (London) were told that they could not be booked beyond Colchester, the ECR's servants affecting ignorance of the EUR. When the train arrived at Colchester, great care was taken that no passenger should proceed beyond or buy another ticket. In another instance, a carriage which was to be sent from Colchester to Norwich was sent to London and thence to Norwich via Cambridge and Ely. The *Ipswich Journal* castigated the EUR for allowing themselves to be so dominated and urged it to break the ECR stranglehold by carrying their passengers between London and Ipswich by steam ship. Even the parliamentary fare was 10/6d from Norwich to London whereas the maximum legal charge was 9/6d. Things got so bad that on 20 September 1850 the EUR gave six months' notice of their intention to terminate the agreement. The ECR suggested that it should be terminated immediately but the directors of the EUR refused to take such a radical step.

In November 1850, the EUR lodged a Bill with parliament to give them running powers over the ECR to London and from Trowse to Yarmouth and Lowestoft over the Norfolk Railway, which, as mentioned previously, was already leased to the ECR in return for running powers over their metals. Traffic arrangements between the companies were to be properly coordinated and disputes referred to arbitration. Cobbold and his fellow directors knew that, even if parliament gave them the powers they desired, it would not be until the summer of 1851, which would be after the notice that they had served on the ECR had expired. No one knew what the ECR might do. Through bookings might be terminated and the ECR, assured of its Norwich traffic via Cambridge, could initiate what would amount to a blockade of the EUR. Eventually, after reflecting on the subject for some weeks, the EUR directors meeting as the Company's Traffic Committee decided to ask the ECR what arrangements they would be prepared to make after the end of March 1851 and suggested that their differences be submitted to arbitration. The full board of the EUR meeting the following week after the Traffic Committee meeting rejected the idea of any communication with the ECR and instructed the EUR's engineer Peter Bruff to prepare plans to meet any eventuality. There was however some communication between the two companies. Joseph Glynn, the vice chairman of the ECR, and some of his colleagues were aware of their own financial problems. Faced with opposing the EUR Bill in parliament, they concluded a new agreement with the EUR and the Norfolk Railway, whose shareholders had always been resentful of the terms on which their railway had been taken over and worked by the ECR. Under the agreement which was provisionally signed by the chairmen of the three companies in January 1851, the ECR was to take over the working of all the lines belonging to the three companies and purchase the rolling stock of the EUR and the Norfolk Railway at sums to be determined by independent valuers. Then, after the ECR had been paid its working costs, the surplus was to be applied to paying interest on the debentures and dividend on the preference shares issued by the three companies with specified maxima in each case. The ECR was to receive three quarters of any surplus and the others an eighth each and the EUR and the Norfolk Railway were each to nominate a director on the ECR Board and an application was to be made to parliament to amalgamate the three companies. Whilst the shareholders of the EUR and the Norfolk Railway ratified the agreement, the ECR's shareholders rejected it on 11 March 1851. On the very last day that the EUR's notice to terminate the agreement expired, a letter was received from the ECR suggesting that the agreement should continue on a monthly basis, subject to a week's notice from either side.

Meanwhile, although the completion of the Norwich extension had brought in more revenue, debts had also increased. The Company made some economies such as cutting the drivers' wages of 7/6d a day to 7s a day, making a few men redundant and discontinuing the practice of allowing office staff to leave the office in the middle of the day to have lunch.

Meanwhile, the EUR's bill had progressed through parliament in the face of stiff opposition from the ECR and became law on 3 July 1851. By then it had lost its teeth. The EUR was merely authorised to make arrangements with the ECR, the Norfolk Railway and the L&BR about rates and through traffic. It had no running powers over lines that it did not own. Disputes were to be referred to arbitration. The maximum fares that could be charged were 3d, 2d and 1½d per mile respectively for the three classes of travel. Cobbold and his colleagues wished to convert their contract debts into special creditors' stock, but in one of the Company's Acts there was a clause that had been inserted by the Railway Commissioners. This was unheard of and the EUR's directors regarded it as an intolerable intrusion into their affairs. The government's auditor was Mr Quilter, who insisted that all available surplus revenue be directly applied to reducing debts incurred during the contract for the building of the company's lines. The EUR did not regard Quilter as an impartial authority and when he first notified the EUR's directors of his intention to go and see its books, the directors resolved that the Chairman should see him and tell him that it would have been more satisfactory if he, the auditor appointed by the Railway Commissioners, had not been connected with the ECR. It seems that Quilter was probably a shareholder in the ECR. In 1851, the Railway Commissioners, and presumably their auditor, disappeared and in 1851 the EUR obtained an Act enabling them, subject only to their shareholders' and creditors' approval, to create £250,000 of this stock at 4 per cent ranking above everything else other than debenture and mortgage interest. Thomas Brassey the contractor was the principal creditor to the tune of £165,000 in addition to holding £60,000 of other stock. He had a greater stake in the Company than the entire board of directors, which he joined in April 1852.

During the spring and summer of 1851, the EUR board and the company's engineer Peter Bruff were preoccupied with negotiating a revised agreement with the ECR. Since February 1850, all traffic receipts between London and Norwich had been divided into two equal parts. The ECR took one portion as representing the route mileage via Cambridge whilst the other portion was divided between the two companies in the ratio of the route mileage which each owned by way of Colchester. The EUR argued that if the Colchester route was organised equitably, it would attract more than half the traffic as it was a shorter route. The ECR naturally wanted to attract as much traffic as possible to the Cambridge route and keep all proceeds. In

December 1851, the EUR gave notice that it wished the dispute to be referred to arbitration in accordance with the provisions of its recent Act. Delays occurred while the ECR looked for an arbitrator (there were to be three with one acting as umpire) and further quibbles over the terms of reference. Before the arbitrators had even met, the ECR decided to terminate the old agreement forthwith, or rather the accounts for the previous half year had been made up a fortnight previously and that was to be that. The ECR's letter to the EUR at Ipswich seems to have been in the post for a week in an era when it was possible to send a letter out in the morning and get a reply that evening. Henceforth, only traffic actually passing through Colchester would actually be divided according to the rules of the Railway Clearing House as from 5 July 1852. The directors of the EUR immediately authorised Cobbold and Bruff to act as they thought best and they arranged a steamer service to London. The service began on 2 August 1852 with the Ipswich Steam Navigation Company paddle steamer *Orwell* sailing to Blackwall whence passengers took an L&BR train to Fenchurch Street. A thrice weekly service was offered. The inclusive fares from Norwich and Bury St Edmunds to London via Ipswich and the steamer were 10s first class and saloon cabin and 6/3d third class and fore cabin. The corresponding fares by rail throughout via Colchester were £1 0s 6d and 8/3d. The journey from Norwich to London by rail, sea and rail took ten hours as opposed to three and a half hours by the ECR via Cambridge. *Bradshaw's Guide* for March 1850 suggests a time wholly by railway of about five hours for Norwich, about four hours for Bury St Edmunds and about three hours for Ipswich. Passengers for the EUR stations west of Ipswich were not able to avail themselves of the facility and were still on the all rail route. In October 1852, the *Orwell* was laid up for the winter and Bruff purchased another paddle steamer, *Pearl,* followed in December by another paddle steamer, *Orion*. There were now two ships on the route and four sailings a week were offered. The services by the ECR with its all-inclusive railway route and the combined

EUR and ECR rail route were daily. The Ipswich Steam Navigation Company went into liquidation in early 1853 and the EUR purchased its ships *Orwell* and *River Queen.* The *Orwell* returned to service in April and the service increased to five each week. Shortly afterwards another ship, *Prince Albert,* was acquired by Bruff and a daily Down service was inaugurated from London. There was no Up service on Saturdays. For a short time, the service was advertised under the name of the Eastern Union Steam Navigation Company, but this was quickly dropped to avoid calling attention to the fact that the EUR was only entitled to run steam powered vehicles on land and the name was altered to the New Steam Navigation Company. The ECR realised that the ships constituted a threat to them and retaliated by opening goods and parcels offices at Ipswich, with road wagons plying to and from Colchester. It is alleged, according to one account, that the wagons were first taken to Ipswich by rail! Goods and parcels from stations on the ECR line were intercepted at Colchester and labels altered or replaced and the goods continued their journey by road. The ECR did not put on road vehicles for passengers for places served by the EUR beyond Colchester. According to Cobbold, a friend once invited him to partake of some champagne which had just arrived from London, but when the hamper was opened, it was found to contain castor oil due to the label having been changed. Advertisements appeared in the local press requesting people sending goods to EUR territory to forward them with the addresses of the consignees 'to the care of the Station Master in Ipswich'.

Meanwhile, during this time the arbitrators met. They were George Parker Bidder for the ECR and Charles Locock Webb for the EUR with Isambard Kingdom Brunel as umpire. In April 1853, the arbitrators announced their decision, which was that the EUR was entitled to have reasonable connections for their trains at Colchester. The EUR announced it would run an express or quick train for first and second class passengers only to London, commencing on 18 April. Connections would leave Norwich at 8.15am and Bury

St Edmunds at 8.40am and the combined train would leave Ipswich at 9.30am and arrive at Colchester at 9.55am from where the ECR was ordered to forward the train to London in 1½ hours. The fares were the same as usual and the train would run daily and it was hoped that there would be a similar Down train in the evening. The EUR's advertisement said that passengers would arrive at Colchester in ample time to proceed to London by the ordinary train which left Colchester at 10.25am in case the ECR declined to forward the new train in accordance with the arbitrators' award. When the new train arrived at Colchester there were red flags flying where the tracks of the two companies met. As soon as the train stopped, an official of the EUR, who was apparently closely followed by a reporter from the *Ipswich Journal,* alighted and confronted the local manager of the ECR and asked if the passengers were to be forwarded so as to reach Bishopsgate Station in London in an hour and a half and was told that they would only reach London by the 10.25 train, which was the usual slow train which did not reach London until 12.50. The EUR train backed into a bay (platform), and the 210 passengers stepped out. They did not appear surprised, and the EUR staff asked for their names and addresses as witnesses as to what had happened. In June, the EUR applied to the high court for an injunction compelling the ECR to abide by the arbitrators' award that an express should be run once a day in each direction between London and Colchester with traffic to and from the EUR in in 1½ hours. The ECR claimed that speed was not within the arbitrators' terms of reference, but judgement was given to the EUR. It seems though that the EUR never obtained the 90 minute express to and from London.

As long ago as 1849 the EUR had first proposed the lease of their line to the ECR as a way out of their financial difficulties and had sought parliamentary authority for such a move, but the ECR shareholders, who were unhappy with their company's takeover of the Norfolk Railway, refused to countenance any further involvement of that kind and the EUR had to delete the offending clauses from their bill. A later proposal for the joint working with the ECR was rejected in 1851 by the ECR's shareholders.

Whilst there was a steady increase in traffic on the EUR, working expenses rose from about 50 per cent in 1850 to over 60 per cent in 1853. The creditors' stock aroused the hostility of the EUR's own preference shareholders. The failure of the EUR to gain any satisfaction from the arbitrator's award was the final blow to the company. As 1853 was drawing to a close, talks took place between Thomas Brassey, the principal creditor of the EUR, and David Waddington, the Chairman of the ECR, and since the ECR's working of the Norfolk Railway was due to be renegotiated in 1855, a new agreement was reached between the three boards. Brassey, as the contractor who had built most of the EUR and had been paid mostly in EUR stock, was probably considered by the EUR board to be the most suitable person to negotiate on their behalf. The new arrangement was approved at special meetings of all three companies on 19 December 1853 and the ECR took over all working on 1 January 1854. The agreement was implemented with remarkable speed as it was not formally signed until 6 February 1854. All receipts were to be pooled, with the ECR taking five-sevenths and the other two a seventh each less 46 per cent for working expenses. EUR rolling stock and the steamships were to be purchased by the ECR at a price to be agreed between Peter Bruff and John V. Gooch, the ECR locomotive superintendent. The arrangements were legalised by an Act dated 7 August 1854 which included the proviso that a bill for the complete amalgamation of the three companies, together with the Newmarket and the East Anglian, was to be deposited before the end of 1861. This, of course, in due course led to the formation of the GER. The N&ER was not amalgamated with the GER until 1902, remaining only a financial company until then.

Chapter 12

The Eastern Counties and Other Railways from 1851 to the Formation of the Great Eastern Railway in 1862

The years 1851 to 1862 saw the ECR consolidate its position as the principal railway in the eastern counties, but in addition to it taking over the working of the existing railways within the area, it resulted in the formation of the GER which was incorporated on 1 August 1862. It also saw the arrival of new railways in the area i.e., the London, Tilbury and Southend and the CV&HR. The GNR still remained a threat.

There was also some scandal. In 1851 the Chairman, Edward Ladd Betts, was succeeded as Chairman by the vice-Chairman David Waddington. When John Gooch was appointed Locomotive Superintendent on the ECR, his draconian methods to save money caused chaos, but this was not all. He made an agreement with the Norfolk and Eastern Counties Coal Company, in which they would pay him 3d per ton purchased. Gooch would then sell some of the ECR coal on for further personal gain. In 1856 the shareholders of the ECR finally worked out what was going on and Gooch and Waddington were dismissed. Waddington was succeeded as Chairman by Horatio Love who went on to become the first chairman of the GER, serving that Company from 1862 to 1863. Gooch was succeeded by Robert Sinclair from the Caledonian Railway and who was the Locomotive Superintendent of the ECR from 1856 to 1862 and of the GER from 1862 to 1866.

The interior of Bishopsgate station in about 1850. Observe that the train in the foreground has, in addition to luggage being put on the roofs of the carriages, a luggage tender. One hopes that the luggage on the carriage roofs was secured tightly to the roofs. (Author's collection).

This is the often shown only known photograph of the exterior of Bishopsgate station. Like so many of the original London termini it was somewhat distant from the centre of London and this ultimately led to the building of the first underground railways. (Author's collection).

A view of the second Chelmsford station which was built in 1856 when the Royal Agricultural Society held its annual exhibition in the town. The two platform building replaced an earlier island platform building. As well as two platform roads there was also a through line between the two lines. (Author's collection).

The year 1851 saw the Great Exhibition of the Works of Industry of All Nations or the Great Exhibition as it is now commonly called, which was held in Hyde Park in London from 1 May to 15 October. The Exhibition provided a golden opportunity for the railways in the form of excursion traffic.

The ECR ran special cheap excursion trains to London to enable people to visit the Exhibition and both it and the EUR provided special cheap rates for people wanting to visit the exhibition.

On the line from Cambridge to Hitchin, the section from Shelford to Shepreth opened on 1 August 1851. The working timetable of the ECR for September 1856 shows a service of three passenger trains a day in each direction from Cambridge to Hitchin on Mondays to Saturdays and two in each direction on Sundays. There was additionally a passenger train from Baldock to Cambridge on Saturdays only and on Wednesdays only a passenger train from Royston to Cambridge worked by a locomotive that had run light from Cambridge to Royston. There was a goods train in each direction on Mondays to Saturdays. On Mondays to Saturdays there was a goods train in each direction from Cambridge to Baldock, but in the reverse direction it did not run on Saturdays. The locomotive of the up goods hauling the Saturday's only passenger train from Baldock to Cambridge.

The line was built single but with provision for doubling. John Wrottesley in *The Great Northern Railway: volume I: Origins and Development* (B.T. Batsford Limited, London, 1979) says that the Board of Trade Inspecting Officer sanctioned opening only on the condition that the ECR could use the Royston and Hitchin Railway turntable at Shepreth. It seems that through carriages were worked between King's Cross and Cambridge. The ECR paid £300 per annum for use of Hitchin station but was always well behind in payment of rent. Towards the end of the lease period, the GNR gave consideration to taking over the Royston and Hitchin Railway Company, but there was obstruction from the GER about the GNR actually reaching Cambridge over its lines from Shelford Junction. During the lifetime of the lease, the Bedford and Cambridge Railway had opened its line to Cambridge on 7 July 1862. This Railway was worked by the London and North Western Railway and according to Robin Leleux in *A Regional History of the Railways of Great Britain: volume IX: The East Midlands* (David and Charles, Newton Abbot, 1976), the London and North Western Railway was at that time friendly to the GNR. The GNR therefore put forward two alternative proposals: one envisaged running powers from Shepreth to Cambridge, doubling of the track between Shepreth and the main line, use of the GER's Cambridge station and a one mile extension to a separate terminal; the alternative was to be an extension from Shepreth to the Bedford and Cambridge Railway, joining it 1½ miles east of Lord's Bridge, with running powers over that line to the outskirts of Cambridge, and then a new two-mile branch would run to the town centre.

The GER saw that if the second choice materialised it would be left in possession of a useless short branch that ended at Shepreth, and they agreed to the GNR's wishes, signing an agreement with it on 2 May 1864. An Act in that year conceded to the GNR full running powers to Cambridge station, where all facilities and a separate platform would be provided; double track capable of carrying express services was promised between Shepreth and Shelford by 31 March 1866, the last day of the lease, on the expiration of which the Royston and Hitchin Railway would be returned to the GNR.

The Hertford and Welwyn Junction Railway was formed to build a line from the ECR terminus at Hertford (converting it to a through station) via Cowbridge station near the centre of Hertford to a new Welwyn Junction station, at the south end of Digswell Viaduct on the GNR. There was to be a triangular junction there, and the new company would have running powers into Welwyn station. The Company got its Act on 3 July 1854. Authorised capital was £65,000. The line was opened to goods traffic on Sunday, 28 February and to passengers on Monday, 1 March 1858. From the start it was worked jointly by the GNR and the ECR, and there were some through bookings between their respective stations. The line also provided a useful route to the London docks for goods traffic to and from the GNR; there were sidings at Welwyn Junction where the traffic was to be exchanged. There were to be running powers for Great Northern Railway goods trains as far as Ware. When the line was constructed, these intentions were altered. A new Welwyn Junction station was opened immediately on the north side of Hunter's Bridge, which nowadays carries Bridge Road over the railway. This was considered a preferable interchange place for the branch, and the proposed north curve of the triangle was never built.

1855 saw the formation of the Luton, Dunstable and Welwyn Junction Railway, which received its Act on 16 July that year. The Railway ran from a junction with the London and North Western Railway at Dunstable to a junction with the GNR at Welwyn. The Company had difficulty in raising money, which delayed the acquisition of land for the building of the Railway. The Directors approached the London and North Western Railway in the hope of leasing their Railway to the larger company, but it was not interested. The next idea was for it to merge with the Hertford and Welwyn Junction Railway, which could be joined by crossing the GNR linking the two instead of connecting into the latter Railway. This proposal was opposed by the GNR, who saw that it might lose control of the local lines, and that possibly the London and North Western Railway would get access from Leighton Buzzard over the line into GNR and ECR territory. The GNR made it quite clear that they would demand onerous conditions for the construction of the bridge, and some of the Luton, Dunstable and Welwyn Junction Railway shareholders opposed the merger of the two Companies for that reason; however, the opposition was voted down and the motion to merge the companies was carried, on 26 January 1858. In fact, the bridge was never built. The Railway was opened from Dunstable to Luton for goods traffic on 5 April 1858 and to passengers on 3 May 1858. This section was worked by the London and North Western Railway. The section from Luton to Welwyn was opened to passenger and goods traffic on 1 September 1860. Previously, an Act dated 28 June 1858 had amalgamated the Hertford and Welwyn Junction Railway with the Luton, Dunstable and Welwyn Junction Railway to form the Hertford, Luton and Dunstable Railway.

Following the opening of the Hertford and Welwyn Junction Railway, the ECR worked a night goods train with docks traffic from 1 March 1858 to 31 August 1860. This and the ECR working over the line from Hertford to Welwyn ceased after 31 August 1860 following a request by the Hertford, Luton and Dunstable Railway for it to do so.

The Norwich and Spalding Railway, despite its name, was a Railway promoted to build a line from Spalding on the GNR to Sutton Bridge and from there to Wisbech, which had been reached by both the ECR and the EAR. Norwich was an aspiration for later rather than an immediate intention. The Company obtained its Act on 4 August 1853 which stated that the other parts of the proposed Railway could not be opened until genuine progress was being made on the section to Wisbech. Obtaining money to build the Railway was not easy, particularly as the Crimean War broke out on 16 October that year and lasted until 30 March 1856. The Company only managed to reach as far as Holbeach which was 7½ miles from Spalding. The stipulation about the section to Wisbech would appear to have been overlooked for the time being. The line was opened for goods on 9 August 1858 and passengers on 15 November 1858. On 13 August 1859, the Company obtained another Act to extend to Sutton Bridge; the earlier powers to do this had expired. The extension was opened on 1 July 1862.

Although the Norwich and Spalding Railway did not directly link with the ECR, it could be seen as a thrust into the latter Company's territory. It was worked by the GNR.

At Victoria Park and Bow, the L&BR platforms closed on 26 September 1850, but those of the ECR closed on 6 January 1851. Briefly, the ECR severed the physical connection between the two Railways there. Relations between the ECR and the L&BR were not in those early days particularly good, though they later improved.

On 1 January 1853 the East and West India Docks and Birmingham Junction Railway changed its name to the North London Railway. Previously, on 1 January 1852 the Railway opened a line from a junction at Bow (Bow Junction) to Poplar and from there to Blackwall and the East India Docks. This section was purely for goods.

In 1856, the L&BR viaduct between Fenchurch Street and Stepney was widened and provided with an additional up line.

The LT&SR came about, according to J.E. Connor in *Stepney's Own Railway* (2nd edition Connor and Butler 1987), when at a special meeting of the L&BR shareholders on 24 November 1851 it was resolved to apply jointly with the ECR to build a railway from the ECR near Ilford via Barking to Tilbury and Leigh to Southend.

This materialised into the LT&SR, which obtained its Act on 17 June 1852. The junction with the ECR was called Forest Gate Junction. The opening of the first section of the line to Tilbury via Barking and Grays took place on 13 April 1854 – Maundy Thursday. The Tilbury station was a terminus. On 14 August, the Railway was extended to Stanford-le-Hope. On 7 June 1855, a branch line off the Railway between Tilbury and Stanford-le-Hope was opened to Thames Haven. So, at last, Thames Haven got its railway. On 1 July 1855, the Railway was extended from Stanford-le-Hope to Leigh via Pitsea and Benfleet and further extended from Leigh to Southend on 1 March 1856. The route to Southend was somewhat rather roundabout.

According to *Bradshaw's Railway Manual* for 1869, the 'Company was originally an incorporation of acquiescing shareholders of the ECR and London and Blackwall' railways. The management of the Railway was in the hands of a committee of four ECR directors and four L&BR directors. There were no actual shareholder directors. The directors were: for the ECR, Lord Alfred Paget, David Waddington (who was at the time the Chairman of the ECR), Richard Patterson (who was at the time the Deputy Chairman of the ECR) and Samuel Anderson; for the L&BR, James Nugent Daniel (who was at the time the Chairman of the L&BR), William Haigh (who was at the time the Deputy Chairman of the L&BR), Joseph Bishop and Josiah Wilson. The Railway was leased by its promoters to the contractors who built it – Peto, Brassey and Betts – to build and to manage the line for a period of 25 years, which was later reduced to 21 years. The operators arranged for the ECR to provide the engines, carriages and wagons. Therefore, the Railway was jointly owned by two Companies leased to its contractors, but with one of the owning companies running the train services as agents to the lessees. Originally, trains ran from and to Fenchurch Street and Bishopsgate stations and joined and divided at Stratford, but in 1856 a line was promoted from Gas Factory Junction on the L&BR to Barking via Bromley and East Ham. The Act authorising this was obtained on 7 July 1856 and the line opened on 31 March 1858. From then on, all trains ran from Fenchurch Street via the new line with the ECR providing a connecting service from Bishopsgate. To round things off in regard to openings, in 1861 a cut-off at Tilbury avoiding the terminal station was opened.

In 1861, although the LT&SR was reckoned to be a separate Company, it was in fact an undertaking jointly owned by the ECR and the L&BR.

The acquiescing shareholders of the ECR and L&BRs clearly felt a need for the LT&SR to become a distinct company in its own right. On 17 December 1861 a special meeting was held at which a Bill was promoted constituting the LT&SR as a separate company, providing for the separation of capital and stock from that of the two promoters of the Railway. At the Half yearly meeting of the ECR on 23 February 1862, the Chairman reported under the heading:

> LONDON, TILBURY, AND SOUTHEND RAILWAY. A Bill has been introduced this Session into Parliament having for its object the incorporation of the Proprietors of the shares in the above line, and to give to such Company the power to appoint an equal number of Directors with this Company and the Blackwall Company. This Directors feel bound to oppose.

Despite the opposition from the Directors of the ECR, the bill became law on 16 May 1862. Following the passing of the Act, the LT&SR became a de facto separate company. This had the effect that those who were not shareholders of the ECR and L&BRs could now buy shares in the LT&SR. This could and would, as the Directors of the ECR realised, have consequences in the future.

The CV&HR came about because by 1856 it had become clear to the inhabitants of Halstead that the line authorised in the Colchester, Stour Valley and Halstead Railway's Act was not going to be built. By this time, the ECR had taken a lease of the EUR, which had worked the Colchester, Stour Valley and Halstead Railway prior to the ECR taking over the working of it. At first it was thought that Halstead might be served by a railway from Braintree, but this proposal was discarded, partly because of the difficulties of construction and partly because of the opposition from the ECR, the EUR and the Colchester, Stour Valley and Halstead Railway. What emerged under the CV&HR's Act of 30 June 1856 was for a railway from Chapel to Halstead. Construction proceeded quite quickly, and the Railway opened to Halstead for all traffic on 16 April 1860.

Having reached Halstead, the CV&HR was interested in extending its line and schemes were discussed for extending it to Shelford, which was on the ECR main line from London to Cambridge, but after consideration it was decided to extend the line only to Haverhill, which did not have a railway. An Act enabling the CV&HR to extend its line to Haverhill was passed on 13 August 1859. Construction of the Railway proceeded fairly quickly, and the line was opened to Castle Hedingham on 1 July 1861, to Yeldham on 26 May 1862 and to Haverhill on 10 May 1863. Having reached Haverhill, the Railway looked about extending further. From Haverhill it looked to extending to Cambridge and from Chapel to Colchester. In 1860 it promoted a bill for such lines.

The ECR was not happy about this, as it was perceived to be competition. The CV&HR made a deal with the London and North Western Railway, which was the prospective lessee of the Bedford and Cambridge Railway which received its Act on 6 August 1860. The deal was for the CV&HR to extend to join the Bedford and Cambridge Railway south of Cambridge and to build a separate line to Colchester nearer the town. The CV&HR's proposed line would have diverged from its existing line and its station at Chapel would have been at right angles to the viaduct and about fifty feet below it. The bill for the extensions was rejected by parliament. Had the bill been accepted, one wonders whether the London and North Western Railway would have tried to have taken over the working of the CV&HR and gained a cross country line that would have extended from Oxford in the west via Bedford and Cambridge to Colchester.

At the same time that the CV&HR was promoting its bill to construct lines from Haverhill to Cambridge and from Chapel to Colchester, the ECR promoted bills for the construction of lines from Sudbury to Long Melford, Long Melford to Clare, Clare to Shelford, Long Melford to Bury St Edmunds and a connecting line at Haverhill between the CV&HR and the ECR. The Act for these lines was passed on 22 July 1861.

The EUR in 1847 had obtained powers to build a line from Ipswich to Woodbridge but these lapsed in 1850 although some land had been acquired. The genesis of the line which was ultimately built from Ipswich to Lowestoft and Yarmouth began with the Haddiscoe, Beccles and Halesworth Railway, which was incorporated on 5 June 1851 to build a railway from Haddiscoe on the Reedham to Lowestoft line of the Norfolk Railway via Beccles to Halesworth, where it was expected to join the proposed EUR line to Woodbridge although the latter Company had not obtained powers to build a line beyond Woodbridge to Halesworth. In 1851, the EUR obtained an extension of time to build the branch to Woodbridge.

Under the Haddiscoe, Beccles and Halesworth Railway's Act, it was empowered to make a working agreement with the Norfolk Railway, which as mentioned previously had been worked by the ECR since 1848. Construction of the Railway proceeded quite quickly and by the beginning of September 1854 was ready for inspection by the Board of Trade. The Railway was inspected by Colonel Yolland of the Board of Trade on 14 September. Unfortunately, he found a number of detailed shortcomings which needed attending to before he would allow it to be opened for passenger traffic. When these had been attended to, the Railway was opened for goods traffic on 20 November and passenger traffic on 4 December. The new Railway included a swing bridge at Beccles and was in a curious position of being notionally worked by the

Norfolk Railway, but in practice worked by the ECR, which worked the Norfolk Railway. The Company offered to sell its line to the ECR, but at a meeting of the latter's shareholders on 13 July 1855, the offer was turned down. On 3 July 1854, the Haddiscoe, Beccles and Halesworth Railway had changed its name to the East Suffolk Railway (ESR).

In 1852, when it became clear that it would be quite some considerable time before the EUR built its branch from Ipswich, the Haddiscoe, Beccles and Halesworth Railway as it then was, seeing that its proposed southern terminus at Woodbridge would be insufficient, decided to build the line from Woodbridge to Ipswich itself. The original route proposed was via Framlingham, but the Duke of Hamilton objected as the line would cross his land and he felt that it would diminish his enjoyment of it. Whilst the Duke of Hamilton was not happy with the original proposed route of the Railway, the ECR was not happy at all with it as it would divide traffic with the EUR Ipswich to Norwich line via Haughley of which it had gained control, its General Manager going to public meetings to speak against the proposed line. Sir Samuel Morton Peto one of the chief promoters of the Railway wrote to the ECR on 27 September 1853 that the Norfolk Railway's board backed the idea of a line from Halesworth to Woodbridge and hoped that the ECR and EUR would take it over either during or after its construction.

On 3 July 1854, the Haddiscoe, Beccles and Halesworth Railway obtained an Act authorising the extension, also changing its name to the ESR. The new line was to run via Saxmundham, Wickham Market and Melton to Woodbridge. At the station called Wickham Market, which in practice was two miles away at Campsea Ash, there was to be a branch line to Framlingham. From Saxmundham there was to be a branch line to Leiston. From Snape Junction there was to be a branch line to Snape Bridge.

As originally built, the Haddiscoe, Beccles and Halesworth Railway was single track, but following the decision to extend it to Ipswich, the decision was made to double it. Whilst this was being done, the train service was suspended from 15 July 1858 to 1 June 1859 and a replacement horse bus service put on instead.

At this time, Sir Samuel Morton Peto became both the dominant shareholder and the contractor for the line. Peto lived at Somerleyton Hall.

In 1855, the people of both Lowestoft and Yarmouth were connected to London by the ECR via Norwich, Ely and Cambridge and noted the Haddiscoe, Beccles and Halesworth Railway and perceived that by building connecting lines to it would give them a more direct route to London.

A meeting was held in Lowestoft on 26 October 1855 to promote a railway connecting to the Haddiscoe, Beccles and Halesworth Railway at Beccles. The Lowestoft terminus of the Railway was planned to be near to St John's church in South Lowestoft. The Lowestoft and Beccles Railway, as the Railway came to be known, got its Act of Authorisation on 23 June 1856.

In Yarmouth, a meeting of business people was held on 10 November 1855 to promote a railway to connect that town to the Haddiscoe, Beccles and Halesworth Railway, and ultimately via the hoped-for extension of the EUR to Woodbridge, a direct route to London. The Yarmouth and Haddiscoe Railway, as the Railway came to be known, received its Act of Authorisation on 7 July 1856. The Railway was to connect with the ESR at Haddiscoe. In Yarmouth, there were to be branches to the docks. One of the chief promoters was Sir Samuel Morton Peto.

Peto had business interests in Lowestoft and could see that the ESR would give a much more direct route from Lowestoft and also Yarmouth to London than the existing route via Norwich. He wanted the ECR to work the ESR. His way of doing so can only be described as a grand deception. He promoted a railway from Pitsea on the LT&SR, which he worked along with Thomas Brassey and Edward Betts, to Colchester via Maldon – the Tilbury, Maldon and Colchester Railway (TM&CR). According to Peter Kay in Volume 1 of his history of the LT&SR, the scheme first became public on

24 September 1856 at a meeting between Peto and Colchester Borough Council. A week later, Peto met with Yarmouth Borough Council and told them that he would not be satisfied until he had what amounted to an independent route from Yarmouth to London. This implies that he would promote a parallel line from Colchester to join the ESR. The length of the TM&CR was 45 miles. The distance from London (Fenchurch Street station) to Colchester via the LT&SR and the TM&CR would have been 78¼ miles as opposed to 51¼ by the ECR from Bishopsgate station in London. The proposed railway also included a branch line from Cold Norton to Burnham-on-Crouch. The plans for the TM&CR were deposited with parliament in November 1856. There was support for the Railway in both Maldon and Colchester, which towns were not happy with the service the ECR was providing for them. The board of the L&BR also supported the proposed railway. The ECR retaliated by promoting lines from Shenfield to Pitsea, Maldon to Pitsea, Maldon to the Chelmer Navigation Basin and Rayleigh to the River Crouch opposite Burnham-on-Crouch. What happened was that Peto's partner Thomas Brassey had talks with Horatio Lowe who was the Chairman of the ECR and on 8 April 1857 there was a special meeting of the ECR's Board at which Brassey put forward 'Heads of Agreement' including extremely detailed proposals for the future split of the Yarmouth and Lowestoft revenue after the ESR line to Ipswich opened, on the basis that Peto would withdraw the TM&CR scheme and that the ECR would agree to work the ESR and that the ECR would withdraw its counter plans for lines. This was agreed and made public in *The Times* of 9 April which reported that Peto had got his way, but there was much anger in Maldon and Colchester.

Because Peto controlled or heavily influenced the ESR, the Lowestoft and Beccles Railway and the Yarmouth and Haddiscoe Railway, he was able to bring about their amalgamation, which took place on 23 July 1858 under the name East Suffolk Railway. Peto leased both the original ESR, the Lowestoft and Yarmouth companies and the new ESR between 1855 and 1861, when its termination was made a condition of entry into the soon to be formed GER.

Meanwhile, the EUR's proposed line to Woodbridge had been amended to make an end on junction with the ESR at Woodbridge and in 1854 it obtained renewed powers to build the Ipswich to Woodbridge line under an Act dated 16 June 1854.

Construction of both the ESR and the EUR's lines started in the spring of 1856. Initially, it was hoped that both would be completed after about a year, but that on the EUR section of the line was lagging behind that of the ESR section of the line, because the works on the former section were heavier than on the latter section. During the construction of the line a bizarre incident occurred at Woodbridge in June 1858. A lane which crossed to the tide mill at Woodbridge was recorded as a public highway and led to an ancient ferry. When the navvies building the line reached there, they were amazed to see men building what has been described as a shed right in the path of the railway. It is possible that it was only a wall as otherwise traffic to adjacent wharves would have been obstructed. The owner claimed that it was private land and that the Company's powers to compulsorily buy it had expired. Luckily, the Company had a bill going through parliament and a clause was inserted in it to overcome the obstruction. On 23 July 1858, the Company's Act of that date gave it until 1 September to buy the plot of land. Meanwhile, on 12 July 1858 the first locomotive had reached Woodbridge along the line of the ESR.

On 7 March 1859, Captain Tyler of the Board of Trade made the necessary inspection to enable passenger traffic to be able to start. Tyler found a number of shortcomings of a technical nature and the Board of Trade did not receive an undertaking as to the method of operation of the ESR. Furthermore, some of the cast iron beams of the underbridges were not considered adequately strong so approval was withheld. On 5 May, Tyler revisited the line after a rather defensive statement had been put out by the company's engineer, George Berkly. This read:

> Captain Tyler has today seen that the slight alterations he required to be made to some of the signals have been completed. You are aware that these alterations were made nearly two months since, but [we] waited till he was in the neighbourhood inspecting the line from Ipswich to Woodbridge before they could conveniently be seen by Captain Tyler.

However, Tyler this time was satisfied with the technical issues. The ESR had indicated that the line would be operated by the one engine in steam system. That is the working of just one train over the whole length of the line. On 27 May 1859, they announced that the entire ESR line would open on 1 June 1859. On the same day, the ECR announced that its line to Woodbridge, the former EUR line, would open on the same day.

The *Ipswich Journal* of 4 June 1859 reported on the opening on the official opening day:

> Opening of the East Suffolk Railway: Whatever may have been the delays from time to time in completing this line of railway, and from whatever causes they may have arisen, we are glad to state that all difficulties have at length been overcome, and that the whole has been thrown open to the public; and a most excellent line it is. It consists of a main line between Ipswich and Yarmouth (53 miles in length), with branches to Framlingham, Leiston, Snape, and Lowestoft.

The opening of the Framlingham branch from Wickham Market station to that town ended in tragedy. The *Ipswich Journal* of 4 June 1859 reported on the opening on the official opening day:

> The bells rang merrily throughout the day, a cricket match was played, and tea was provided by Mr. John Pipe of the Crown Inn, in his usual style, of which 40 of the gentry and inhabitants of the

> town partook; appropriate speeches were made, songs sung, and a merry and convivial evening spent.

Unfortunately, an evening concert at the Corn Exchange was cancelled as the band leader Edward Plantin was involved in a serious accident at the station and died of his injuries a few days later. Frustratingly, no details are available as to quite what happened to the poor musician.

Of the branch to Leiston, there is not a great deal to say. The line, whilst supported by Peto, was supported by the Leiston agricultural machine manufacturer, Richard Garrett. It opened to Leiston on 1 June 1859 and was extended on 12 April 1860 to the coastal town of Aldeburgh. At Leiston there was a branch line to Garrett's works, which was originally worked by horses.

The Snape branch, which also opened on 1 June 1859, never had a passenger service. The supporters of the line to Snape Bridge proposed it in order to secure the support of the owner of Snape Maltings, Newsom Garrett, and as a way of securing malted barley traffic for the burgeoning brewery trade in London. At Snape Junction, a station was proposed and appeared in public timetables for some years during the 1860s. *Bradshaw's Railway Guide* for February 1863 shows it, albeit only in the timetable for the Down direction and with no trains stopping there. A road leading to the site of the proposed station was constructed, as was a building still known as 'Station House', and there have been references to the site as 'Tunstall Station'.

In 1850, the Waveney Valley Railway Company was promoted to build a railway from Tivetshall on the Norwich line via Bungay to Beccles and from Bungay to Halesworth and from Bungay to the Lowestoft Railway at Raveningham. These plans had to be pruned and the Company's Act of 3 July 1851 only authorised to build a railway from Tivetshall on the EUR line from Haughley Junction to Bungay, the Railway to be worked by the EUR. Another Act was obtained in 1853 which sanctioned the Company to extend its line to Beccles on the

ESR. Investing members of the public declined to take up shares and the story of the Company was one of Acts to extend the time for completing the line. Nothing seems to have happened about the actual construction of the Railway until December of 1855, when a local committee was set up in Harleston. A contract was let for the building of the line to that town, to which it opened on 1 December 1855, a distance of 6¼ miles from Tivetshall. It is claimed that when the line opened, services were worked by the Company's only locomotive named *Perseverance*. This was a 2-2-2 tank locomotive built by Sharp, Stewart and Co (Manchester). And it did not perform particularly well. On 2 November 1860 the railway was extended from Harleston to Bungay. The extension from Bungay to Beccles opened on 2 March 1863. The total length of the line was 19½ miles. When the line opened, it was originally intended that the EUR should work it for 50 per cent of the receipts, but when the time came for the trains to run, the ECR, which had taken over the working of the EUR, demanded 75 per cent of the receipts and even retained the balance to settle a disputed debt. The dispute dragged on for several years with mounting discontent over the service provided. At last the Waveney Valley Railway directors gave notice that they intended to work the Railway themselves from 15 September 1860. The ECR promptly offered to reduce its charge to 50 per cent of receipts, but the offer was refused. Meanwhile, it had originally been intended to build the Railway on the Suffolk side of the River Waveney between Bungay and Beccles, but the offer of cheaper land on the Norfolk side of the river caused the Company to decide to build the line on that side instead. The Bill for the new route was thrown out by the House of Lords in June 1858 on representations from hostile local landowners who claimed that the Company had no capital available for the works, having been unable to issue a single share, the powers to reach Bungay were about to expire and the whole line was unremunerative. The Bill became an Act in 1859. Back to 1860. It would seem from the evidence that it was only then did the Waveney Valley Railway acquire its locomotive. As to how long

Perseverance had sole command of the line is not known. The absolute minimum number of locomotives needed to work a short railway is two; one out working the services and one in repair, but three is a better number, enabling one to be kept in reserve should the one out working the services fail. It is fairly certain that when *Perseverance* was out of service for some reason, a locomotive would have been hired from the ECR. D.I. Gordon in *The Regional History of the Railways of Great Britain – the Eastern Counties Railway* says that it was from 1861 until the day of the opening of the section to Beccles. On that day, the Waveney Valley Railway was taken over by the GER.

The Wells and Fakenham Railway was incorporated in 1854 and was promoted by local landowners and some of the directors of the Norfolk Railway to build a line from Fakenham to Wells-next-the-Sea. Although the works on the line were completed by June 1857, the line was not opened until 1 December. According to the *Norfolk Chronicle* of 5 December, a public holiday was declared in Wells. In the evening there was a dinner of about 90 gentlemen at the Crown Inn in Wells under the presidency of Lord Leicester. A short branch to Wells Harbour was built in 1859.

Hunstanton is said to be the only west facing seaside resort in the Eastern Counties. Its origin as a resort goes back to 1845 when efforts were made to promote the town as a seaside resort. By the mid-1850s, businesses were keen to attract visitors. The EAR subsidised two omnibus services to and from Lynn to the town, despite the fact that in 1861 the town had a population of fewer than 500 people. The distance from Lynn to Hunstanton was 16 miles. A railway from Lynn to the town was projected and the Act for it received the Royal Assent on 1 August 1861. The Lynn and Hunstanton Railway, as the Railway was known, was incorporated with authorised capital of £60,000. The terminus of the Railway was at New Hunstanton, south of the old centre where development was possible. The first sod was cut on

13 November 1861. Construction over the relatively flat terrain was completed in ten months within budget.

The inspection by the Board of Trade required for passenger operation, took place in September 1862, and the line opened for traffic on 3 October 1862, just over two months after the formation of the GER. *The Times* of 6 October 1862 reported:

> Railway Intelligence ... Lynn and Hunstanton: This line was opened for traffic on Friday. The first train started at a little after noon, and conveyed the directors, contractors, and officers of the company, shareholders and others, to the number of about 150. A luncheon was served at the Hunstanton terminus. The line is 15 miles in length from the junction with ... the Great Eastern [Railway] at Gaywood [immediately north of King's Lynn], and its cost amounted altogether to only £80,000. The stations are at North Wootton (near Castle Rising), Wolferton, Dersingham, Snettisham, Heacham and Hunstanton.
>
> The Wolverton station is on the estate of the Prince of Wales (through which the line runs for nearly three miles) and is to be enlarged at the expense and for the accommodation of his Royal Highness. The Hunstanton terminus is near the verge of the cliffs. The line is worked by the GER Company.

There were a few other lines that were opened during the period of this chapter. 26 November 1855 saw the opening of the Victoria Dock. The plans for this were first announced in 1849. The owning company was the Victoria Dock Company. This was a deepwater dock larger than any other in London and was the first to be adequately served by rail. As the entrance to the dock was near Bow Creek, it was necessary for the railway to be carried over it on a swing bridge. Because traffic would be interrupted as ships moved in and out, an avoiding line was built, at the expense of the Dock Company, along the northern and eastern edges of the dock. The line branched off the original route at Thames Wharf Junction and joined it again at Silvertown, about three quarters of a mile west of the terminus at North Woolwich. Under the statutory title of 'the Woolwich Abandoned Line', the abandoned section passed to the Dock Company. The avoiding line with its intermediate station at Custom House opened on 26 November 1855. A second intermediate station was opened at Tidal Basin in February 1858. To service the new dock, in 1854 the ECR opened a 1½ mile link line between the North London Railway at Victoria Park and the North Woolwich line at Stratford. At first this only carried goods traffic. On 16 October 1858, passenger traffic started when the North London Railway started a service between Victoria Park and Stratford Bridge. Interchange was made with ECR main line trains via a new Low Level station at Stratford which became known to travellers as the North London Station.

From 1 June 1854 to 15 October 1854 and again from 1 May 1855, the ECR operated a Fenchurch Street-Stratford Bridge-North Woolwich service. On 31 March 1858, following the construction of the LT&SR line from Bow to Barking, a curve was opened between it and the North Woolwich line, the respective junctions being Abbey Mills Upper Junction on the LT&SR and Abbey Mills Lower Junction on the North Woolwich line. From 1 June, trains ran alternately via Stratford Bridge and via Bromley by Bow on the LT&SR.

Another new line that was opened during this time was that from Stratford to Loughton on 22 August 1856.

An early scheme for a railway to Epping from the L&BR at Stepney, and another scheme from the ECR at Ilford, came to nothing. In 1852, the Woodford Railway was promoted to run from the North London Railway at Victoria Park to Woodford. At the same time, the ECR had put forward to parliament for a Woodford and Loughton branch to run from Stratford. The ECR Bill won the day, but with the stipulation under its Act of 1853 that the Loughton branch could not be opened until an additional line of rails had been laid between the ECR and North Woolwich Railway junction at Stratford and the junction at Bow between the ECR and the L&BR. Construction seems to have been fairly easy and the line was opened on 22 August 1856. Loughton was 12 miles from Fenchurch Street and 11¼ miles from Bishopsgate. The staff timetable of 1 September 1856 shows all the trains on Mondays to Saturdays running to and from Fenchurch Street, but two of these in each direction had a portion to and from Bishopsgate. On Sundays, all the trains ran to and from Bishopsgate. There is no goods service shown and it is not known when the goods service started. Apparently, there was no telegraph until 1858. The staff timetable for 1 June 1863 shows Loughton, but only Loughton, as having a goods service. That for October 1866 does not show any goods service whilst that for October 1870 does show a goods service.

It has been said that during the Crimean War (October 1853 to February 1856) that the branch lines from Witham to Maldon and Witham to Braintree were singled and the surplus line used to build the Grand Crimea Central Railway though there is no clear evidence one way or the other.

A new station was erected in Chelmsford in 1856 when the Royal Agricultural Show was held in the town. A new Corn Exchange was also built. The new station replaced the existing timber framed island platform building and was built on a site 200 yards to the south west of it at a cost of £4,462.

At Ipswich, the station was re-sited to its present location in 1860. The Italianate style of the station is a design by Sancton Wood, the architect, who submitted it as part of a competition. Princes Street, linking the station to the town, was created at the same time. Originally, the station had a single main through platform with some shorter bay platforms at the north end. We know from the Ways and Works report in the Directors report to the shareholders at the 36th half yearly meeting of the ECR held on 29 August 1854 that the viaduct at Bishopsgate had been widened.

The earliest mention of complete amalgamation of the Eastern Counties, Norfolk and EURs with the Newmarket Railway and the EAR is in the Half Yearly Meeting of 29 August 1856; by the Half yearly Meeting of 27 February 1857 the talk of amalgamation is definitely in the air. At the Half year Meeting on 25 August 1859 the Chairman, Horatio Dove, said that the directors were fully aware of the importance of proceeding with the measure as only by the fusion of the interests of all the Companies could the differences be avoided. They had under consideration the terms under which such an amalgamation could be made and when they were in a condition to do so would bring forward a bill for the purpose.

At the half Yearly meeting on 23 February 1860, the Chairman reported that the Directors had given it their most careful consideration. The Board had 'adopted certain principles as the basis of the Amalgamation, which principles they believe to be equitable to all the Associated Companies'. The Norfolk Railway and the EUR had declined to consider them and the N&ER had objected. The whole matter 'in conformity with the Act of Parliament have to be submitted for the decision of the Board of Trade, to which tribunal are to be referred for settlement all questions that may arise between Companies as to the terms of Amalgamation'.

At the Half Yearly meeting on 23 August 1860, the Chairman reported that since the last Half Yearly Meeting, the 'Heads of Amalgamation referred to in the Directors' Report of the 16th February last have been submitted to the Board of Trade'. The Board had called upon the other Companies:

> ... to submit, within a limited time, any observations they may have to offer on the Heads of Amalgamation as proposed by this

> Company. Your Directors will continue to watch your interests in regard to this very important subject; and will endeavour to obtain such terms as shall be equitable to all the Companies concerned. The preliminary steps are being taken to prepare the requisite Bill in compliance with the Act of Parliament.

At the Half yearly meeting on 21 February 1861, the Chairman reported that the Board of Trade had determined that 'the Bill for the proposed amalgamation should be first prepared and submitted to the other Companies', and that then any points of difference would be determined by the Board. The Draft was 'now before Counsel, and your Directors fully hope to be in a position to introduce it in Parliament for the next Session'.

At the Half Yearly Meeting on 29 August 1861 the Chairman reported that the Bill for carrying out the amalgamation of the Associated Companies would be submitted to Parliament in the next session:

> Your Directors have much satisfaction in being able to state that they are co-operating with the Norfolk and Eastern Union Companies in the necessary arrangements for this important measure upon the most friendly footing, and with every prospect of an amicable settlement of the terms upon which the amalgamation is to be effected … Your Directors entertain a confident hope that at the termination of this half-year the pressure on the agricultural districts will have ceased, and that it may reasonably be anticipated that the traffic will show more elasticity. It is satisfactory to know that the period is drawing nigh when there will be a fusion of interests by the Amalgamation, and that the entire concern may then be conducted with greater benefit to the advantage of the public.

At the half yearly meeting of the Company on 23 February 1862 the Chairman reported that:

Your Directors have, for some time past, been earnestly engaged in endeavours to arrange with the other Companies the terms for their amalgamation. They are happy to state that they have been able to agree with the Norfolk Company upon terms which they consider fair, as between that Company and the other Companies to be amalgamated; but they regret to state that, up to the present time, they have been unable to effect any amicable settlement, either with the Eastern Union or with the East Anglian Companies. The negotiations for this purpose with those Companies were continued to so late a period that it was not possible to bring the matter under the consideration of the Board of Trade before the period arrived for depositing the bill. And your Directors had, therefore, no alternative but to deposit a bill embodying the terms of the arrangement with the Norfolk Company, to which that Company had expressed its assent, making such provision with regard to the two other Companies as your Directors believe would meet the fair claims of those two Companies. Unless, therefore, some amicable arrangement can in the meantime be come to, it will be necessary that the terms for the Amalgamation of the Companies should be settled by the committees of the two Houses of Parliament. Until, therefore, the Bill shall have passed the House of Commons, it will not be possible to bring the matter under the consideration of the Proprietors. They will then, however, have the opportunity of considering the whole matter, and full notice and information upon the subject will be furnished to the Proprietors before the meeting takes place.

This Undertaking, after years of constant care and attention, as regards the Permanent Way and Works, the Rolling Stock, the Train Service, and the Working generally, has been placed on a footing with the first Railways in the

> country; and your Directors cannot close their report without expressing their satisfaction at the improved aspect of your affairs, and they confidently believe that when the Bill for the Amalgamation of the several Companies shall have been passed, and the whole united into one Corporate body, great advantage will result.

At the Half yearly Meeting on 27 August 1862, the Chairman reported:

> The Act for the Amalgamation of this Company with the Norfolk, Eastern Union, East Anglian, and Newmarket Companies has at length, after a protracted contest, been carried through both Houses of Parliament, and received the Royal assent. As finally passed, it is substantially to the effect of the Bill submitted to the Proprietors in the month of June last, when it received their sanction.
>
> As the Meetings about to be held will be the last of the ECR Proprietors, and as a new Board will be elected by the Shareholders of the GER Company, your Directors have only to express their fervent hope and expectation, that by the union of interest which will now prevail, by the entire removal of any conflict with regard to working expenses, there will be but one object in view, namely, that of obtaining the largest amount of receipts with the least possible expenditure, having due regard to the efficient working of the Lines, and the economical conduct of the service.

The Railways in East Anglia had had a long and tortuous road to follow in their first thirty years or so and it did not end there – the story continues in the companion volume to this book, *The Great Eastern Railways, The Late 19th and Early 20th Century, 1863–1924.*

Appendix

Locomotives, Rolling Stock and Ships of Constituent Companies from 1838 to 1862

Tank locomotives – those which have their water tanks and coal bunkers on the locomotive as opposed to locomotives having separate tenders – are described as saddle tank for those having their water tank in a saddle over the boiler, well tank for those having their water tank under the coal bunker and side tank for those having their water tanks in tanks on each side of the boiler.

Locomotives of the ECR

As some of the classes introduced by that Company were later built for the GER, there will be some overlap.

A total of 254 locomotives were built for the ECR. Their order here is based on *British Locomotive Catalogue 1825-1923 – Volume 6 – GER, North British Railway, Great North of Scotland Railway, Midland and Great Northern Joint Railway, Remaining Companies in the LNER Group* – compiled by the late Bertram Baxter and edited by the late David Baxter and Peter Mitchell (Kestrel 2012).

The first locomotive superintendent of the ECR was William Fernihough, who held the post from 1839 to 1846. He was succeeded by John Hunter, who held the post from 1846 to 1850 and was succeeded by John Viret Gooch, who was the brother of Sir Daniel Gooch and had previously held that post on the London and South Western Railway. Gooch held the post from 1850 to 1856 when he was dismissed and was succeeded by Robert Sinclair, who held the post until 1866, latterly from 1862 on the GER, when he retired.

Unless indicated otherwise, all locomotives had inside cylinders, i.e., cylinders within the frames as opposed to outside cylinders which were outside the frames.

The first locomotives for the ECR were four 0-4-0 locomotives built by Braithwaite, Milner and Company and delivered in 1838, named *Essex, Middlesex, Norfolk* and *Suffolk*. Of these, the first three were scrapped by 1846, but *Suffolk* was rebuilt by Kitson as an 0-4-2 saddle tank locomotive and was sold sometime between 1856 and 1865. In 1848, *Suffolk* was numbered 188. There is some confusion on the numbering of these locomotives, as according to Baxter they were originally numbered 151-4 in 1839.

A further two unnamed locomotives were built by Braithwaite, Milner and Company in June 1839. They were originally numbered

One of the two 0-4-0 goods locomotives built for the ECR in 1839 by Messrs Braithwaite, Milner and Company. Originally numbered 7 and 8, in 1845 they were renumbered 92 and 93. In 1846 they were again renumbered 141 and 142. (Author's collection).

7 and 8 but were then renumbered twice – firstly 92 and 93 and then 141 and 142. Both were sold in 1849.

Some of the first four locomotives were according to contemporary newspaper accounts employed in the building of the first section of the ECR. In June 1839, Braithwaite, Milner and Company delivered six 2-2-0 locomotives to the ECR. These were numbered 1 to 6. Nos 1-4 and 6 were replaced in 1852. Disposal is not known. No 5 was replaced in 1846 and disposal is not known.

In 1840 Walter Hancock of Stratford tried on the Railway a steam carriage which had a vertical boiler. It was not acquired by the Railway and nothing further is known of it. This could be held to be the ancestor of what later became known as rail motors.

In 1840, Edward Bury and Company built three 2-2-0 locomotives, Nos 9 to 11. These had the typical Bury 'haystack' sort of firebox. No 10 was lent to the MR for a period from October 1846.

The following year, Jones, Turner and Evans built four 2-2-0 locomotives of similar appearance, but of different dimensions – Nos 12 to 15. Nos 12 and 15 were lent to the MR for a period from October 1846. Withdrawal took place between 1850 and 1861. Not all dates are known.

Two 2-4-0s numbered 16 and 17 were supplied by Stothert and Slaughter in 1841. Withdrawal took place between 1850 and 1861.

In 1842 Bury, Curtis and Kennedy supplied another eight 2-2-0s, Nos 18 to 26. Of these No 26 was said to be of smaller dimensions than the others, whilst No 25 was later rebuilt as a 2-2-2. Withdrawal took place between 1850 and 1861. There was some renumbering of these locomotives. Nos 9 and 10 were renumbered 121 and 122. No 14 was renumbered 123. No 16 was renumbered twice – first 94 and then 143. No 17 was renumbered four times, 95, 144, 218 or 219 and 169. Nos 18, 19, 21 and 22 were renumbered 126-9, whilst No 23 was firstly renumbered 5 and then 118. No 24 was renumbered 6 and then 119. No 25 was renumbered 16 and then 124. No 26 was renumbered 17 and then 125.

All of the above locomotives were built to the gauge of 5ft and were converted to 4ft 8½in on the change of gauge in 1844. In total 31 locomotives were built to the wider gauge.

In 1845-6, Jones and Potts delivered nine 2-2-2 locomotives to the Railway (Nos 41 to 50), but No 50 on delivery was immediately transferred to the Norfolk Railway, becoming that Company's No 12. These locomotives had haystack fireboxes and outside cylinders. Withdrawal took place between 1847 and 1861.

Stothert and Slaughter delivered ten 2-2-2s in 1845 which had the dome on the firebox. They were numbered 51 to 60 and had outside cylinders. Withdrawal took place by 1862. The following year the same Company delivered seven similar locomotives but having a shorter wheelbase and inside cylinders– Nos 61 to 67. They were withdrawn between 1873 and 1879. Their GER numbers were the same as their ECR numbers.

In 1847, E.B. Wilson and Company supplied two long boilered 2-2-2s, Nos 116 and 117. They had outside cylinders. They were rebuilt as 2-4-0 saddle tanks in 1855 and renumbered 18 and 19 by the GER. They were scrapped in 1870 and 1871. Another two 2-2-2s followed – Nos 103 and 104 followed by three more in 1848 – Nos 105 to 107. It is not known whether the last five had inside or outside cylinders. They were scrapped between 1867 and 1874. These last five locomotives retained their ECR numbers under the GER.

In 1845, R. and W. Hawthorn had supplied to the Railway a 2-2-2-0 locomotive of the Crampton sort, in which the driving wheels were placed at the extreme rear end. The number of this locomotive was 8. This was renumbered 120 about 1853 and withdrawn by 1862. Ten more Crampton type locomotives of the 2-2-2-0 wheel arrangement followed in three batches in 1846-7 from Jones and Potts. These were Nos 88 to 90 in 1846-7, Nos 91-3 in 1847 and Nos 94-7 in 1847. Of these, Nos 94 and 97 had a rear trailing wheel added and became 2-2-2-2s. In all instances, the first pairs of wheels were not on a bogie, but separately connected to the locomotive frame, otherwise they would have been 4-2-0s or 4-2-2s. All these locomotives were withdrawn by 1862.

In 1846-7, Robert Stephenson and Company supplied five outside cylindered 2-2-2-2 Crampton type locomotives – Nos 98-102. They were later rebuilt as 2-2-2s. All had been withdrawn by the end of 1866. The GER inherited Nos 99 and 101 and they retained these numbers on that company.

In 1848, E.B. Wilson and Company supplied five outside cylindered 2-2-2-2 Crampton type locomotives – Nos 108-12. In 1854-5, the boilers of these locomotives were used on five locomotives of the 0-6-0 wheel arrangement of the 234 class. Their new numbers were 233 to 237. The reason the class was called 234 because the boiler of old No 109 was the first one to be used on a member of the new class – locomotive No 234.

In 1845, Jones and Potts delivered a 2-4-0 with outside cylinders. This locomotive had originally been ordered as a 2-2-2, No 50. It retained its number under the GER. It was scrapped in 1868. In 1846, the same company delivered a 2-4-0, No 48. By 1850 it had been renumbered 203, which number it retained under the GER; it was scrapped in 1876. In 1848, the Company delivered two long boilered 2-4-0s, Nos 102 and 103. In about 1847 they were renumbered 170 and 171, which numbers they retained under the GER. They were scrapped in 1879 and 1877 respectively.

In 1846, Robert Stephenson and Company delivered three long boilered 2-4-0s, Nos 68-70. They were withdrawn between 1868 and 1878. They retained their numbers under the GER.

In 1847 an outside framed 2-4-0, No 140, was delivered to the Railway. It had been built by Robert Stephenson and Company for the North Midland Railway, which then became part of the MR from whom the locomotive was transferred. In 1861, it was sold to the CV&HR. It was renumbered 217 in 1854 and 95 in 1856.

In 1846-7, Jones and Potts supplied five outside cylindered 2-4-0s, Nos 79 to 81 and 182, the latter having been numbered 82 in error as a number 82 already existed. They were withdrawn between 1869 and 1881.They retained their numbers under the GER.

In 1846-7, E.B. Wilson and Company supplied five outside cylindered long boilered 2-4-0s, Nos 37 to 41. They were scrapped between 1878 and 1882. They retained their numbers under the GER.

In 1847, Robert Stephenson and Company supplied seven outside cylindered 2-4-0s, Nos 71 to 77. They were scrapped between 1859 and 1881. No 74 was scrapped in 1859 after an explosion at Ilford that year. The rest were scrapped between 1869 and 1881. The rest retained their numbers under the GER.

In 1847 the Vulcan Foundry supplied ten outside cylindered, 2-4-0s, Nos 172 to 181. They were scrapped between 1862 and 1879. They originally retained their numbers under the GER, but Nos 71, 72 and 75 were renumbered 710, 720 and 750 in the duplicate list in 1876.

In 1847, Robert Stephenson and Company supplied one outside cylindered 2-4-0, No 189. In 1849 the same company supplied three similar outside cylindered 2-4-0s, Nos 190 to 192. They were scrapped between 1868 and 1870. They retained their numbers under the GER.

In 1847-8, B. Hick and Son under sub-contract from Robert Stephenson and Company supplied six outside cylindered 2-4-0s, Nos 82 to 87. It seems that they were originally intended to be Nos 182 to 187 and according to Baxter were probably delivered with those numbers before being renumbered. They were withdrawn between 1868 and 1871. They retained their numbers under the GER, except No 87 which was renumbered 870 in the duplicate list in 1868.

In 1848, Jones and Potts supplied five outside cylindered 2-4-0s, Nos 183 to 187. They were scrapped between 1868 and 1876. They originally retained their numbers under the GER, but Nos 185, 186 and 187 were renumbered 1850, 1860 and 1870 in 1872.

In 1848-9, E.B. Wilson and Company supplied eight 2-4-0s, Nos 193 to 200. They were scrapped between 1868 and 1871. They retained their numbers under the GER.

In 1846, Longbridge and Company supplied two long boilered outside cylindered 0-4-2s, No 104 and 105. In 1848-9, they were respectively rebuilt as long boilered outside cylindered 2-4-0s by Kitson and Company. They were withdrawn by 1862. In 1847/8 they were renumbered 145 and 146.

In 1846, Stothert and Slaughter supplied five 0-6-0s, Nos 97 to 101. They were withdrawn between 1865 and 1873. The ECR renumbered them 155-9. They retained their numbers under the GER.

In 1846, Kitson and Company supplied a long boilered 0-6-0, No 90. This was withdrawn by 1862. It was renumbered 149 in about 1847.

In 1846, Tayleur and Company supplied an 0-6-0, No 91, which was transferred on delivery to the Norfolk Railway. This was withdrawn by 1862. It was renumbered 50 in 1847.

In 1846-7, Jones and Potts supplied two long boilered 0-6-0s, Nos 151 and 152. No 151 was withdrawn by 1862 but No 152 did retain its number under the GER, but was transferred to the duplicate list as No 1520 in 1864 and was scrapped in 1873.

In 1847, Robert Stephenson and Company supplied an 0-6-0, No 188. This was renumbered 154 in 1848 and withdrawn by 1862.

In 1847-8, Stothert and Slaughter supplied ten 0-6-0s, Nos 160 to 169. Nos 162, 164 and 169 were returned to Stothert and Slaughter in dispute. The rest were scrapped between 1865 and 1867. These retained their numbers under the GER.

In 1846 a long-boilered 0-6-0 built by P. Rothwell and Company for the Midland Railway as part of that Company's 86 Class was transferred on delivery to the ECR and became that Company's No 106. It was renumbered 153 in 1846 and was sold in 1857.

In 1847, Kitson and Company supplied two 0-6-0s, Nos 170 and 171, which were similar to 0-6-0 No 90 already supplied by them to the ECR. Both were replaced by 1865 but seem to have been withdrawn by 1862 as there is no mention of their GER numbers.

In 1847, W.B. Adams supplied an 0-2-2 vertical boilered steam powered carriage seating seven people. It was originally named *Little*

Wonder but was also known as 'Lilliputian', which according to Baxter was possibly a nickname. Its other name was *Express.* It was not numbered in the ECR locomotive stock and its disposal is not known.

In 1849, W.B. Adams supplied an outside cylindered 2-2-0 well tank locomotive plus four wheeled carriage rail-motor seating 42 passengers named *Enfield.* As mentioned earlier, this early rail-motor originally worked on the Enfield branch. The locomotive and carriage were later separated and the locomotive part rebuilt as a 2-2-2 well tank locomotive. It was not numbered in the ECR locomotive stock and its disposal is not known.

In 1849, W.B. Adams supplied a 2-2-0 outside cylindered well tank locomotive named *Cambridge.* It was not numbered in the ECR locomotive stock but is known to be in use a stationary boiler in 1872.

This covers the locomotives built to the designs or at least order under the tenures of William Fernihough and John Hunter. In relation to the locomotives obtained in 1838-9, one would suggest that they were built to the design of or built to the order of John Braithwaite. The following lists the locomotives built to the design of John Gooch.

Gooch's first locomotives were nine outside cylindered 2-2-2 well tank locomotives, Nos 20 to 25 and 4 to 6, built in 1851-2. Nos 20 to 25 were built at the ECR's Stratford Works, with No 20 being the first locomotive built there by the Company. Nos 4 to 6 were built by R.B. Longbridge and Company. These locomotives were later classified Class A by Robert Sinclair. They were withdrawn between 1871 and 1879. They retained their numbers under the GER, but No 22 was renumbered 022 in 1878 and was withdrawn in 1879.

In 1852, E.B. Wilson and Company supplied three 0-2-2 well tank locomotives, Nos 1 to 3, which had originally been ordered by the Norfolk Railway. All were withdrawn by 1862.

In 1853 to 1855, Stratford Works built sixteen outside cylindered 2-2-2 well tank locomotives, Nos 7 to 12 and 250 to 259. Sinclair later classified these locomotives Class B. No 8 was rebuilt in 1874 as a 2-2-4 well tank locomotive attached to an inspection saloon and in 1876 was further rebuilt as a 4-2-4 saddle tank. George Dow in *London, Tilbury and Southend Album* (Ian Allan 1981) says that these locomotives were the first to work on the LT&SR when it opened. He also says that Nos 250 to 259 were specifically designed to work on that Railway and were of different dimensions to Nos 7 to 12. Kay says that by July 1855 the ECR had built ten passenger tank locomotives and two tender goods locomotives for the LT&SR. This suggests that Nos 250 to 259 were working the latter Railway. All were withdrawn between 1871 and 1883. They retained their numbers under the GER, but Nos 8, 250, 252, 253, 255, 258 and 259 were later renumbered 08, 0250, 0252, 0253, 2550, 2580 and 2590.

In 1854-5, Stratford works built five outside cylindered 0-6-0s, Nos 233 to 7. They were known as 'Floating Batteries' and used the boilers of the previously described Cramptons Nos 108-12. I would hazard a guess and say that as Nos 234 and 237 were built in late 1854 and that Nos 233, 236 and 235 were not built until after July 1855, the first two were the two tender locomotives working the LT&SR. This is not proven, so it is very probable that different goods locomotives worked on the LT&SR at different times. They were withdrawn between 1882 and 1884. They retained their numbers under the GER but were later renumbered 0233-7.

In 1855-6, eighteen outside cylindered 2-4-0s were built for the ECR. Of these, Nos 238 to 243 were built by Sharp, Stewart in 1855, whilst Kitson and Company built Nos 244 to 249 in 1855. Brassey, Jackson and Betts built Nos 214 to 219 in 1856. These locomotives were known as 'Butterflies'. They were withdrawn between 1873 and 1879. They retained their numbers under the GER, but Nos 249, 214, 215, 217 and 219 were later renumbered 0249, 2140, 2150, 2170 and 2190.

Between 1855 and 1859 twelve outside cylinder 2-2-2s were built for the Company. Of these, Nos 274-9 were built by Brassey, Jackson and Betts in 1855-6, whilst Stratford Works built Nos 27, 94 and

280-3 in respectively 1856, 1857 and 1859. Sinclair later classified these locomotives Class C. They were withdrawn between 1874 and 1879. They retained their numbers under the GER, but Nos 280-3 were later renumbered 2800, 2810, 2820 and 2830

Robert Sinclair, who was the Locomotive Superintendent of the ECR from 1856 to 1862 and of the GER from 1862 to 1866, designed the following locomotives. Sinclair originally came from the Caledonian Railway. All of the locomotives built in Sinclair's time for the ECR retained these numbers when the GER was formed in 1862.

As during Sinclair's period of office the GER was formed, the following list mentions not only those locomotives that were built to his design prior to the formation of that Company but also afterwards.

During Sinclair's time, six outside cylindered 2-4-0s, Nos 301 to 6, were built by P. Rothwell and Company in 1858. These were Class Z. They were withdrawn in 1873-5.

Between 1859 and 1866, a total of 110 outside cylindered 2-4-0s, Nos 307 to 416, were built by the following builders: Nos 307 to 326 by Neilson and Company; Nos 327 to 341 by Robert Stephenson and Company; Nos 342 to 356 by R. and W. Hawthorn and Company; Nos 357 to 381 by Kitson and Company; Nos 382 to 406 by the Vulcan Foundry Company; and Nos 407 to 416 by Schneider and Company. These locomotives were Class Y. No 327 was exhibited at the International Exhibition in London in 1862. Some of these locomotives were the first locomotives on the GER to be fitted with cabs for the enginemen. Originally, locomotives were not fitted with cabs and the enginemen were exposed to the elements from both the front and rear, and also from above. Later a weatherboard or spectacle plate was provided at the front as a windscreen for the enginemen. On some tank locomotives this was also provided at the front of the rear coal bunker. Later cabs of varying sorts were fitted on the locomotives. Ten of the Y Class were rebuilt to Class U13 in 1882. Amongst other things, this involved increasing the diameter of their driving wheels from 6ft 1in to 6ft 3in. These were Nos 307, 321, 328, 341, 344, 356,376, 379, 382 and 384. Twenty were rebuilt as 4-4-0s in 1876 to 1878. These were Nos 308, 311-2, 314, 317, 320, 324-5, 327, 329, 342, 349, 360, 366, 370, 381, 385, 406, 412 and 416. All of the Y Class locomotives were withdrawn between 1883 and 1894. All of the U13 Class locomotives were withdrawn in 1892 to 1894. A lot of the locomotives of Classes Y and U13 were renumbered into the duplicate list in 1888 and 1890. The duplicate numbers were 0307-9, 0311-2, 0314-7, 0319-21, 0324-5, 0327-32, 0335-6, 0339-41, 0344-5, 0349, 0351-2, 0355-62, 0365-6, 0370, 0372-3, 0375-80, 0382, 0384-6, 0389, 0393, 0396-7, 0405-9, 0411-6.

In 1862, Stratford Works built five 2-4-0 well tanks, Nos 120 to 124 of Class X. The boilers of these locomotives were built by Slaughter Grunning and Company. They were all withdrawn between 1880 and 1884, but number 122 was used as a stationary boiler until 1907. No 121 was possibly renumbered 121A, whilst No 122 was renumbered 1220 in 1884.

In 1864-5 Neilson and Company built twenty 2-4-2 well tanks, Nos 140 to 159 of Class V. They were known as 'The Scotchmen'. All were withdrawn between 1883 and 1888. In 1880 Nos 140-9 were

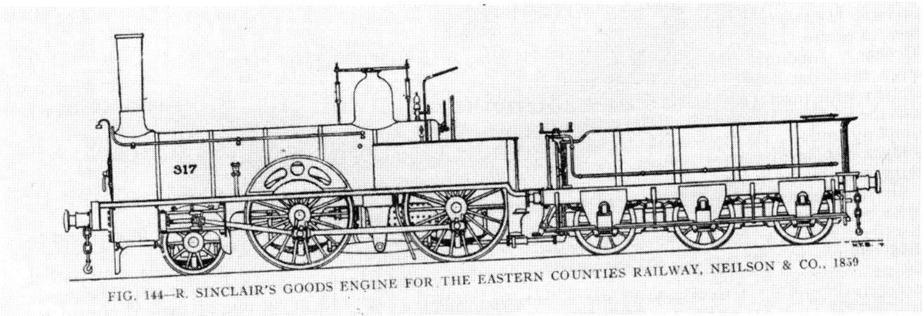

Sinclair Y Class 2-4-0 No 317 of the ECR as built by Neilson and Company in 1859. Unlike later members of the class, the locomotive does not have much protection for the enginemen. The class was built by both the ECR and the GER. (Author's collection).

renumbered 1400, 1410, 1420, 1430, 1440, 1450, 1460, 1470, 1480 and 1490.

Between 1862 and 1867, thirty-one outside cylindered 2-2-2s of Class W were built as follows. Nos 284-8 by William Fairburn and Sons. Nos 51-60 by Slaughter Grunning and Company, Nos 289-09 by Kitson and Company and Nos 87-90 and 299-300 by Schneider and Company. No 284 was painted cream for the wedding of the Prince of Wales and Princess Alexandra of Denmark and hauled the Royal Wedding Train from London to Wolferton after their marriage in Westminster Abbey on 10 March 1863. No 87 was exhibited at the Paris Exhibition in 1867. No 54 was scrapped after being involved in the Thorpe accident of 10 September 1874. The W class had a reputation of performing satisfactory work and of being much steadier riding than many contemporary outside cylindered locomotives.

In the late 1860s, Patrick Stirling, the Locomotive Superintendent of the GNR, was in the process of contemplating designing a large express locomotive. Norman Groves in *Great Northern Locomotive History Volume 2 – 1867-95 – The Stirling Era* (RCTS) says that Stirling seems to have originally contemplated building an outside cylindered 2-2-2. In 1868, Stirling approached Samuel Waite Johnson who had succeeded Robert Sinclair as the Locomotive Superintendent of the GER in 1866 and asked to borrow a W class locomotive for the purpose of testing the merits of an outside cylindered locomotive having large driving wheels within a short wheelbase on the GNR main line. From the end of August 1868, trials lasting some weeks were conducted in comparison with GNR 2-2-2s of Stirling and Sturrock designs having similar driving wheel dimensions to the W class between Peterborough and London in charge of GNR driver Lloyd. The W Class locomotive in question was No 293. The result of the trials led Stirling to produce his 8ft driving wheeled outside cylindered 4-2-2s - built from 1870 to 1895. Two of the W class, Nos 51 and 291, were rebuilt as 4-2-2s in 1873. Other than No 54 scrapped in 1874, the rest were withdrawn between 1883 and 1894.

These locomotives underwent a certain amount of renumbering. In 1878, Nos 87-90 were renumbered 301-4 and in 1880 Nos 51-3 and 55-60 were renumbered 275-83. In 1886 the following renumbering of the then existing members of the class took place. The new numbers were: 0275-8, 0280-6, 0288-92, 0295-7, 0299-301.

Locomotives of the N&ER

Longridge and Company supplied between 1840 and 1842 seven inside cylindered outside framed 2-2-2s. After being taken over by the ECR, they were withdrawn between 1850 and 1862 prior to formation of the GER. Their ECR numbers were originally 23, 25, 29, 30, 35 and 36, but Nos 23, 35 and 33 were later renumbered 26, 27 and 28.

Tayleur and Company supplied three 2-2-2s in 1840-1. After being taken over by the ECR, they were withdrawn between 1850 and 1852. Their ECR numbers were 27, 28 and 34.

Robert Stephenson and Company supplied two 2-2-2s in 1841. In the same year the same Company supplied a long boilered 2-2-2. After being taken over by the ECR they were withdrawn between 1850 and 1852. Their ECR numbers were 31, 32 and 24.

In 1843, Bury, Curtis and Kennedy supplied an inside cylindered, outside framed 2-2-2, which at an unknown date was rebuilt as a 2-4-0 saddle tank and was withdrawn by 1862. Its ECR number was 26, but it was renumbered 143 in 1852 and either 218 or 219 in 1854 and finally 129 in 1856. All these locomotives were originally built to the 5ft gauge and converted to the 4ft 8½in gauge in 1844.

A total of fourteen locomotives were taken over by the ECR in 1844.

Locomotives of the Norfolk Railway

The Norfolk Railway had two locomotives built in 1844 of which nothing is known other than their numbers 1 and 2 and which were, it would seem, ex-contractor's locomotives acquired by the Yarmouth and Norwich Railway and sold prior to the ECR taking over the working of the Norfolk Railway.

In 1844 Robert Stephenson and Company supplied three outside cylindered 2-2-2s, Nos 3 to 5. In 1848 Nos 3 and 5 were sold to the Liverpool, Crosby and Southport Railway. No 4 was withdrawn in 1868. Its ECR number and GER number was 45. These first three locomotives were, it would seem, built for the Yarmouth and Norwich Railway, which latter Company had ordered five outside cylindered 2-2-2s from Robert Stephenson and Company and which were delivered to the Norfolk Railway in 1845 as that Company's Nos 6 to 11. All appear to have been withdrawn by 1862. Their ECR numbers were 46-8 in the case of Nos 6-8 and 140-2 in the case of Nos 9-11.

Locomotive No 12 has been mentioned previously under the ECR. As mentioned, it was an outside cylindered 2-2-2 built by Jones and Potts in 1846. This was withdrawn by 1862. Its new ECR number was firstly 204 and then in 1856 No 124.

In 1845 Tayleur and Company delivered four long boilered 0-6-0s, Nos 21 to 24. Of these No 24 was sold to the Royal Danish Railways in 1853. The others were withdrawn at various dates between 1867 and 1883. Their ECR numbers were for Nos 21-3 – 225-7, which they retained on the GER. No 24 retained its Norfolk Railway number 24 prior to being sold to the Royal Danish Railways. The following year

Yarmouth and Norwich Railway locomotive No 4, built by Robert Stephenson and Company in 1844. The locomotive is of the long boilered outside cylindered sort having the firebox behind all of the locomotive's wheels. (Author's collection).

(1846) Tayleur and Company delivered three outside cylindered 2-2-2-0 Cramptons, Nos 13 to 15. They were withdrawn between 1856 and 1868. Their ECR numbers were 42 and 143 and 144. No 42 is known to have kept its number on the GER. I can find no mention of the others having GER numbers. That same year (1846) the same Company delivered an 0-6-0, No 20. This was withdrawn in 1882. This was renumbered 224 by the ECR and kept the number under the GER prior to being renumbered 2240 in 1877. Finally in 1846 the Company delivered nine long boilered 0-6-0s, Nos 16 to 19 and 25 to 9. No 16 was immediately on delivery transferred to the ECR and became that company's locomotive No 91. They were withdrawn between 1862 and 1881. Their ECR numbers were 220-3 and 228-32 which they retained on the GER. Nos 221-3 and 231 were later renumbered 2210, 2220, 2230 and 2310.

In 1846-7, Robert Stephenson and Company delivered ten long boilered outside cylindered 2-4-0s, Nos 30 to 29. They were withdrawn between 1866 and 1882. Their ECR and GER numbers were 130-9, but numbers 135 and 138 were later renumbered 1350 and 1380.

In 1849, J. and E. Headley Brothers delivered a 2-2-0 well tank named *Eagle*. It was later converted to a 2-2-2 well tank with a built in saloon and was always used as an Engineer's locomotive and was never numbered. This was withdrawn in 1868.

A total of 40 locomotives were taken over by the ECR.

Locomotives of the EUR

Sharp Brothers supplied thirteen 2-2-2 outside framed locomotives between 1846 and 1849. They were numbered 1 to 6, 14 to 19 and 26. Nos 1 to 6 were named. According to Baxter there is some confusion over the names, stating a discrepancy between the names given in a series of articles in *The Locomotive Magazine* and *East Anglia's First Railway* by Hugh Moffat (Terence Dalton 1987). No 1 was either *Ipswich* or *Colchester*, No 2 was either *Bury* or *Ipswich*, No 3 was either *Colchester* or *City of Norwich*, No 4 was either *Diss* or *Bury St Edmunds*, No 5 was either *Stowmarket* or *Orwell* and No 6 either *Haughley* or *Stour*. Moffat also states that Nos 1 to 3 were intended for the Blackburn and Preston Railway. They were withdrawn between 1873 and 1880. Their ECR numbers were in 1854, 260-72, but in 1855 Nos 271, ex-19, and 272, ex-26, were renumbered 116 and 117. The numbers that they had when taken over by the GER were the numbers that they retained under that Company, except that Nos 260, 262, 264 and 267 were later renumbered 2600, 2620, 2640 and 2670.

In 1846, Stothert and Slaughter supplied four 2-2-2s, Nos 7, 8, 20 and 21. In 1852 all were rebuilt as 2-4-0s. They were withdrawn between 1860 and 1868. Their ECR and GER numbers were 205, 206, 209 and 210.

In 1846 to 1849 Stohert and Slaughter supplied six 0-4-2s, Nos 9 and 10 and 22 to 25. No 9 was either named *Suffolk* or *Essex*. All had been withdrawn by the end of 1867. Their ECR numbers were 207, 208 and 211-4. No 214 was renumbered 204 in 1856. All retained these numbers under the GER.

In 1846, R. and W. Hawthorn and Company delivered three 2-2- 2s, Nos 11 to 13, which had originally been ordered by the I&BR. All had

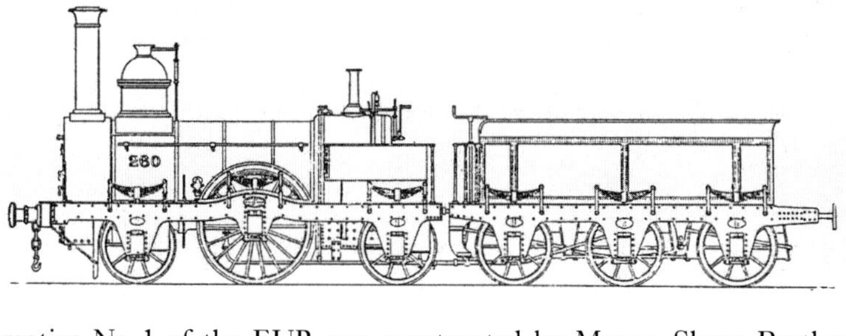

Locomotive No 1 of the EUR was constructed by Messrs Sharp Brothers of Manchester and was of standard Little Sharpie type. The locomotive was twice renumbered by the ECR to 260 and 2600 and survived until December 1879. (Author's collection).

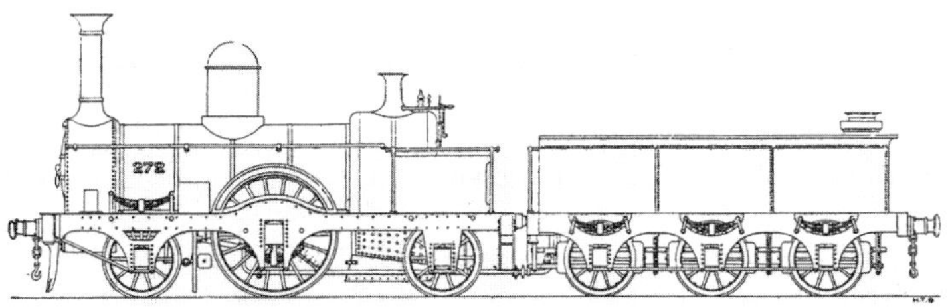

107

EUR locomotive No 13 was one of three 2-2-2s built by Messrs R. and W. Hawthorn and Company in 1846 and had originally been ordered by the I&BR. All had been withdrawn by 1862 when the GER was formed. (Author's collection).

been withdrawn by 1862. They were renumbered 273-5 in 1854, but in 1855 Nos 274 and 275 were renumbered 271 and 272.

In 1849, Sharp Brothers delivered a 2-2-2 well tank, No 27. Baxter says that the locomotive may have been converted from an undelivered I&BR locomotive. This was withdrawn in 1871. Its ECR and GER number was 14.

In 1851, Kitson, Thompson and Hewitson delivered a 2-2-0 well tank, No 28, named *Ariel's Girdle* and which was later rebuilt as a 2-4-0 side tank locomotive. This was withdrawn in 1879. Its ECR and GER number was 17, but in May 1875 it was renumbered 17A.

In 1854, Sharp Brothers delivered three 2-2-2s, No 29 to 31. They were all withdrawn in 1871. Their ECR and GER numbers were 13-5.

A total of thirty-one locomotives were taken over by the ECR.

Locomotives of the Newmarket Railway

The Newmarket Railway had six outside cylindered 2-4-0s built by Gilkes, Wilson and Company in 1848. They were named but not numbered. Their names were *Beeswing, Queen of Trumps, Van Tromp, Flying Dutchman, Eleanor* and *Alice Hawthorn*. Their ECR and GER numbers were 31-6. A further six locomotives were ordered by the

Company, but were never delivered to it and instead went to the Stockton and Darlington Railway. As I understand it their names were *Newmarket, Priam, Orion, Brunswick, Clarendon* and *Alarm.*

A total of six locomotives were taken over by the ECR. All were withdrawn between 1866 and 1870. They retained their ECR numbers under the GER.

Locomotives of the EAR

In 1846-8, Sharp Brothers supplied eight 2-2-2s named *Eagle, Vulture, Ostrich, Falcon, Hawk, Kite, Raven* and *Heron.* They were withdrawn between 1867 and 1870. The same Company in 1848 supplied two 0-4-2s named *Lion* and *Tiger.* They were withdrawn in 1871 and 1872. A total of ten locomotives were taken over by the ECR. Their ECR and GER numbers were for the 2-2-2s 108-15 and for the 0-4-2s 162 and 164. No 162 was renumbered 1620 in July 1872.

There was one other form of motive power and that was horses. Their main use was for shunting or hauling a single wagon on a short branch line saving the need for a locomotive, but they were in the early days used to haul a single passenger carriage on a lightly used branch line.

It is the carriages of the railways with which passengers are most acquainted after stations. In the early days, whilst first class passengers enjoyed the luxury of a closed carriage, third class and sometimes second class passengers did not enjoy the luxury of having a roof over their heads. Second class had seats and third class were standing. Gladstone's Act of 1844 compelled railway companies to run one train a day providing covered accommodation for third class passengers.

In the early days, carriages were with a few exceptions four wheeled compartment vehicles. The number of compartments depended on the class. There were exceptions. Regarding the railways of the eastern counties, on the North Woolwich branch of the ECR there was to be found some jointed eight wheeled carriages built in 1847 by W. Bridges

Adams of Bow. These carriages were not eight wheelers in the true sense but jointed four wheelers.

Ships

River Queen was an iron paddle steamer built by Ditchburn and Mare of Blackwall in 1839 and owned by the Ipswich Steam Navigation Company and which sailed between Ipswich and Harwich in arrangement with the EUR in 1849. It was sold in 1853 to Alfred Cobbold when the Ipswich Steam Navigation Company was liquidated.

Railway was another paddle steamer built by Ditchburn and Mare, in 1842, and which was owned by the L&BR and sailed between Ipswich and Harwich for a few months in 1850 with an agreed division of receipts between that Company and the EUR. I can find no other mention of any L&BR steamships.

Peter Bruff was the owner of the following ships which were sold to the ECR in 1854. The iron built paddle steamer *Atlanta* was built at Deptford in 1841 and purchased by him from London owners in 1850. The iron paddle steamer *Cardinal Wolsey* was built at Beddington Ironworks, Northumberland in 1845 and purchased by Bruff from London owners in 1850. This ship was sold to the ECR in 1854. The GER in turn sold it to a Middlesbrough owner in 1863. The replacement was the paddle steamer *Ipswich* which was built by James Ash of Cubitt Town on the Thames and entered service in August 1864, being sold out of service in 1873.

The wooden paddle steamer *Prince* was built for Bruff by Harvey and Son of Ipswich in 1852.

The wooden paddle steamer *Pearl* was built at Blackwall in 1835 and purchased by Bruff from Milford Haven in 1852.

The iron built paddle steamer *Orion* was built by Read and Page of Ipswich in 1841 and purchased by Bruff from Goole owners in 1852.

The iron built paddle steamer *Prince Albert* was built by Walker-on-Tyne in 1842 and purchased by Bruff from London owners in 1853.

The iron paddle steamer *Orwell* was built by Ditchburn and Mare of Blackwall in 1839 and owned by the Ipswich Steam Navigation Company and sold in 1853 to Alfred Cobbold when the latter Company was liquidated. In turn it was sold to the ECR in 1854 and resold by them in 1857.

According to D.J. Payne in *The History of the Woolwich Free Ferry* (2006), in 1847 two steam ferries were built at Barking and ran in connection with the trains from London to North Woolwich. They were named *Essex* and the *Kent* and were both built at Barking. They were described as small tug like, open decked, paddle boats with wooden hulls and weighing 65 tons. Later a third boat was added, *Middlesex*. According to the Newham Story website of the London Borough of Newham, the price to cross the river was 1d, with the ticket office being on the southern side, which not only sold ferry tickets, but tickets to various destinations on the ECR.

Bibliography and Sources

Firstly, I wish to thank the members of the GER Society for their help in answering my questions. Without their help I could not have written this book.

I also wish to thank Keith Ronaldson for proofreading the manuscript of this book.

Additionally, I wish to thank John Scott-Morgan for his help with the book.

Aldrich, C. Langley, *Locomotives of the Great Eastern Railway 1862-1962* Privately published, 1962

Allen, Cecil J., *The Great Eastern Railway*, Ian Allan, 1967

Boyles, John and Russell, Ronald, *The Canals of Eastern England*, David and Charles 1977

Bradshaw's Railway Guide – Especially for July 1845 and March 1850 and February 1863

British Locomotive Catalogue 1825-1923 Volume 6 GER, North British Railway, Great North of Scotland Railway, Midland and Great Northern Joint Railway, Remaining Companies of the LNER Group (Kestrel 2012)

British Railway Journal

British Railway Journal – Great Eastern Edition

Brown, Arthur, *Essex People 1700-1900* ERO 1972

Brown, F.A.S., *Great Northern Locomotive Engineers Vol 1 1846-1881*, Allen and Unwin 1966

Clark, Ronald H., *A Short History of the Midland and Great Northern Joint Railway*, Goose 1967

Connor, J.E., *All Stations to Poplar*, Connor and Butler 1980

Connor, J.E., *Stepney's Own Railway*, Connor and Butler 1987

Connor, J.E., *The Tottenham Joint Lines*, Connor and Butler 1993

Cooper John M., *The East Suffolk Railway*, Oakwood 1982
Directors' reports to shareholders of the Eastern Counties, Great Eastern and London and North Eastern railways.
Dow, George, *London, Tilbury and Southend Railway Album*, Ian Allan 1981
Dow, George, *The First Railway in Norfolk*, LNER 1947
Great Eastern Journal
Glover, John, *Essex and the Industrial Revolution*, ERO 1972
Gordon, D.I., *The Regional History of the Railways of Great Britain – Volume 5 - Eastern Counties*, David and Charles 1968
Hilton, H.F., *The EUR 1846-1862*, LNER 1946
Jackson, Alan A., *London's Local Railways,* David and Charles 1978
Jackson, Alan A., *London's Termini*, David and Charles 1969
Kay, Peter, *The London, Tilbury and Southend Railway – a History of the Company and Line. Volume 1*, Privately published
Klapper, Charles, *London's Lost Railways*, RKP 1976
Lake, G.H., *The Railways of Tottenham* 1945
Local Transport History Library
Moffat, Hugh, *East Anglia's First Railways*, Terrance Dalton 1987
Phillips, Charles, *The Great Eastern Railway in South Esse*x, Pen and Sword 2019
Riley, R.C., *Great Eastern Album*, Ian Allan, 1968
Robbins, Michael, *The North London Railway*, Oakwood Press, 1983
Swindale, Dennis, *Branch Lines to Maldon*, EARM 1977
The British Newspaper Archive
The Great Eastern Journal
White, H.P., *The Regional History of the Railways of Great Britain – Volume 3 – Greater London*, Phoenix 1963
The Times Archive
Welch, H.D., *The London, Tilbury and Southend Railway*, Oakwood Press, 1951
Whitehead R.A. and Simpson, F.D., *The Colne Valley and Halstead Railway* Oakwood Press, 1988
Working Timetable of the ECR for 1856
Wrottesley, A.J., *The Great Northern Railway Vols, 1, 2 and 3*, Batsford 1979-1981
Wrottesley, A.J., *The Midland and Great Northern Joint Railway* David and Charles, 1970

Index